# Table of Contents

Acknowledgements (in no particular order) .................................................. ix
A (Brief) Introduction to this book ........................................................... xi

**Chapter 1: A Brief History of Neurotechnology** ........................................... 1
    1.1    The Late 1800s ................................................................. 1
    1.2    First Half the 20th-Century .................................................. 2
    1.3    Post-War ........................................................................ 3
    1.4    The Decade of the Brain and Onwards ................................... 5
    1.5    Neurotechnology Today ....................................................... 6

**Chapter 2: Electroencephalography (EEG)** ................................................. 9
    2.1    Introduction ..................................................................... 9
    2.2    Brief History of EEG ......................................................... 10
    2.3    How It Works .................................................................. 10
    2.4    Properties ...................................................................... 14
    2.5    Hardware Properties ......................................................... 14
    2.6    Ready to Find Meaning: Software & Analysis Options ................ 18
    2.7    Notable Uses .................................................................. 20
    2.8    Logistics ....................................................................... 21
    2.9    Conclusion .................................................................... 23

**Chapter 3: Magnetoencephalography (MEG)** ............................................. 27
    3.1    Introduction ................................................................... 27
    3.2    How It Works .................................................................. 28
    3.3    History ......................................................................... 36
    3.4    Properties ...................................................................... 37
    3.5    Logistics ....................................................................... 38
    3.6    Risks and limitations ........................................................ 38
    3.7    Conclusion .................................................................... 39

## Chapter 4: Functional/ Magnetic Resonance Imaging (f/MRI) ................ 43

- 4.1 Introduction/The Basics ................ 43
- 4.2 How It Works ................ 43
- 4.3 Typical Usage ................ 46
- 4.4 History ................ 46
- 4.5 Properties ................ 47
- 4.6 Logistics ................ 49

## Chapter 5: Near-Infrared Spectroscopy (NIRS) and Functional Near-Infrared Spectroscopy (fNIRS) ................ 53

- 5.1 Introduction ................ 53
- 5.2 History of NIRS and fNIRS ................ 54
- 5.3 NIRS Overview ................ 55
- 5.4 fNIRS Overview ................ 58

## Chapter 6: Positron Emission Tomography (PET) ................ 69

- 6.1 Introduction ................ 69
- 6.2 How Does it Work? ................ 70
- 6.3 History ................ 73
- 6.4 Properties ................ 75

## Chapter 7: Intracranial electroencephalography (iEEG) ................ 85

- 7.1 Introduction ................ 86
- 7.2 Historical aspects ................ 86
- 7.3 iEEG Properties ................ 87
- 7.4 Signal processing to infer functionality ................ 94
- 7.5 Usability ................ 98
- 7.6 Conclusion ................ 100

## Neuroimaging Devices Comparison Chart ................ 105

## Chapter 8: Transcranial Electrical Stimulation (tES) ................ 109

- 8.1 Introduction ................ 109
- 8.2 Historical development of tES devices ................ 110
- 8.3 Basics of tES devices and dose ................ 112
- 8.4 Design aspects of tES electrodes ................ 114
- 8.5 Indications for tES use ................ 117

8.6 Current Flow Modeling Informs Electrode/Device Design and Set-up ............................................................ 118
8.7 Safety and Tolerability of tDCS Devices ........................... 119
8.8 Home-based tDCS Devices ............................................. 121
8.9 Conclusion ........................................................................ 121

## Chapter 9: Transcranial Magnetic Stimulation (TMS) ............ 127

9.1 Introduction ..................................................................... 127
9.2 How It Works .................................................................. 128
9.3 Typical Usage .................................................................. 129
9.4 History ............................................................................. 132
9.5 Risks and adverse effects ................................................. 134
9.6 Costs & Setup .................................................................. 136
9.7 Conclusion ....................................................................... 136

## Chapter 10: Deep Brain Stimulation ......................................... 141

10.1 Introduction ..................................................................... 141
10.2 How It Works .................................................................. 141
10.3 Typical Usage .................................................................. 144
10.4 History ............................................................................. 145
10.5 Properties ........................................................................ 147
10.6 Logistics ........................................................................... 148
10.7 The Future of DBS .......................................................... 151

## Chapter 11: Focused Ultrasound ............................................... 155

11.1 Introduction/The Basics ................................................. 155
11.2 How it Works .................................................................. 155
11.3 Typical Usage .................................................................. 156
11.4 History ............................................................................. 157
11.5 Properties ........................................................................ 159
11.6 Logistics ........................................................................... 160
11.7 Future of FUS .................................................................. 162

## Chapter 12: Hybrid Neurotechnology Systems ........................ 165

12.1 Introduction ..................................................................... 166
12.2 The Rationale for Hybrid Systems ................................. 166
12.3 Concepts of hybrid BCIs ................................................. 167
12.4 Applications ..................................................................... 170
12.5 Final considerations ........................................................ 173

Brain Stimulation Methods Comparison Chart ............................................. 179

## Chapter 13: Market Drivers ................................................................. 183

13.1 Neurotechnology is Going Noninvasive and Pervasive ..................... 183
13.2 Noninvasive neurotechnologies provide a new and scalable avenue to monitor and harness that promise. ................................. 185
13.3 Pay attention to these ten areas of expected rapid growth ................. 188
13.4 Big Data-enhanced diagnostics and treatments ............................... 189
13.5 Help us promote responsible innovation and wise adoption ............ 191
13.6 Fortunately, multiple stakeholders are already working hard on this. 193
13.7 Conclusion .................................................................................... 193

## Chapter 14: The Neurotech Ecosystem ................................................ 197

14.1 10 Companies in the Spotlight ...................................................... 197
14.2 Academia ...................................................................................... 202
14.3 Notable Individuals ....................................................................... 204
14.4 Government Brain Initiatives ........................................................ 207

## Chapter 15: Challenges in the Field ..................................................... 211

15.1 Overview ....................................................................................... 211

## Chapter 16: An Introduction to Neuroethics and the Neuroethical Considerations of Neurotechnology ......................... 219

16.1 Introduction .................................................................................. 219
16.2 The "Self" consciousness, autonomy, and identity ........................... 220
16.3 Ownership and Consent ............................................................... 221
16.4 Neurohype, Neuroseduction, Overtrust, and Dishonest Marketing ... 224
16.5 What does this mean for neurotechnology? ................................... 226

## Chapter 17: The Future of NeuroTechnology ..................................... 229

17.1 Companies driving the future of Neurotech ................................. 229
17.2 Researchers ................................................................................... 234
17.3 Government Led Initiatives .......................................................... 240
17.4 Brain Data on the Blockchain? ..................................................... 244

## Chapter 18: Where to Start .................................................................. 251

18.1 Getting started with hardware ...................................................... 252
18.2 Data and Software ........................................................................ 252

18.3 Hackathons, competitions, and conferences ................................... 253
18.4 DIY Projects and the Neurotechnology Community ........................ 253
18.5 NeuroTechX ........................................................................... 254

# Acknowledgements (in no particular order)

This book would not have been possible without the support of the NeuroTechX community. In no particular order, we would like to thank the following people:

Sheida Rabipour, Paniz Tavakoli, Jed Meltzer, Benjamin De Leener, Raymundo Cassani, Thomas Funck, Chaim N. Katz, José Zariffa, Taufik A. Valiante, Niranjan Khadka, Marom Bikson, Shreyas Harita, Frank Mazza, John D. Griffiths, Irene E. Harmsen, Tiago H. Falk, Hubert Banville, Lucas Trambaiolli, Alvaro Fernandez, Lohit Velagapudi, Sunidhi Ramesh, Yannick Roy, Adam Sefler, and Zane Russom.

Additionally, we would like to thank the following people for reviewing the book and giving feedback. Anaelle Haddad, Ashish Srikanth, Bingyi Wu, Christelle Bitar, Han Nguyen, Ingrid Xu, Katherine Cheung, Lucas Roldos, Vanessa Correia, and Sydney Sue.

Finally, a big thank you to Ahmed Osmanovic and Mary Vanko for illustrating and editing this book, respectively.

A special shout-out goes to Jen Wang and Maria Marano, who were the foundation of this book. Without their support, there is a good chance that this would not exist in the first place.

**Sydney Swaine-Simon:** *Project Lead for the NeuroTech Primer*

**Lukas Shannon:** *Assistant Project Manager for the NeuroTech Primer*

# A (Brief) Introduction to this book

## Sydney Swaine-Simon

Sydney is a Montreal native with a strong desire to grow the cities innovation ecosystem. Having completed his studies in Psychology and Computer Science he developed a strong passion for Biotechnology, AI, and Open Innovation. In 2012 Sydney became one of the co-founders of District 3, one of Quebec's largest innovation centers.. His responsibilities as the AI Fellow included supporting and recruiting teams for the AI XPRIZE, helping to organize the AI for Good Summit which is hosted by the ITU, and supporting AI startups. Sydney also co-founded NeuroTechX, a non-profit organization which has built the largest international network of neurotechnology enthusiasts. The organization has created a community of over 10,000 people worldwide and has supported multiple open source neurotech projects. In his spare time, Sydney is a core organizer of the DEF CON Biohacking Village, a conference which brings biohackers from across the world to share their projects and experiences.

When we decided to write our first book, our goal was to create something that made it easy for anyone to learn about the subject and develop a strong grasp of what the ecosystem is like and how to get involved. What we didn't realize was how much of an undertaking something like that would be. The field of Neurotechnology has a history going back a hundred years, but only a small portion of the world is aware of it.

Awareness and interest in Neurotechnology increased once the emergence of consumer-focused products came in the mid-2000s. It all started with an open-source version of EEG (electroencephalogram) back in the 90s. The consumer brain-computer interface (BCI) market was eventually formed by innovators like Tan Le of Emotiv, KooHyoung Lee, and Jongjin Lim, who co-founded one of the first consumer neurotechnology devices, along with Steve Castellotti who brought brain-controlled toys to the masses.

As the field grew and public interest started to grow, it led to a variety of grassroots communities from across the world who were interested in using the technology to control everything around them, from brain-controlled cars to those that wanted to use brain stimulation as a way to increase their focus. This growth in public interest eventually led to the creation of NeuroTechX as people across the globe searched for a community to connect with.

With more people outside of neuroscience showing an interest, one of the biggest issues was a lack of material that allowed people to learn about the field. The majority of information would either be too complex or would consist of so much scientific jargon that it was not user-friendly to the general public. Most people were also not aware of its history, the inventors, its market size, and the ethics associated with the new trends in Neuroscience.

This book was put together by our community to address these needs. The Neurotech primer represents the collaboration of 20+ authors and editors. What makes this book unique, from our perspective, is that you will learn from authors with a variety of backgrounds. As a reader, you will get the chance to learn enough about the field to understand its ecosystem. This book is your step on a journey to find a domain that truly interests you and a way to get involved.

This book is structured to first talk about the technologies in part one. Part two discusses the Neurotech ecosystem and the key players in the space. It also includes world initiatives that help grow the field, the major contributors to the field, the companies developing these technologies, open initiatives, challenges of the field, and the ethics involved. To conclude, we provide additional resources and ways for you to get involved in the space. This book is not large enough to go into depth about everything, but it does have a little bit of everything for whoever wants to learn more about the field.

As a final note, it took us two years to put this together, so some of the information may not be up to date. If you find anything that is no longer accurate, please let us know.

We hope you enjoy!

# 1 A Brief History of Neurotechnology

**Jen Wang**
*Jen Wang is a recent graduate from McGill University where she studied neuroscience and computer science. She has a passion for science communication and strongly believes in making scientific concepts accessible to everyone, whether that be through articles or educational infographics. Having joined the NeuroTechX community in 2018, her interests vary between AI, neurotech, and mental health.*

The history of neurotechnology starts with the tumultuous and ongoing journey of understanding the brain itself. Like many other scientific fields, the journey was not straight and narrow but a winding path of wrong — and then gradually, slightly less wrong — observations.

As is expected with the nature of the subject, the study of neurology started in tandem with religious beliefs and hinged on concepts of the soul, or "life energy." Only as the field transitioned into what we now consider modern neurology in the 1700s did the scientific community begin to shed ties between the brain and the soul. The constant uphill battle of understanding the brain, always having been an interdisciplinary field, developed with more advanced scientific tools. The debunking of one paradigm created vacuums that others rushed to fill with newer theories.

The theory of localization — the idea that different parts of the brain give rise to certain brain functions — gained traction in the scientific community in the late 1700s and early 1800s.[1]

## 1.1 The Late 1800s

Dr. William Macewen was among the first to use localization to his advantage. He carried out several operations and studies — on the living and the dead, from the mid-1860s to the mid-1880s.[2] Although Dr. Macewen was accredited with having performed one of the first successful intracranial neurosurgeries, Dr. A. Hughes Bennett and Richman J. Godlee also used localization to successfully locate and excise a brain tumor from symptoms alone in 1884. Their findings were well-documented and were published in the August 1962 issue of Journal of Neurosurgery entitled, "Case of Cerebral Tumor."

At around the same time, in the field of neurophysiology, Dr. Angelo Mosso invented a peculiar device in 1882 that he dubbed the "human circulation balance." Mosso laid his participants on a large, human-sized scale and noted that mental stimulation would cause the scale to tip toward the head, effectively "weighing brain activity."

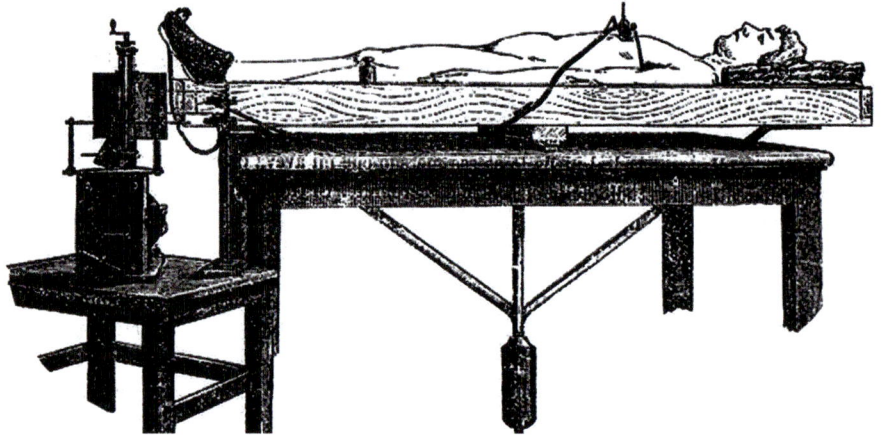

Figure 1.1 Angelo Mosso's human circulation balance

Citing his results, in 1890, Charles Smart Roy and Sherrington theorized that blood flow and brain activity were coupled. These findings laid the foundation for what was to become the imaging techniques of PET and MRI. However, after the initial surge of interest, a lack of technology prevented the pursuit of this line of research until the 1920s.

The newly theorized electrical properties of the brain were also being explored. In particular, Richard Caton, in 1875, described his experiments with a highly sensitive galvanometer.[3] Placing one electrode on the skull's surface and another on the brain's grey matter in rabbits and monkeys, he proved the existence of electrical currents for the first time.[4] Caton found that stimulation to different sensory areas, such as intense light to the eyes, caused increased electrical activity in certain brain regions. Notably, Caton found that these electrical currents increased during the dying process and then lessened, leading to the eventual absence of the current after death.[5]

## 1.2 First Half the 20th-Century

The well-known experiments of Hans Berger helped to change the face of neuroscience as the inventor of the electroencephalogram (EEG), coining the term in 1929.[6] Berger also discovered alpha and beta waves. Berger's findings are described further in chapter 2 of this book. His findings were dismissed at first, especially by the neurophysiology community. However, Edgar Douglas Adrian published his own experiments that proved Berger's findings in 1934.[7] Around the same time, further excitement for this new technique grew as Gibbs and Lennox proved the usefulness of EEG in measuring epilepsy.[8]

In the late 1930s, Wilder Penfield at the Montreal Neurological Institute developed a technique that obtained EEG recordings directly from the pial matter of the brain, also known as electrocorticography (ECoG). More background on this development can be found in chapter 7.

On the physiological side of things, the rise of x-rays became standard in clinical settings worldwide. Infamous Portuguese neurologist Egas Moniz developed cerebral angiography in 1927, a revolutionary technique that allowed for a high-contrast visualization of blood vessels in the cerebrum. Before this development, clinicians used air ventriculography and air encephalography techniques comprised of the injection of air into the lateral ventricle of the brain for greater contrast in x-rays. Though this was a breakthrough on its own, it was considered relatively dangerous.

Moniz's development arose after he experimented with different "radiopaque" solutions. After some (painful) experiments with lithium bromide and strontium bromide, Moniz settled on the quick and relatively painless 25% solution of sodium iodide. Still, sodium iodide was considered hazardous, and thorium dioxide replaced it in 1931. Despite this, angiography became widely adopted until the invention of the computerized tomography (CT) scan took its place.

After Roy and Sherrington's findings in the late 1800s, the first quarter of the century saw very little study into the link between brain function and blood flow. In 1928, however, the topic was revisited when a patient of neurophysiologist John Fulton reported abnormal vascular murmurs in the back of his head. These murmurs, described by the medical term "bruits," grew louder only with effortful visual tasks — tasks that required the patient to make a mental effort to visually distinguish between different objects. He also found that other senses did not trigger the same events. Again, however, the significance of this finding was largely dismissed until the 1940s, especially since EEG had captured the interest of the scientific world.

## 1.3  Post-War

After World War II, the development of nuclear research gave us safe radioisotopes and laid the foundation for what would eventually become Positron emission tomography (PET).[9] In 1948, Seymour Kety and his colleagues at the University of Pennsylvania and the National Institutes of Health re-sparked interest in the blood flow versus brain function line of questioning by using x-ray images of radiolabeled tissue (also called autoradiography). With it, they were able to visualize blood flow in cats after visual stimulation. Kety's student, Louis Sokoloff, went on to study a longer-lasting radiotracer called DG (carbon-14 deoxyglucose) and eventually synthesized FDG (2-[18F] fluoro-2-deoxy-d-glucose), which is still used in PET today.

As EEG grew in popularity, so did its flaws. In particular, the subpar conductivity of the scalp created distortion and "smearing" of EEG signals, which made it hard to pinpoint where the activity originated. As a result, research into the magnetic properties of the brain captured the interest of the scientific community. However, magnetic signals were extraordinarily weak compared to electric signals, so the development of what became Magnetoencephalography (MEG) required further development within the field of physics.[10,11] More information about the advancement of signal analysis, including the advent of Superconducting Quantum Interference Devices (SQUIDs), can be found in the MEG chapter of the book, chapter 3.

From the beginning of the "digital revolution," which started in the 50s, came unprecedented computational and data handling power. With this came two more revolutionary imaging techniques still in use today.

One of these technologies was computerized tomography (CT), which leveraged both x-rays and computing. The entire technique was nearly single-handedly created by English electrical engineer Godfrey Newbold Hounsfield in the late 1960s. Having been interested in computer design for more than a decade, Hounsfield had the idea of taking several x-ray images of the brain from different angles and reconstructing them with a computer that allowed for previously elusive soft tissue visualizations. The first official CT scanner was built and installed in London, England in 1971, and its first scan was completed in 1972, which revealed a large, circular brain tumor in the subject.[12]

The second of these pivotal inventions, which arrived swiftly after the advent of the CT scan, was that of magnetic resonance imaging (MRI). The technique depended on the concept of nuclear magnetic resonance — that protons moved with an angular momentum or "spin." More details can be found in the MRI section of the book in chapter 4.

In the midst of this exciting era, the Society of Neuroscience was formed in 1969. Their first meeting took place in 1971 in Washington, DC. Before then, neuroscience was a motley collection of separate disciplines. Thus, the society brought together neurologists, anatomists, psychiatrists, and physiologists, creating the interdisciplinary field it is today.[13]

At this point of extensive study into *imaging* the brain, interest in *stimulating* the brain began to gain footing. The use of electrical and magnetic stimulation in medicine dates back to Michael Faraday's findings from the 1830s that outlined the relationships between electrical currents and magnetic flux.[14] In the 1970s, Dr. Anthony T. Barker began experimenting with short-pulsed magnetic fields on human peripheral nerves to eventually develop transcranial magnetic stimulation (TMS) in 1985 in Sheffield, England. After its conception, TMS was primarily used for mood disorders, especially in depressed patients.[15]

In 1973, Belgium scientist Jacques J. Vidal published an integral paper and coined the term "Brain-Computer Interface" (BCI), describing it as "utilizing the brain signals in a man-computer dialogue."[16] The concept gained traction, especially in its projected ability to aid people with motor impairments. The P300 speller, a machine that allowed the spelling of letters and words via Event-Related Potentials (ERPs) with EEG, was described a decade and a half later by Farwell and Donchin and became the most widely-known example of BCI in action.[17]

Near-infrared spectroscopy, which uses wavelengths of 780 nm to 2500 nm, was primarily used in agriculture in the 1960s. However, in the late 70s, non-invasive spectroscopy specialist Frans Jöbsis discovered that these same wavelengths could be used on brain tissue to create high transparency and detect hemoglobin oxygenation. Thus, near-infrared spectroscopy (NIRS) was conceived in 1985 to study newborns and cerebrovascular patients.[18] More details about its conception and early usage can be found in the NIRS section, chapter 5.

## 1.4 The Decade of the Brain and Onwards

The past two to three decades saw exponential growth in neurotechnology. As the 1990s approached, the U.S. Congress designated January 1st, 1990 to be the beginning of the Decade of the Brain (DOB)[19] in an attempt to "enhance public awareness of the benefits to be derived from brain research."[20] Bipartisan in its interest, this period saw an increase in public awareness of brain research and advocacy groups.

By this time, however, the field of neurotechnology, and especially neurostimulation, was under heavy scrutinization and regulation. The Food and Drug Administration (FDA) was often considered a gatekeeper, and the field was constantly being pushed and pulled between the FDA and rapidly developing neurotechnology possibilities. The success of therapeutic neurostimulation was hard to quantify and often dismissed. In the 1980s, however, French scientist Alim-Louis Benabid and his team had the tools and expertise to conduct clinical trials of chronic stimulation as a therapy for Parkinson's Disease (PD). After a few more trials and tribulations, deep brain stimulation (DBS) for tremors and PD symptoms was approved by the FDA in 1997.[21]

With the completion of the Human Genome Project (HGP) in the early 2000s came more insights into the field of neurogenetics, giving neurologists tools to study hereditary psychiatric disorders — especially depression, schizophrenia, Parkinson's, and Alzheimer's disease. 2003 also saw the formation of the Allen Institute for Brain Science, which aimed to map the brain just as HGP had mapped the human genome. Other notable mentions of this decade include the breakthrough of optogenetics by Ed Boyden — the ability to activate neurons via light, intensive research into neuroplasticity, development of neural implants, and a focus on mental illnesses such as bipolar disorder and schizophrenia.

The field transitioned in the 2010s, bringing the lesser-known *International Decade of the Mind*. This initiative brought in Europe and Asia in later years, in an atmosphere where "each nation contributes to the overall scientific effort with its own indigenous scientific expertise."[22] It focused on four broad topics: mental health, research on high-level cognitive functions, education, and computational applications. The United States, on its own, sought more than $4 billion to fund this new undertaking. Here the field experienced a shift in its study. Whereas areas like motor control and perception were studied extensively in the years before, scientists started to focus on "higher-level" functions such as memory, cognition, and emotions. The Brain Research through Advancing Innovative Neurotechnologies® (BRAIN) initiative was also launched in 2013, aiming to map the entire brain at the level of individual cells.

## 1.5   Neurotechnology Today

Neuroscience and neurotechnology have come a long way since their early roots and are now forging ahead with fervor and funding like never before. In the last decade, we've seen a rise in commercial and academic interest in the field and increased international governmental interest.

The next few sections of the book will feature government brain initiatives, emerging startups, and innovative labs.

# Endnotes

1. Zola-Morgan, Stuart. "Localization of brain function: The legacy of Franz Joseph Gall (1758-1828)." *Annual review of neuroscience* 18, no. 1 (1995): 359-383.

2. Kirkpatrick, Douglas B. "The first primary brain-tumor operation." *Journal of neurosurgery* 61, no. 5 (1984): 809-813.

3. Haas, Lindsay F. "Hans berger (1873–1941), richard caton (1842–1926), and electroencephalography." *Journal of Neurology, Neurosurgery & Psychiatry* 74, no. 1 (2003): 9-9.

4. Caton, Richard. "Electrical currents of the brain." *The Journal of Nervous and Mental Disease* 2, no. 4 (1875): 610.

5. Berger, H. "Uber das elektroenkephalogramm des menschen (On the Encephalogram of Man)." *Arch Psychiatrics* 101 (1931): 452-459.

6. La Vaque, T. J. "The history of EEG hans berger: psychophysiologist. A historical vignette." *Journal of Neurotherapy* 3, no. 2 (1999): 1-9.

7. Adrian, Edgar Douglas, and Brian HC Matthews. "The Berger rhythm: potential changes from the occipital lobes in man." *Brain* 57, no. 4 (1934): 355-385.

8. Gibbs, Frederic A., William G. Lennox, and Erna L. Gibbs. "The cortical frequency spectrum in epilepsy." *Archives of Neurology & Psychiatry* 46, no. 4 (1941): 613-620.

9. Portnow, Leah H., David E. Vaillancourt, and Michael S. Okun. "The history of cerebral PET scanning: from physiology to cutting-edge technology." *Neurology* 80, no. 10 (2013): 952-956.

10. Cohen, David. "Magnetoencephalography: detection of the brain's electrical activity with a superconducting magnetometer." *Science* 175, no. 4022 (1972): 664-666.

11. Noohi, Sima, and Susan Amirsalari. "History, studies and specific uses of repetitive transcranial magnetic stimulation (rTMS) in treating epilepsy." *Iranian journal of child neurology* 10, no. 1 (2016): 1.

12. Mould, Richard Francis. *A century of X-rays and radioactivity in medicine: with emphasis on photographic records of the early years.* CRC Press, 1993.

13. Raichle, Marcus E. "A brief history of human brain mapping." *Trends in neurosciences* 32, no. 2 (2009): 118-126.

14. Al-Khalili, Jim. "The birth of the electric machines: a commentary on Faraday (1832) 'Experimental researches in electricity'." *Philosophical Transactions of the Royal Society A: Mathematical, Physical and Engineering Sciences* 373, no. 2039 (2015): 20140208.

15. Fitzgerald, Paul B., and Z. Jeff Daskalakis. "The history of TMS and rTMS treatment of depression." In *Repetitive transcranial magnetic stimulation treatment for depressive disorders*, pp. 7-12. Springer, Berlin, Heidelberg, 2013.

16. Lotte, Fabien, Chang S. Nam, and Anton Nijholt. *"Introduction: Evolution of Brain-Computer Interfaces."* (2018).

17. Kübler, Andrea. "The history of BCI: From a vision for the future to real support for personhood in people with locked-in syndrome." *Neuroethics* (2019): 1-18.

18. Ferrari, Marco, and Valentina Quaresima. "A brief review on the history of human functional near-infrared spectroscopy (fNIRS) development and fields of application." *Neuroimage* 63, no. 2 (2012): 921-935.

19. Tandon, P. N. "The decade of the brain: a brief review." *Neurol India* 48, no. 3 (2000): 199-207.

20. Jones, Edward G., and Lorne M. Mendell. "Assessing the decade of the brain." *Science* 284, no. 5415 (1999): 739-740.

21. Gardner, John. "A history of deep brain stimulation: Technological innovation and the role of clinical assessment tools." *Social Studies of Science* 43, no. 5 (2013): 707-728.

22. Olds, James L. "For an international decade of the mind." *The Malaysian journal of medical sciences: MJMS* 18.2 (2011): 1.

# 2
# Electroencephalography (EEG)

**Sheida Rabipour, PhD**
*Dr. Sheida Rabipour received her Bachelor and Master of Science degrees in Neuroscience from McGill University, and her PhD in Experimental Psychology from the University of Ottawa. She then completed a post-doctoral fellowship at the Douglas Hospital Research Centre, affiliated with McGill University. Her research examines factors that influence and enhance cognitive function, as well as applied neuromodulation interventions that may help optimize brain function throughout life. Her work, cited more than 500 times to date, has been supported by funding from agencies such as the Natural Sciences and Engineering Research Council of Canada, the Fonds de Recherche Québec - Santé, and the Centre for Research on Brain, Language, and Music. Dr. Rabipour is also passionate about science communication and community outreach. Her first popular science book, How (Not) To Train The Brain, was published in 2019 by Oxford University Press.*

**Paniz Tavakoli, PhD**
*Dr. Paniz Tavakoli recieved her PhD in Experimental Psychology from the University of Ottawa. She then completed postdoctoral fellowships at both the Children's Hospital of Eastern Ontario (CHEO) and McMaster University. Her research utilizes event-related potentials (ERPs) to study impairments of cognitive functioning in a variety of clinical populations, including depression, suicide, concussion, and coma. Her work has been supported by funding from various agencies such as the Natural Science and Engineering Research Council of Canada, Canadian Institute of Health Research, and the McMaster University Arts Research Board.*

## 2.1 Introduction

### 2.1.1 What is EEG?

Digital technology has increased and simplified our ability to study the living brain in action using affordable and efficient tools. Electroencephalography (EEG) is one noninvasive technique used to visualize electrical brain activity. Advanced analytic methods enable researchers and clinicians to translate these electrical signals into meaningful information about different brain states, helping monitor, diagnose, and treat conditions of the human brain and body. This chapter explores the origins of EEG and provides a brief overview of use cases, application procedures, and some advantages and disadvantages of the technique.

## 2.2 Brief History of EEG

### 2.2.1 First Release and Inventors

German physiologist and psychiatrist Hans Berger (1873-1941) was the first to record the electrical activity of the human brain using EEG in the 1920s. Over the next decade, Berger began using more powerful and sophisticated methods allowing for more precise and sensitive recordings of electrical signals. His first report of the human EEG signal was published in 1929.[1]

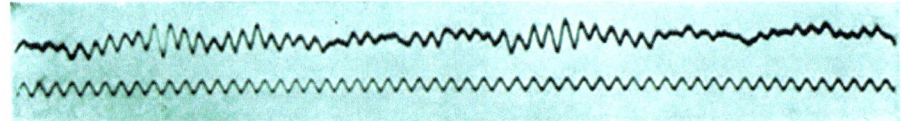

Figure 2.1 Hans Berger's first EEG in 1924 (Wikipedia Commons).

Neurophysiologists of the era assumed that the rhythmic "brain waves" Berger observed were a result of noise or artifact and did not truly reflect brain activity. Several years later, however, numerous other physiologists began to observe the human EEG signal and confirmed the details of Berger's studies. These corroborations led to the acceptance of EEG as a real phenomenon. The term *electroencephalogram* was hence used to refer to the measure (-gram) of the electrical (electro-) activity of the human brain (encephalon).

## 2.3 How It Works

### 2.3.1 Precision and Accuracy

Brain cells (neurons) communicate by sending nerve impulses from one cell to another to transfer messages around the brain and the body. This communication results in changes in the electrical charge of the brain cells. These brain cells use electrical signals to communicate and emit electricity as a result. Electrodes placed on the head pick up this electrical activity, sometimes called brain waves, due to the signal's rhythmic and periodic nature. However, scalp electrodes cannot detect electrical signals from individual neurons because the electrical charge they produce is far too small. Instead, EEG records the electrical activity from thousands of brain cells firing in unison within a particular area of the brain. Because brain waves are generated and propagated in biological tissue, the delay between electrical activity in the brain and potentials recorded at the scalp is negligible — hence the high temporal precision of the technique. Notably, EEG indicates the presence or absence of brain activity in a general brain region; interpretation of what the signal reflects is up to specialists to determine.

Neuronal activity produces a flow of current in localized regions. These localized current flows, termed local field potentials, are generated by groups of brain cells that fire synchronously. The electrical activity of local field potentials is *oscillatory*, often (although not always) following a sine-wave-like pattern at frequencies typically ranging from approximately 0.01-100 Hz in humans and may contribute to communication between cells within the brain.

The parameters of brain waves (e.g., their shape, amplitude, frequency of oscillation, alignment with other brain waves) can provide information about a person's wakefulness, arousal, health, and chemical and cognitive processes.[2] In healthy adults, the amplitudes and frequencies of such signals change from one state to another such as wakefulness and sleep. The characteristics of the waves also change with age and in clinical conditions. There are five canonical brain waves, distinguished by their frequency ranges and the processes with which they are commonly associated (Table 1) Mu waves, typically observed in the alpha/beta frequency range, are associated with motion-related activity.

Table 2.1 The Five Canonical Brain Waves.

| Symbol — Name | Wave Range | Processes |
| --- | --- | --- |
| δ — delta | <4Hz | commonly associated with deep sleep and comatose states[4] |
| Θ — theta | 4-8Hz | the most common waves during sleep and certain memory processes[5] |
| A — alpha | 8-13 Hz | commonly associated with drowsiness, sleep onset, attention, memory, and visual processes[6] |
| B — beta | 13-30Hz | associated with cognitive function often requiring rigorous mental activity and concentration[7] |
| Y — gamma | 30-80Hz | associated with attention processes and heightened states of perception[8] |

The traveling current propagated by brain cells generates an electrical field over the scalp. EEG systems measure the voltage difference between at least two different locations, captured by a minimum of two scalp sensors or "electrodes." Specifically, EEG measures currents that flow during the excitation of a layer of brain cells called pyramidal neurons, located on the brain's surface (the cerebral cortex). The captured current is generated within branch-like structures of a neuron called dendrites. Only large populations of active neurons can generate sufficient electrical activity to be recordable at the scalp surface. Thus, despite being generated by a large number of cells, the electrical signals detected by scalp electrodes are relatively weak and must be massively amplified before being visualized as a waveform on the computer screen.

EEG is a relative measure. In other words, the voltage measured by EEG is always compared to a reference point. Ideally, the reference point should be a location where no activity of interest is expected to occur (i.e., a "neutral" location). Choosing the best reference point depends on your research question, but common references include mastoids, earlobes, nose, or an average of all electrode sites.[4] Historically, when the voltage registered at a particular electrode site is more positive than the reference, the EEG waveform points *downwards* to indicate a relative *positivity* and vice-versa. More recently, many researchers have opted to shift the direction of positivity upwards and negativity downwards, following mathematical convention. However, because no prevailing convention or rule currently exists, it is important to verify axis labels when viewing EEG graphs.

EEG activity can be "evoked," "induced," or "spontaneous." *Evoked* potentials refer to electrical currents generated in response to a stimulus and are therefore synchronized to the time of its emergence. Importantly, evoked potentials can be triggered by external events (i.e., exogenous) such as hearing a tone or seeing an image, or by internal processes (i.e., endogenous) such as generating a motor response. Conversely, *induced* potentials are related, but not time-locked, to a slowly changing input. In other words, induced potentials vary over time and reflect general cognitive states or changes in functional neural processes. Finally, spontaneous or ongoing potentials reflect electrical brain activity with no temporal relationship to an external event.

## 2.3.2 Event-Related Potentials (ERPs)

As the EEG procedure is noninvasive and painless, it is widely used to study the brain organization of cognitive processes such as perception, memory, attention, language, and emotion in neurotypical adults and children. For this purpose, one of the most useful applications of EEG recording is the event-related potential (ERP) technique.

ERPs are significant voltage fluctuations resulting from evoked neural activity. They represent the time-locked electrical activity of the brain in response to external stimulation (e.g., visual, auditory, tactile stimulation) or internal psychological events (e.g., memory, decision-making, etc.):[5] in other words, they represent the EEG signal generated, for example, by viewing an image or hearing a sound. ERPs consist of a series of positive and negative-going deflections or "components," reflecting different hypothetical stages of cognitive processing and can be classified as either "exogenous" or "endogenous," as described in the previous section.[6]

A major advantage of ERPs is that they provide a measure of ongoing information processing in the brain. This level of nuance is not possible through traditional performance measures such as the speed and accuracy of behavioral responding.

The ability to measure ongoing processes permits in-depth analysis of the "stages" of processing affected by a given experimental manipulation.[7] Secondly, ERPs can study cognitive processes with very high temporal resolution (millisecond precision) not feasible with other neuroimaging techniques such as functional magnetic resonance imaging (fMRI). Mental operations, such as those involved in perception, selective attention, language processing, and memory, proceed over time ranges in the order of tens of milliseconds. Whereas positron emission tomography (PET) and fMRI can localize regions of activation during a given mental task, ERPs can help define the time course of these activations. For this reason, ERPs are a suitable methodology for studying the aspects of cognitive processes in both typical and atypical development (e.g., in neurological or psychiatric disorders).

### 2.3.3 Steady-State Visual Evoked Potential (SSVEP)

The repetitive presentation of a stimulus generates a so-called steady-state response. Steady-state visual evoked potential (SSVEP) responses occur when oscillatory brain activity becomes linked or "entrained" to the frequency of a rhythmically presented visual stimulus (e.g., while observing a flickering light source). In other words, the frequency at which the stimulus appears determines the frequency of the SSVEP response.

First discovered in the 1930s and further developed in the 1960s, SSVEPs can be elicited at a wide range of frequencies, from as low as 1Hz to as high as 100Hz. As stimulus frequencies increase, the intervals at which each stimulus is presented decrease; at a certain point, the time interval between stimulus presentations becomes shorter than the time it takes to generate the SSVEP response. This interval decrease results in an overlap between the SSVEP and an individual stimulus, leading to a general lowering of SSVEP amplitude. The stimulation frequency at which one can elicit the largest SSVEP appears to be a function of the stimulus type and the recording site. For example, flickering lights appear to elicit the strongest SSVEP at 10Hz.[8]

SSVEP responses are useful for both the study and potential modulation of brain function and have several advantages. Because the SSVEP can occur in the absence of observed behavior, the response can help evaluate cognitive processes in populations that are typically difficult to study, including infants and clinical populations. More recently, SSVEP responses have been used in brain-computer interfaces to aid in communication with relatively high accuracy.

### 2.3.4 Invasiveness

Because EEG measures brain activity *noninvasively* from the scalp's surface, patients, including typically developing children and adults, can receive repeated applications with virtually no risk. EEG has been used in clinical and research settings for a number of purposes — from detecting signs of brain-based disorders (e.g., epilepsy, sleep disorders) to communicating and controlling objects with the mind. However, the downside of surface recording is that the signal must travel through different levels of brain tissue and bone before reaching the scalp. Once at the surface, EEG signals are also prone to the influence of the scalp's condition (e.g., oiliness, dryness, sensitivity, presence of hair product, etc.). These factors create the need for specific considerations in the design and application of EEG tools, as well as the interpretation of signals.

## 2.4 Properties

### 2.4.1 Temporal and Spatial Resolution

Brain imaging techniques are generally classified into two categories: metabolic (PET, fMRI, NIRs) and electrophysiological (MEG, EEG). Metabolic techniques are sensitive to changes in oxygenated blood flow and provide high spatial resolution (i.e., accuracy in space). However, as changes in blood flow operate in time ranges of several seconds, these techniques provide poor temporal resolution (i.e., accuracy in time).

Electrophysiological techniques, on the other hand, have excellent temporal resolution, occurring at the millisecond (ms) scale (see Brule et al., [2015] for a review.[9]). However, at a scale of approximately 10cm2, EEG provides less spatial resolution compared to MEG, MRI, and PET.[10] The high temporal resolution of EEG makes it a very useful tool for understanding the foundations of cognitive functions, which occur in fractions of a second. By combining these techniques (e.g., EEG-MRI), researchers can better glean the spatial and temporal course of mental activity.[10]

### 2.4.2 Setup Requirements

EEG recordings are ideal for studying events with high temporal precision. However, the signals are prone to noise from the environment. These can include electrical outlets, light fixtures, and other equipment. Moreover, sound and other distractors from the surrounding areas may interfere with a participant's performance and affect the integrity of collected data.

## 2.5 Hardware Properties

This section describes the hardware required to record EEG signals. The study of EEG signals can be divided into two separate systems for data acquisition and data analysis.

The data acquisition system involves:

1. Electrodes that record electrical brain activity through the surface of the scalp.
2. Amplifiers to view and interpret the signal.
3. A computer that integrates and projects the amplified signal captured by the electrodes.

## 2.5.1 Electrodes

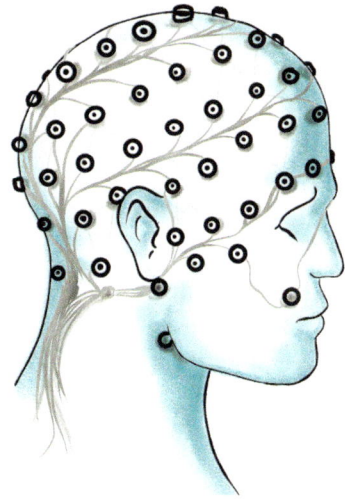

Figure 2.2 Subject ready for EEG recording at the phonetics lab, Stockholm U.

Electrodes are placed on the scalp at specific positions to obtain EEG signals from various localized sources of the brain. The placement of these electrodes on the scalp is called the "montage." A standardized placement and naming system called the "10-20 system" was developed in the early days of EEG recordings.[12] This conventionally used montage divides the head into proportional distances from prominent skull landmarks such as the nasion (i.e., the topmost end of the nasal bone or bridge of the nose), the inion (i.e., the outward projection at the base of the skull), and the middle of the two ears (i.e., the pre-auricular points) to provide adequate coverage of all regions of the brain. The label "10-20" refers to the proportional distances between electrodes relative to these landmark points. For example, the electrode closest to the inion along the center of the scalp, electrode Oz, is located 10% of the distance from the inion to the nasion at the base of the skull. The next electrode, toward the nasion along the center, is Pz and is set 20% anterior to Oz. Additional electrodes are placed in incremental distances of 20% from each other, as shown in Figure 2.3.

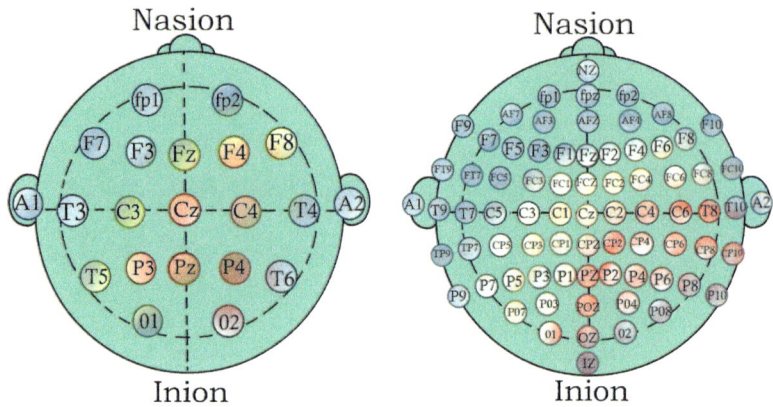

**Figure 2.3** The international a) 10-20 and b) 10-10 systems of electrode.

Electrode letters correspond to the major regions of the brain (FP = Frontal Polar, F=Frontal, C= Central, P = Parietal, T=Temporal, O=Occipital) followed by a number indicating the distance from the midline (designated by "z") and whether the electrode is over the left (odd numbers) or right (even numbers) hemisphere. For example, electrode position F7 is located over the left frontal region, more lateral (or farther) from the midline than electrode F3.

The original 10-20 system did not allow for electrodes that were closely spaced for denser coverage across the skull. Modified systems have since emerged to permit intermediate positions providing greater coverage (American Electroencephalographic Society, 1991). The 10-10 system is an example of such modified positioning, accommodating twice the number of electrodes as the 10-20 system.

### 2.5.1.1 Wet vs. Dry Electrodes

Wet electrodes are currently the gold standard of EEG scalp electrodes. These types of electrodes require the application of a conductive substance (e.g., electrolyte gel or paste) in the space between the electrodes and the scalp, typically secured using a tight-fitting elastic cap. Wet electrodes have the advantage of providing higher quality data but require longer setup times, are less comfortable for participants (e.g., discomfort during application and requirement to wash hair afterward), and can dry out after prolonged testing periods leading to increased impedance and reduced signal quality.

With rapid setup and no cleanup, dry electrodes have the advantage of comfort and practicality. These electrodes can be classified by the way they contact the scalp and include spiky, non-contact or capacitive, and other heterogeneous types of electrodes.[13] Spiky electrodes, as the name implies, contact (or sometimes pierce) the scalp with an array of small spikes at the nanometer, micrometer, or millimeter scale. Non-contact or capacitive electrodes avoid physical scalp contact altogether, leading to large impedances and low signals that greatly limit their usefulness for most EEG applications. Perhaps most commonly, dry electrodes leverage a combination of flexible material, a stable structure, dry conductive surface (e.g., ink coating or conductive metal), and a sophisticated algorithm to extract the EEG signal and separate it from biological and environmental noise.

### 2.5.1.2 Active vs. Passive Electrodes

Active electrodes enable amplification of the EEG signal directly at the scalp before reaching the amplifiers. This pre-amplified signal decreases the influence of environmental noise (e.g., from electrical outlets or appliances in the recording space). Conversely, passive electrodes involve distal amplification that occurs away from the scalp surface. Typically, passive electrodes connect to the amplifiers through long cables that can carry environmental noise. Therefore, minimizing electrode impedance (resistance within the electrical current) is particularly important for passive systems. Traditionally, EEG recordings have relied on passive electrodes, which are more affordable than active systems. However, active electrodes are becoming increasingly prevalent due to their ability to deliver superior signal quality.

## 2.5.2 Amplifiers

The EEG signal is minuscule, measured in units such as millivolts (mV), microvolts (μV), or nanovolts (nV). For this reason, the EEG signal must be amplified and converted to a digital signal that can be processed and viewed on a computer display. However, amplifiers must provide amplification selective to the physiological signal, reject noise and interference signals, and guarantee protection from damages through voltage and current surges for both patients and electronic equipment.

## 2.5.3 Recording computer

The EEG recording computer can be any laptop or desktop, provided it has sufficient power and processing speed to keep up with the vast amount of incoming data points from the amplifier. Most advanced EEG laboratories often have 2-3 computers for the EEG recording. One computer presents stimulation (if required for the experiment), usually a visual or auditory task. A second computer then records the EEG signal. Finaly, a third computer may be used to provide real-time information about the performance of the individual on task. When multiple computers are used, it is very important that the computers communicate with each other.

Most importantly, the EEG computer must know what stimuli are being presented and at precisely what moment they occur. This communication is often done in real-time through a cable connection between computers and event codes (or triggers) sent from one computer to the next. Alternatively, it is also possible to synchronize the stimuli and EEG recordings using time stamps.

Data recording software is used to store the incoming EEG signals onto the computer. One of the limitations of EEG recordings is due to high storage requirements. For example, a typical 1-hour recording using a dozen electrodes placed on the scalp occupies around 200 MB of the memory.

## 2.6 Ready to Find Meaning: Software & Analysis Options

Analysis of EEG signals requires specialized software to preprocess the raw signal. EEG analysis software can be categorized as open-source vs. proprietary/commercial. Commercial software offers different general-purpose options for data quantification. Some researchers, however, choose to write their own ERP analysis program, often using open-source software. These have the obvious advantage of being low cost and provide many of the same quantification procedures available in the commercial systems, albeit perhaps not as "user friendly" or as readily comparable to other EEG recordings if the analyses are fundamentally different from standard methods. Regardless of the software, the same preprocessing steps apply to most analysis approaches.

### 2.6.1 Filtering

EEG signals are noisy. Eliminating sources of noise when possible — using a shielded room that blocks external electromagnetic signals (e.g., a Faraday cage), minimizing motion, keeping the testing environment cool and dry to minimize skin potentials, etc. — is the best way to maximize the EEG signal.[14] However, when used properly, filtering raw EEG data improves the signal-to-noise ratio by removing frequency bands that are not of interest and increases the interpretability of data.

Filtering also bears a cost. By definition, each added filter distorts the signal and, if applied inappropriately, can lead to severe misinterpretation of the data.[15] To avoid excessively biasing raw data, filters must be used carefully and adjusted based on the specific parameters of a particular experimental setup.

### 2.6.2 Data Inspection & Artifacts

Artifacts refer to interference in a signal due to essential procedural requirements (e.g., study setup, location, sample characteristics) and not due to a naturally occurring phenomenon. In the context of EEG, artifacts refer to signals that are present in the electrical recording but unrelated to brain activity. Sources of noise can introduce artifacts into the EEG signal. For example, an individual's blood pressure, heart rate, blinks, and other eye movements, and muscle tension (especially in the jaw) are common causes of distortion to EEG data. Correcting for these artifacts is, therefore, necessary to ensure the interpretability of the signal.

Inspection of EEG data is a critical step to ensure that unwanted artifacts or segments of noisy data are eliminated from analyses. Artifacts can be corrected to preserve trials or rejected to remove noisy segments from the data completely. Commonly occurring artifacts such as those emerging from eye blinks, for example, can be isolated and corrected using algorithms that separate the complex, noisy signal into its component parts (e.g., using independent component analysis). Other artifacts, such as motion or other muscle spasms (e.g., during a cough or sneeze), are more sporadic and difficult to anticipate. For such sources of noise, rejection is best.

EEG analysis software typically has automated artifact rejection tools. Such tools generally offer the option of manually rejecting artifacts or noisy data segments or automating the process by simply selecting an upper and lower threshold value. Optimal parameters for rejection are crucial: if a voltage threshold is too high, the risk of including noisy trials and obtaining false positives increases, but if the voltage threshold is too low, there is a risk of losing good data and inducing false negatives.

### 2.6.3 Analyzing EEG Data

Once raw data have been preprocessed, it is time to select an appropriate analytic method to help glean insights of interest. Aside from clinician-based judgment and diagnosis of brain-based conditions, EEG analyses largely rely on quantifying the digitally recorded EEG waveform into mathematical parameters, including voltage, amplitude, and frequency. Broadly, these analyses are termed quantitative EEG (QEEG). QEEG may involve identifying particular waveform components or patterns, or correlating specific EEG parameters to observed behavior compared to population norms. QEEG-based analyses can evaluate the frequencies at which EEG varies most commonly within the time frame of interest (i.e., power spectral density), the time at which specific frequency waves are present, or the evolution of frequency power over time (i.e., wavelet analysis). The appropriate analytic method depends on the nature of the information desired and should be carefully selected before proceeding with the analysis.

## 2.7 Notable Uses

### 2.7.1 EEG Biofeedback

EEG biofeedback or "neurofeedback" is a method to self-regulate one's brain activity in real-time, to alter the underlying neural mechanisms of cognition and behavior. This technique, used in research and clinical contexts since the 1960s, converts EEG signals into visual or audio representations (e.g., colored bars or tones) that users can try to control and change voluntarily.[16] On the user end, neurofeedback converts raw EEG data into information that users can easily understand, showing moment-to-moment changes in EEG. Neurofeedback lies on the theoretical premise that, with proper feedback from this moment-to-moment brain wave activity, users can learn to alter and control electrical brain wave patterns to a significant degree and thereby improve behaviors that draw on such brain activity.

Neurofeedback is promising yet engulfed in controversy. The approach has been increasingly advertised and used for cognitive enhancement in the healthy as well as a therapeutic tool for clinical conditions. Most commonly, neurofeedback is applied to aid with symptoms of a brain-based condition (e.g., for impulse-control impairments such as ADHD). However, research on the effectiveness of neurofeedback remains mixed. On the one hand, studies have shown that neurofeedback can help treat conditions such as ADHD, seizure disorders, anxiety, and related conditions (e.g., obsessive-compulsive disorder, generalized anxiety disorder, post-traumatic stress disorder, phobias), depression, reading disabilities, and substance use disorders. On the other hand, criticisms of the technique point out important flaws in studies on which the field is largely based, including failure to account for the effects of repeated exposure, practice, or the passing of time, and lack of meaningful improvements in comparison to fake ("sham") feedback protocols.[17] These studies suggest that neurofeedback responses may result from a placebo effect rather than mechanisms specific to the technique; if this is accurate, some have suggested using neurofeedback as a non-deceptive suggestion-based therapy.[18,19]

In response to the controversies surrounding neurofeedback mechanisms and efficacy, a team of scientists published the Consensus on the Reporting and Experimental Design of Clinical and Cognitive-Behavioural Neurofeedback Studies.[20] The checklist provided in this Consensus aims to improve the scientific rigor and reporting of neurofeedback studies to determine the specific and non-specific effects of such therapy.

### 2.7.2 EEG & Brain-Computer Interfaces

Brain-computer interfaces (BCIs) acquire brain signals through EEG, analyze them, and translate them into commands relayed to output devices that carry out desired actions. Researchers and professionals use BCI primarily to replace or restore useful functions to people affected by neuromuscular disorders such as ALS, cerebral palsy, stroke, or spinal cord injury. BCI technology is the focus of a rapidly growing research and development enterprise that is exciting to scientists, engineers, clinicians, and the general public. BCI systems use signal-acquisition hardware that is portable, safe, and able to function in all environments. EEG-based BCI systems have the added advantage of being noninvasive, although using scalp-based systems increases noise in the signal and can result in loss of data from the brain to the EEG sensor. Analysis methods, including the classification of EEG signals into interpretable commands, are becoming increasingly accurate and efficient. Among many promising applications is the use of BCI in people with paralysis or disabilities to help control devices (e.g., wheelchairs, digital cursors, etc.) and communicate through typed speech.

## 2.8 Logistics

### 2.8.1 How Much Does It Cost?

Research-grade EEG devices are expensive. A full system is typically on the scale of tens of thousands of dollars, with variations depending on the company and devices desired. Access to analytic software, software updates, and client consulting services are typically included. Despite the seemingly steep cost, EEG is relatively cheap and low-maintenance compared to other research-grade imaging devices, which may require several millions of dollars to set up and maintain (e.g., MRI). Research-grade devices are built for in-lab use to address the needs of researchers. These devices primarily target scientific laboratories and typically focus on technical parameters and reliability.

Consumer-grade EEG devices are much less expensive. Such devices typically offer fewer recording options (e.g., fewer recording channels), sometimes with less control over collected data. Although consumer-grade EEG devices decrease the flexibility of possible recording parameters, they are typically less bulky and transportable, permitting the collection of data in real-world settings. However, ethical issues, as well as those of privacy, become prominent in the context of consumer devices. Because these devices target individual consumers rather than research laboratories and academic institutions, companies selling consumer-grade EEG systems often integrate web or mobile applications. These companies also make claims surrounding the systems' ability to improve concentration, relaxation, meditation, sleep, and other medical benefits, touting evidence directly or indirectly tied to their product.[21] Importantly, many direct-to-consumer EEG companies lack readily available validation of their recording systems.[22]

## 2.8.2 Accessibility for researchers

One notable problem with commercial software is that purchased packages do not always provide the tools researchers may need for their specific research questions. A possible compromise in such a situation would be for researchers to write their own software using systems designed for numerical processing. MATLAB is one such system. MATLAB software is designed specifically for the types of mathematical computations involved in EEG analysis. There are currently three open-source libraries developed within MATLAB that allow for EEG analysis, EEGLAB, BrainStorm, and Fieldtrip.[23-25] Aside from MATLAB — itself a proprietary software and, therefore, not accessible to all users — several open-source platforms have emerged to enable free, customizable, and shareable analysis options. Notable examples include Open BCI,[26] which sells low-cost devices and freely available software, and the Python MNE platform.[27] Both have garnered a sizeable user community, providing analysis scripts as well as support. The main limitation for creating fully customized solutions is that users must know how to write and implement code, at least to some extent, in the programming language selected.

## 2.8.3 Limitations

Although extremely insightful when used appropriately, EEG is not suitable in all cases. In contrast to its excellent temporal resolution, EEG is less effective when seeking high spatial resolution, particularly true of montages involving fewer electrodes, providing only a general indication of where a signal was recorded. Notably, even in high-density EEG montages, the precision of recording location does not necessarily provide accurate information regarding the signal's origin. For example, brain activity generated from deep brain locations may relay to the scalp, only then recorded by EEG electrodes.

Similarly, EEG is ill-suited to detect brain activity on smaller, "mesoscopic" scales (e.g., at the level of individual neurons or small clusters of neurons). EEG records electrical brain activity but cannot capture signals from chemical interactions or hemodynamic responses. However, EEG can be combined with other techniques such as fMRI, optical imaging, single-unit recordings, or multi-electrode arrays to provide greater insights into the nature and precision of brain activity. Practical limitations also present challenges to EEG use. For example, surface electrical activity becomes increasingly noisy with increasing age and in clinical conditions, making it more difficult to collect "clean" data and accurately interpret the signal. Skin quality (e.g., oiliness, dryness, presence of scabs or irritation, etc.) may make it difficult or impossible to record from a particular region. Moreover, although EEG is a relatively safe and painless procedure, differences in scalp sensitivity or motion control (e.g., in children or people with psychiatric or neurological conditions) may hinder the ability to perform adequate setup or signal de-noising.

## 2.9 Conclusion

The brain generates spontaneous rhythmic activity and more refined patterns of activation in relation to events in the internal or external environment. EEG signals provide a very useful tool in both scientific and clinical applications. The clinical utility of EEG spans a wide variety of neurological and psychological disorders. Because of its excellent temporal resolution, EEG is particularly well suited to studying biological phenomena that occur over very rapid (i.e., millisecond) periods and applications that rely on real-time user feedback. EEG can be combined with other techniques such as magnetic resonance imaging, optical imaging, single-unit recordings, or multi-electrode arrays to provide greater insights into the nature and precision of brain activity.

Several existing books and reviews describe in greater detail the cases in which EEG measures have provided valuable insight (see, for example, Luck, 2005; Nilad & Malik, 2014; Tong & Thakor, 2009). Here we discuss select cases that have gained increased popularity over the last decades; we encourage readers interested in gleaning insights on EEG use beyond this introduction to pursue more detailed resources.

Recommended additional readings:
- *An Introduction to the Event Related Potential Technique (2nd ed., Luck, 2014)*
- *Rhythms of the Brain (Buzsaki)*

## Endnotes

1. Berger, Hans. "Über das elektroenkephalogramm des menschen." *Archiv für psychiatrie und nervenkrankheiten* 87, no. 1 (1929): 527-570.

2. Cole, Scott R., and Bradley Voytek. "Brain oscillations and the importance of waveform shape." *Trends in cognitive sciences* 21, no. 2 (2017): 137-149.

3. Pfurtscheller, Gert, Ch Neuper, Doris Flotzinger, and Martin Pregenzer. "EEG-based discrimination between imagination of right and left hand movement." *Electroencephalography and clinical Neurophysiology* 103, no. 6 (1997): 642-651.

4. Luck, Steven J. *An introduction to the event-related potential technique*. MIT press, 2014.

5. Picton, Terence W., Otavio G. Lins, and Michael Scherg. "The recording and analysis of event-related potentials." *Handbook of neuropsychology* 10 (1995): 3-3.

6. Sutton, Samuel, Margery Braren, Joseph Zubin, and E. R. John. "Evoked-potential correlates of stimulus uncertainty." *Science* 150, no. 3700 (1965): 1187-1188.

7. Luck, Steven J., Geoffrey F. Woodman, and Edward K. Vogel. "Event-related potential studies of attention." *Trends in cognitive sciences* 4, no. 11 (2000): 432-440.

8. Norcia, Anthony M., L. Gregory Appelbaum, Justin M. Ales, Benoit R.Cottereau, and Bruno Rossion. "The steady-state visual evoked potential in vision research: A review." *Journal of vision* 15, no. 6 (2015): 4-4.

9. Burle, Boris, Laure Spieser, Clémence Roger, Laurence Casini, Thierry Hasbroucq, and Franck Vidal. "Spatial and temporal resolutions of EEG: Is it really black and white? A scalp current density view." *International Journal of Psychophysiology* 97, no. 3 (2015): 210-220.

10. Nunez, P. L., R. B. Silberstein, P. J. Cadusch, R. S. Wijesinghe, A. F. Westdorp, and R. Srinivasan. "A theoretical and experimental study of high resolution EEG based on surface Laplacians and cortical imaging." *Electroencephalography and clinical neurophysiology* 90, no. 1 (1994): 40-57.

11. Nunez, Paul L., and Ramesh Srinivasan. "A theoretical basis for standing and traveling brain waves measured with human EEG with implications for an integrated consciousness." *Clinical neurophysiology* 117, no. 11 (2006): 2424-2435.

12. Jasper, HH. "The ten-twenty electrode system of the international federation." *Electroencephalogr. Clin. Neurophysiol.* 10 (1958): 370-375.

13. Lopez-Gordo, Miguel Angel, Daniel Sanchez-Morillo, and F. Pelayo Valle. "Dry EEG electrodes." *Sensors* 14, no. 7 (2014): 12847-12870.

14. Luck, Steven J. *An introduction to the event-related potential technique.* MI press, 2014.

15. Widmann, Andreas, Erich Schröger, and Burkhard Maess. "Digital filter design for electrophysiological data–a practical approach." *Journal of neuroscience methods* 250 (2015): 34-46.

16. Congedo, Marco, Joel F. Lubar, and David Joffe. "Low-resolution electromagnetic tomography neurofeedback." *IEEE Transactions on Neural Systems and Rehabilitation Engineering* 12, no. 4 (2004): 387-397.

17. Thibault, Robert T., and Amir Raz. "The psychology of neurofeedbackClinical intervention even if applied placebo." *American Psychologist* 72, no. 7 (2017): 679.

18. Thibault, Robert T., Michael Lifshitz, and Amir Raz. "Neurofeedback or neuroplacebo?." *Brain* 140, no. 4 (2017): 862-864.

19. Thibault, Robert T., Samuel Veissière, Jay A. Olson, and Amir Raz. "Treating ADHD with suggestion: neurofeedback and placebo therapeutics." (2018): 707-711.

20. Ros, Tomas, Stefanie Enriquez-Geppert, Vadim Zotev, Kymberly D. Young, Guilherme Wood, Susan Whitfield-Gabrieli, Feng Wan et al. "Consensus on the reporting and experimental design of clinical and cognitive-behavioural neurofeedback studies (CRED-nf checklist)." (2020): 1674-1685.

23. Wexler, Anna, and Robert Thibault. "Mind-reading or misleading? Assessing direct-to-consumer Electroencephalography (EEG) devices marketed for wellness and their ethical and regulatory implications." *Journal of Cognitive Enhancement* 3, no. 1 (2019): 131-137.

24. Wexler, Anna, and Robert Thibault. "Mind-reading or misleading? Assessing direct-to-consumer Electroencephalography (EEG) devices."

25. Delorme, Arnaud, and Scott Makeig. "EEGLAB: an open source toolbox for analysis of single-trial EEG dynamics including independent component analysis." *Journal of neuroscience methods* 134, no. 1 (2004): 9-21.

26. Baillet, Sylvain, Line Garnero, Gildas Marin, and J-P. Hugonin. "Combined MEG and EEG source imaging by minimization of mutual information." *IEEE transactions on biomedical engineering* 46, no. 5 (1999): 522-534.

27. Oostenveld, Robert, et al. "FieldTrip: open source software for advanced analysis of MEG, EEG, and invasive electrophysiological data." *Computational intelligence and neuroscience* 2011 (2011).

28. Tools, OpenBCI-Open Source Biosensing. "Openbci. com. retrieved 24 february 2019." (2019).

29. Gramfort, M. Luessi, E. Larson, D. Engemann, D. Strohmeier, C. Brodbeck, R. Goj, M. Jas, T. Brooks, L. Parkkonen, M. Hämäläinen, MEG and EEG data analysis with MNE-Python, *Frontiers in Neuroscience*, Volume 7, 2013, ISSN 1662-453X, [DOI]

# 3
# Magnetoencephalography (MEG)

**Jed A. Meltzer, Ph.D.**

*Dr. Jed Meltzer is a cognitive neuroscientist studying the basic science of language processing from a neurobiological perspective, with applications to the diagnosis and treatment of acquired neurological disorders such as stroke and dementia. His work has helped to characterize the role of neural oscillations in healthy aging and disease. Affilliations: Canada Research Chair in Inteventional Cognitive Neuroscience; Senior Scientist, Rotman Research Institute of Baycrest; Associate Professor, University of Toronto, Psychology and Speech-Language Pathology; Baycrest Site Director, Canadian Partnership for Stroke Recovery*

## 3.1   Introduction

Synaptic currents within synchronously active neurons produce electric fields large enough to measure from the scalp using electroencephalography (EEG), and at the same time, also produce magnetic fields.[1] Through the technique of magnetoencephalography (MEG), the measurement of these magnetic fields has been an important part of the toolkit of cognitive neuroscience for the past few decades. MEG has achieved greater prominence in recent years, accompanied by technological advancement, improvements in access to the hardware, and the proliferation of techniques and tools (often open access) for the analysis of the rich datasets produced by a modern MEG machine.

Despite this increased prominence, MEG remains one of the more esoteric and unfamiliar neuroimaging methods for many in the neurotechnology space. The combination of high cost, the necessity for specialized resources and expertise, and lack of adaptation into mainstream medical applications has relegated MEG to a few highly specialized research centers. Nonetheless, the use of MEG is ever-increasing, and novel clinical applications are rapidly emerging. Most importantly, MEG can provide unique insights into neural dynamics that can be incorporated into neurotechnology projects even if the final product will not itself involve the measurement of magnetic fields. Therefore, this chapter aims to demystify MEG for the curious neurotechnologist or interested layman. It is assumed that the reader has some basic familiarity with EEG (see Chapter 2), as this chapter will emphasize how MEG is different, along with its relative advantages and disadvantages. Since MEG signals can vary considerably, depending on the design of the machine, some references will be made to specific manufacturers currently in business at the time of this book's publication — the reader should keep in mind that these details may change as the market evolves.

Since neuronal currents generate both EEG and MEG signals at the same time, one may ask — why use MEG at all when EEG is much cheaper and more widely available? There are several advantages to measuring magnetic fields instead of, or in addition to, electrical fields, as we will detail below. However, one particular application drives the vast majority of interest in MEG: source localization of the underlying neural generators within the brain that produce the signal measured from the surface. The reason that MEG is preferred over EEG for the localization of neuronal electrical activity is that the human head is relatively "transparent" to magnetic fields — they pass through from the neurons that generate them to the sensors that detect them without the spatial smearing and distortion that occurs with electric fields, allowing source locations to be estimated with significantly greater accuracy and resolution.

Although there are numerous use cases for sensor-level MEG measurements, in the opinion of this author, MEG without source localization is, basically, a very expensive EEG. With source localization, however, MEG becomes a highly sensitive measurement of neural activity that combines the superb temporal resolution of EEG with reasonable spatial precision approaching (but not quite matching) hemodynamic/metabolic imaging methods such as fMRI and PET.

## 3.2 How It Works

MEG depends fundamentally on obtaining a high-quality measurement of a local magnetic field using a highly sensitive detector.[2] MEG sensors measure the amount of magnetic flux passing through a small loop of wire, referred to as a "pick-up coil." The coil is coupled to a device that produces an output signal proportional to the magnetic flux through the wire loop, and the output device itself may be located a meter or more away from the actual coil. Currently, all commercially available MEG systems are based on a detector known as a Superconducting Quantum Interference Device (SQUID). Based on an electronic component known as a Josephson junction, a SQUID can convert magnetic flux into an output voltage that is subsequently digitized as a waveform similar to that obtained with EEG.

Currently, the SQUID is the only widely available sensor with a sufficiently high signal-to-noise ratio to make MEG practical. Unfortunately, SQUIDs only function at very cold temperatures allowing for superconductivity (<4K), requiring the use of expensive cryogenic equipment based on liquid helium, a non-renewable resource in depleting supply. However, the disadvantages of maintaining a steady helium supply are gradually being overcome as helium recycler systems, alternative cryogenic techniques, and ultimately, alternative sensors that do not require superconductivity come to market.

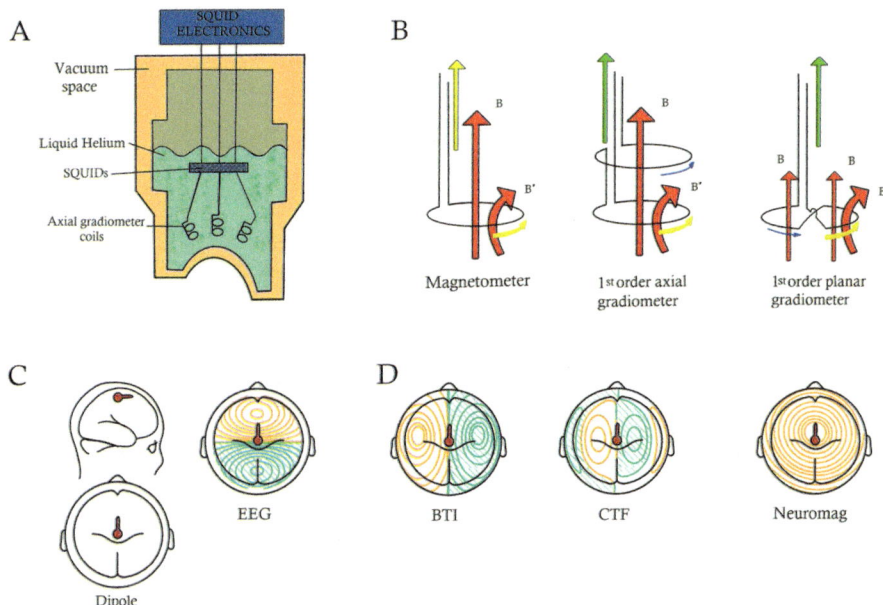

**Figure 3.1** Overview of MEG instrumentation. A) Schematic of the layout of a dewar containing pick-up coils linked to SQUIDS. Three first-order axial gradiometers are shown in a helmet; an actual system would contain 100-300 such sensors arranged around the head. Adapted from (Hari et al., 2018)[3]. B) Illustration of magnetic flux and induced current in three kinds of MEG sensors. In a magnetometer, both an environmental magnetic field B, in which we are not interested, and a neuromagnetic field B' that we want to measure, combine to induce a large current in the wire (yellow arrow). In a 1st order axial gradiometer, both coils pick up the environmental field B to almost the same extent, but the lower coil is far more sensitive to the neuromagnetic field due to its closer proximity, resulting in a larger induced current (yellow arrow) compared to the upper coil (blue arrow). Following the path of the wire through the two loops shows that the current flow in the two coil loops is opposite with respect to the wire path (although identical through space), resulting in cancellation. The final measured current (green arrow) thus reflects primarily the neuromagnetic field. The situation for a 1st order planar gradiometer is similar, such that the measured current reflects the difference between the two loops, which are both the same distance from the scalp. Adapted from (Cheyne and Papanicolaou, 2017)[4]. C) Location of a dipolar current source in the brain and its projected electric field as measured by EEG. Modeled with BESA Simulator. D) Projection of magnetic fields produced by the same dipole, as detected by three MEG systems with different sensor configurations: BTI (magnetometers), CTF (1st-order axial gradiometers), and Neuromag (1st-order planar gradiometers). Note that for the Neuromag system, the field map represents the combination of two sets of planar gradiometers with orthogonal orientations.

MEG sensors come in different configurations, depending on the machine, and the sensitivity profile of different sensor types to a given source generator can vary substantially. Figure 3.1 illustrates the basic layout of a MEG system and the three most common sensor types: a magnetometer (present in BTi and MEGIN systems), that measures magnetic flux through one wire loop, resulting in high sensitivity to deep signal but also to environmental noise, a radial gradiometer (CTF, Compumedics, and Ricoh systems), that measures the difference in flux between two loops placed on top of each other, and a planar gradiometer (MEGIN systems), that measures the difference between two loops placed side to side. Notably, the spatial topography of signals from the same underlying generator detected by these different sensor types varies substantially. Therefore, a reader must keep this in mind when interpreting sensor topographies presented in publications.

The signals recorded from the sensors are usually subjected to additional preprocessing to reduce noise from non-brain sources. The noise reduction is typically built into the system and applied before signals are viewed by the operator, although it can be reversed if necessary. Approaches for noise reduction vary. In most radial gradiometer systems, an additional array of sensors located far from the head measures environmental noise. These reference signals are subtracted from the head sensor signals using sophisticated spatial filtering algorithms, resulting in reduced environmental noise and enhanced sensitivity to sources located right below the head sensors.[5] Alternatively, spatial filtering algorithms can be applied to sensor data to separate activity generated inside the helmet from that generated outside of it, even without reference sensors, as done in the MEGIN system.[6,7]

After these, typically, highly automated preprocessing steps, which require little user input, the resulting signal is quite similar to EEG and can be analyzed in similar ways. As mentioned previously, the main advantage of MEG over EEG is in improved accuracy of source localization. If only a sensor-level analysis is being performed, then there are still some differences between MEG and EEG,[8] but little consensus about which is better (although EEG is certainly more cost-effective in this case). In theory, neural currents generated within a spherical conductor only generate an external magnetic field if they are oriented tangentially to the surface — purely radial sources would generate an EEG signal but no MEG signal. This theory is not completely true in practice because the skull is not a perfect sphere. However, in general, MEG signals are believed to be dominated by neurons oriented tangentially to the skull (i.e., neurons in cortical sulci). An EEG may be equally sensitive to both gyri and sulci. Another difference is that the process of passing through the skull, which is quite non-conductive compared to other tissues, tends to have a low-pass filtering or "smearing" effect on electric fields. Given the transparency of the skull to magnetic fields, the same sources typically produce "tighter" patterns of activity in the sensors, making it easier to infer their sources without formal source localization. Estimating source locations without formal source analysis is easiest for planar gradiometer signals, which produce maximum amplitude directly over a neural source. Radial gradiometers have a more complicated spatial relationship to the sources.

MEG and EEG are, in general, subject to many of the same sources of artifact (e.g., blinks, eye movements, cardiac activity), although there are some differences. MEG is more subject to environmental noise since magnetic fields propagate through space more easily than electrical fields, although this is mitigated by the numerous noise reduction strategies detailed below. On the other hand, MEG may be less sensitive to artifacts generated by scalp muscles,[9,10] which can be an advantage given that muscle activity overlaps in frequency content with neural activity of great interest, particularly in the gamma range (30-100 Hz).[11]

MEG also possesses some practical advantages over EEG. Although it is certainly more expensive and complex to run a MEG facility than an EEG lab, the process of obtaining data from individual subjects tends to be easier with MEG. In addition, no preparation of the scalp is necessary, no gel to conduct electrical current from the scalp to the sensors, no need to abrade the scalp to reduce impedances, and barely any time required to set up. Thus, MEG can be a more practical procedure than EEG for certain patient groups who cannot tolerate long preparations.

The main preparation step is to affix localization coils to the head at key locations to monitor head position within the helmet. Furthermore, since the positions of the sensors are fixed within the helmet, and the head position is measured, there is virtually no uncertainty about the spatial position of the sensors relative to the head, whereas EEG requires an elaborate procedure of digitizing the locations of electrodes to enable detailed source localization.

### 3.2.1 Analysis Strategies

Researchers employ an extremely varied set of analysis techniques for MEG data, resulting in potential confusion for a newcomer to the field. Two studies using the same machine to study the same cognitive task may reach widely different conclusions depending on the analysis used. To simplify this diversity, we would emphasize that analysis approaches differ in two main respects: 1) the aspect of the signal under investigation, and 2) the method of source analysis used. If source analysis worked perfectly, then the results should be identical no matter which method is used, but of course, this is not the case. But in analyzing distinct aspects of the signal, researchers focus on different kinds of neural activity that play different roles, so the diversity of findings is less surprising.

The most traditional signal to analyze is event-related fields (ERFs), the magnetic counterpart to the event-related potentials (ERPs) studied in EEG.

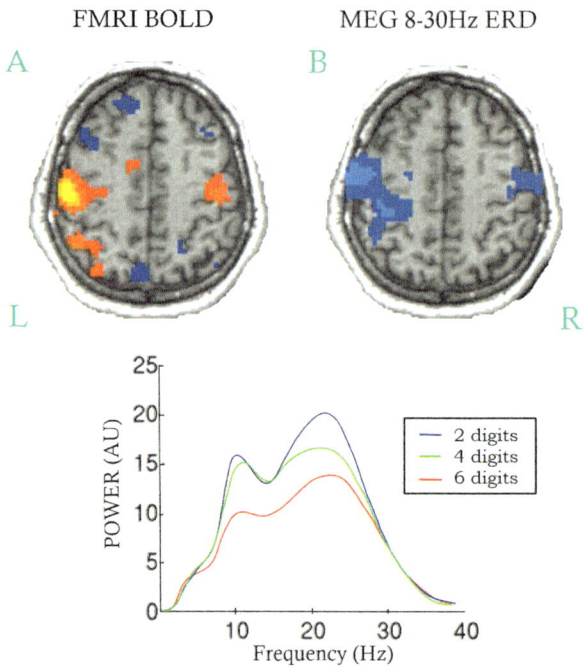

Figure 3.2 Comparison of fMRI BOLD and MEG 8-30 Hz Event-related desynchronization. Both maps represent neural activity during the delay period of a Sternberg working memory task, comparing trials in which participants held 6 digits in memory vs. trials with 2 digits in memory. A) Thresholded difference in fMRI BOLD signal in a single individual. B) Thresholded difference in oscillatory MEG activity in the 8-30 Hz range in the same individual, estimated with the SAM pseudo-t algorithm. C) Power spectrum of activity in a virtual channel estimated in the left precentral gyrus, showing oscillatory power during maintenance of 2, 4, and 6 digits. The negative relationship between 8-30 Hz power and the fMRI BOLD signal (and by inference, neural activity) is apparent. fMRI data adapted from (Meltzer et al., 2007)[12], MEG data from pilot experiments previously unpublished.

Here, time series of magnetic measurements are averaged together across trials, time-locked to an event of interest, resulting in a series of distinct peaks in the signal that may correspond to different spatial generators and cognitive functions. Another form of analysis focuses on increases in the oscillatory power of the MEG signal (termed "event-related synchronization," [ERS]), along with decreases (event-related desynchronization, [ERD]). ERS and ERD occur in distinct frequency bands with conventional definitions, including theta (4-7 Hz), alpha (8-12 Hz), beta (15-30 Hz), and gamma (>40 Hz). Although findings vary across studies, one of the most easily detectable phenomena is ERD in the alpha and beta ranges, which is closely linked to positive BOLD activation in fMRI (see chapter 4) but measurable at greater temporal resolution in MEG (Figure 3.2). Notably, ERFs, ERS, and ERD can be studied either in raw sensor signals or in the source domain after source localization is performed. In addition to these measures that emphasize rapid changes in signal characteristics across time, as seen, for example, in a cognitive task, other measures may emphasize characteristics of spontaneous signals that persist over a long period, such as resting state power spectra.

Besides these techniques that involve activity in a single population of neurons, a wide variety of techniques exist for evaluating connectivity between multiple sensors or sources. Some techniques are based on correlated fluctuations in oscillatory power between signals, and again, these techniques have been most fruitful in the alpha and beta frequency ranges.[13,14,15] Other techniques are based on phase information, detecting consistent leads or lags between multiple signals that suggest information transfer from one region to another. Notably, some of these techniques are more resistant than others to the problem of volume conduction (contamination of multiple signals from a common neural generator, leading to spurious detection of connectivity). Also, some techniques can resolve the direction of information flow, while others are symmetrical measures.[16] Still other techniques consider both amplitude and phase information together, in the form of "cross-frequency coupling," meaning that the phase of one signal (typically lower in frequency) modulates the amplitude of another signal (typically higher). All these measures are far easier to interpret when localized to specific brain areas, making their use in MEG quite popular compared to EEG.

Regarding source localization techniques, three broad families may be identified. The simplest technique is to fit the pattern of magnetic signals across the sensors to a "single equivalent current dipole" located in the brain using a nonlinear optimization process that fits the location, direction, and magnitude of the dipole. Essentially, this method models the magnetic field pattern as arising from an electric current confined to one location in space. It is most applicable to signals that are thought to have a single dominant source, such as an ERF peak or an epileptic spike. A second approach is to compute a distributed linear inverse solution that estimates current magnitude throughout a large grid of points typically spanning the entire brain. This approach may be used on a single pattern of sensor values or on a continuous dataset to yield time series of estimated neural data in source space. A third family of techniques is known as beamforming, spatial filtering, or scanning. Here, a point in the brain is selected, and the algorithm attempts to recover a signal originating at or near this location while canceling out activity rising from anywhere else. This process can then be repeated at multiple points spanning the entire brain, yielding a whole-brain map of activity. However, the estimate at each point is independent of whether other points are also being estimated, unlike a linear inverse solution which depends sensitively on the source space included in the model. All these techniques have pros and cons depending on the goals of an experiment and the nature of the neural activity under investigation.[17,18]

## 3.2.2 Clinical Use

A significant and growing portion of MEG usage is clinical in nature. The number one clinical application is the localization of epileptic foci as a precursor to neurosurgery.[19,20] While the main purpose of such use is to identify epileptogenic tissue for surgical removal, functional mapping of the surrounding tissue for relevance to language and memory functions is an important secondary application that helps the neurosurgeon plan a surgical path that minimizes the chances of postsurgical cognitive deficits.

The use of MEG as a routine part of epilepsy treatment has become established enough that the procedure has been issued reimbursement codes by the American Medical Association and is covered by some health insurance providers in the US and Canada. The clinical use of MEG for other applications is not as well established but is an active topic of research encompassing disorders such as depression, Parkinson's disease, chronic pain, Alzheimer's disease, autism, and stroke. In clinical applications, there is a distinction between direct clinical use, in which a patient might be expected to undergo a MEG procedure as part of their medical treatment, and indirect clinical use, in which MEG may be used in research studies geared toward developing new diagnostics and treatments for neurological and psychiatric conditions. However, patients may not need to undergo MEG themselves to benefit from these advances. Most current topics of clinical MEG research are in the latter category. There is much potential to use the superior localizing power of MEG to identify clinically meaningful signals, determine the optimal parameters for eliciting and quantifying them, and then translate them for use with cheaper and more widely available EEG equipment.

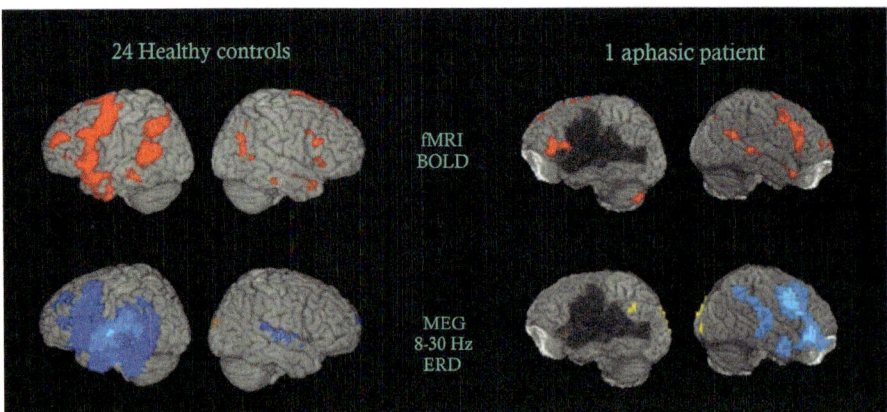

Figure 3.3 Comparison of fMRI BOLD and MEG 8-30 Hz Event-related desynchronization on the group level in healthy volunteers, and on the individual level in a patient with aphasia due to a large left hemisphere stroke. All maps show activity during listening of semantically reversible vs. irreversible sentences. fMRI data adapted from (Meltzer et al., 2010)[21], MEG from (Meltzer and Braun, 2011)[22].

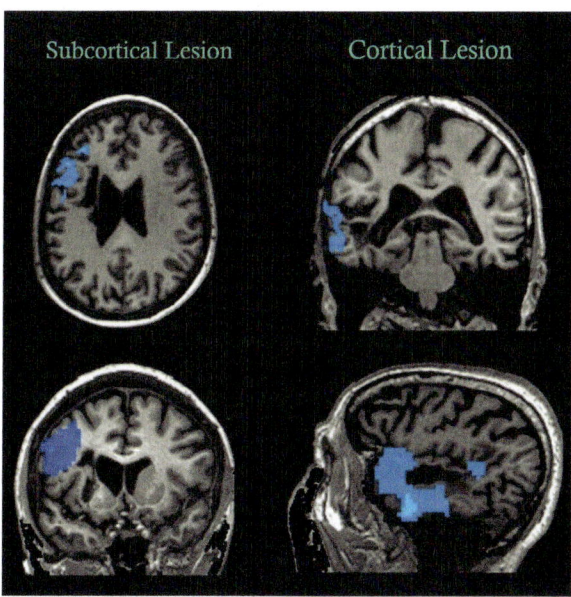

**Figure 3.4** Localization of abnormal spontaneous resting state activity in perilesional cortex. These are thresholded maps identifying voxels in which fine-scale multiscale entropy values are 2 standard deviations below the mean of the entire brain of the individual, superimposed on anatomical MRI. The left column shows a patient with Broca's aphasia caused by a lesion to white matter underlying Broca's area, leaving the cortical tissue structurally intact but functionally compromised. The right column shows dysfunctional activity in cortical tissue surrounding a temporal lobe lesion in a patient with anomic aphasia. Data adapted from (Chu et al., 2015)[23].

To give one example drawn from the author's own work — MEG has proven useful to characterize abnormal electrophysiological activity in patients recovering from aphasia, the loss of speech and language abilities due to a stroke. MEG can reveal changes in recruitment of particular brain regions, such as a shift from left-hemisphere language areas to their right-hemisphere homologs (Figure 3.3), which may be a desirable outcome and a biomarker of successful treatment. Beyond changes in task-induced activity, it is well known that many neurological disorders involve alterations of spontaneous EEG/MEG signals detectable at rest. In stroke and dementia, for example, patients frequently exhibit increased power in delta (1-4 Hz) and theta (4-7 Hz) bands, with decreased power in alpha (8-12 Hz) and beta (15-30 Hz). Although these slowed brainwaves can appear broadly across the scalp in surface-level recordings, the analyses of spontaneous signals in the source space have revealed that slow waves are generated in cortical tissue adjacent to frank structural lesions in disorders associated with focal lesions, including tumor and stroke (Figure 3.4).[24,25,26] In disorders with more diffuse patterns of neuronal injury, the localization of slow waves corresponds to the sites of particular dysfunction. For example, focal MEG slowing is linked to cortical regions suffering from white matter disconnection in traumatic brain injury[27] and areas exhibiting reduced metabolism but not yet atrophy in dementia.[28] Ultimately, the assessment of these focal functional abnormalities may play a role in developing interventions to treat the underlying conditions. Although the anatomical structure of the brain (as assessed by structural MRI) is unlikely to change in response to interventions, the successful treatment of neurological disorders with drugs or brain stimulation is likely to result in changes in electrophysiological signals that could be used as a biomarker to determine the effectiveness of early intervention within an individual.

## 3.3 History

Given that electrical currents have long been known to produce electrical and magnetic fields in the surrounding medium, since the early days of EEG, it was suspected that a magnetic counterpart should also be possible. However, because magnetic fields propagate freely through space without requiring a special conductor (such as the gel and wires involved in EEG), any magnetic detector sensitive enough to pick up brain signals will also be extremely sensitive to noise sources in the environment. Therefore, the development of MEG has been a series of advances in optimizing the signal-to-noise ratio.

MEG was pioneered in the laboratory of David Cohen at MIT in the mid-1960s.[29] Building on observations of magnetic signals generated by the heart (much larger than those coming from the brain),[30] Cohen built the first magnetically shielded room designed to block external noise. He recorded magnetic signals using a room-temperature detector consisting of thousands of turns of copper wire. Because the noise of this detector was still much larger than the brain signal, extensive signal averaging (based on simultaneous EEG) was necessary to detect the strongest signal available in spontaneous EEG, the alpha rhythm. In the early 1970s, employing the recently developed SQUID sensor, Cohen's lab was able to record spontaneous alpha rhythms without averaging and went on to characterize abnormal signals in epilepsy.[31]

Early demonstrations of MEG were largely confined to single-channel detectors. Characterization of the spatial topography of the signals depended on laboriously repeating the measurements at different locations on the head. The first commercial whole-head systems were developed in the late 1980s. The number of channels typically included in such systems has steadily increased over the years to about 100-300 sensors arranged over the head. This number is unlikely to increase further, as it suffices to characterize the MEG signal at a suitable spatial scale and approaches the physical limits of the number of detectors squeezed into the available space of a helmet that fits the average human head with a minimal distance between the brain and the sensors. The design of whole-head MEG systems has remained largely stable since the late 1990s, especially regarding the sensors, although improvements in electronics and algorithms for data processing have enhanced the accuracy and utility of the technique. The next major development in MEG is likely to be the commercialization of alternative sensor types not based on SQUIDs. These sensors may operate at higher temperatures and free users of the need for expensive cryogenics.

## 3.4 Properties

### 3.4.1 Temporal and Spatial Resolution

The temporal resolution of MEG is essentially identical to EEG. Magnetic fields can be sampled as quickly as the electronics will allow — up to 20 kHz or more, but the value of faster sampling declines as relatively little detectable neural activity occurs above a certain frequency range, perhaps 100 Hz. Thus, conventional sampling rates of 500-1000 Hz are entirely adequate. However, one should note that the true temporal resolution of MEG depends on the intrinsic temporal properties of the neural process that one is studying. For example, fast signals, such as oscillations in the gamma band (> 40 Hz), can be detected with greater temporal precision than slowly evolving signals, no matter what apparatus is used to measure them.

The spatial resolution of MEG is a matter of much debate and depends on the intrinsic characteristics of the signal under investigation. However, it is generally agreed that the transparency of the head to magnetic fields results in more accurate inverse solutions when compared to EEG. Studies of early sensory responses to simple visual and tactile stimulation have demonstrated that neural populations corresponding to different retinal locations or fingers can be distinguished on the order of a few millimeters. However, the activity induced by more complicated cognitive manipulations is likely to engage large regions of the cortex and therefore be inherently harder to pin down to such small areas.

Another major factor related to the spatial precision of MEG is the accuracy with which MEG signals can be coregistered with brain structure, typically derived from MRI. A related problem is the issue of participant head motion, which can yield an unstable spatial relationship between brain regions and the MEG sensors. Various strategies exist to track head position and incorporate the information into the analysis.[32,33] Head motion can be reduced through physical means such as custom-fitted face casts.[34,35]

## 3.5  Logistics

A modern commercial MEG machine is a major piece of infrastructure with large setup requirements. It is typically installed within a hospital or research center and made available to a large number of researchers. It is seldom the property of a single lab. MEG requires a shielded room, which may require building modifications due to its weight. A new system typically costs between 1 and 3 million USD, not including renovation costs. Annual operating costs are substantial (100-200K USD) due to the need for preventative maintenance carried out by a skilled technician and a steady supply of helium for cryogenic cooling, although the increased use of helium recycling systems brings this cost down.

A MEG lab also has a personnel requirement for weekly helium refills (in the absence of a closed-loop recycler) and monitoring system performance (including cryogenics). These tasks can be performed by a dedicated technician or by academic researchers within the research facility. Another logistical requirement, in most cases, is access to an MRI scanner. MEG acquisition can, in principle, be performed without an MRI for each individual. However, to take full advantage of the technique's spatial localization capabilities, it is necessary to construct a head model capturing the shape of the skull, most commonly from a high-resolution T1-weighted MRI scan. Most MEG machines are located within major research centers with access to an MRI scanner. However, not all participants are eligible for MRI, and the cost of an MRI scan can strain the budget of an otherwise viable MEG project. To economize, many labs invite participants back for multiple MEG studies once an MRI scan has been acquired.

Most researchers contemplating getting involved with MEG will not be buying a new system but rather paying a user fee for time on an existing system. Fees typically range from 100-600 USD per hour, comparable to fMRI, and training on data acquisition and analysis is usually provided. The number of participants required for a given research study depends on the size of the effect studied, but 15-25 is typical for a cognitive neuroscience experiment.

## 3.6  Risks and limitations

MEG is one of the most patient-friendly and safe techniques in neuroscience. As a passive recording technique, it is noninvasive, with no energy transmitted to the body. There are virtually no risks. In theory, a leak of helium from the dewar could cause asphyxiation, but there are safety measures in place to prevent this, and no such incidents have ever occurred.

There are some limitations on who can have a MEG, but any impediments are related to data quality and not safety. The presence of metallic implants in the body (including some dental hardware, although most fillings are not an issue) can create large artifacts in the signal. Large metallic objects can damage the sensors (reversibly) in some MEG systems. Due to the technique's sensitivity to head motion, it may not be suitable for some special populations (pediatric, geriatric, psychiatric). The sensitivity of MEG to metallic artifacts requires the use of non-metallic peripheral equipment for stimulus delivery and response recording. This necessity can increase costs and result in a slightly compromised quality of stimuli, especially sound, generally delivered through pneumatic tubes or a distant speaker, as normal headphones are not suitable.

Because the MEG sensors are built into a helmet with fixed geometry, it may not fit everyone — occasionally, one finds a participant with a head too large for the helmet. Pediatric populations pose a special challenge, as their neurons will be located much farther from the sensors. It is nonetheless possible to obtain satisfactory data from an adult-sized MEG system with pediatric participants, including infants.[36,37] Additionally, a few research centers in the world maintain specially built systems with smaller helmets designed for children.[38,39]

## 3.7 Conclusion

MEG is a high-tech neuroimaging modality offering an unparalleled combination of temporal and spatial resolution for assessing the electrical activity of the human brain and detects aspects of neuronal information processing inaccessible with other techniques. It requires considerable investment for funding and appropriate facilities. Currently, the best-case scenario is a core facility shared by multiple research and clinical users. MEG can be used directly in neurotechnology projects and provide important insights to inform the design of smaller-scale products. Given recent technological developments, MEG may yet become much cheaper and more widely available.

## Endnotes

1. Nunez, Paul L., and Ramesh Srinivasan. *Electric fields of the brain: the neurophysics of EEG*. Oxford University Press, USA, 2006.

2. Hämäläinen, Matti, Riitta Hari, Risto J. Ilmoniemi, Jukka Knuutila, and Olli V. Lounasmaa. "Magnetoencephalography—theory, instrumentation, and applications to noninvasive studies of the working human brain." *Reviews of modern Physics* 65, no. 2 (1993): 413.

3. Hari R, Baillet S, Barnes G, Burgess R, Forss N, Gross J, Hamalainen M, Jensen O, Kakigi R, Mauguiere F, Nakasato N, Puce A, Romani GL, Schnitzler A, Taulu S (2018) IFCN-endorsed practical guidelines for clinical magnetoencephalography (MEG). *Clin Neurophysiol* 129:1720-1747.

4. Cheyne D, Papanicolaou A (2017) Magnetoencephalography and magnetic source imaging. *The Oxford Handbook of Functional Brain Imaging in Neuropsychology and Cognitive Neurosciences*:13.

5. Vrba, Jiri, and Stephen E. Robinson. "Signal processing in magnetoencephalography." *Methods* 25, no. 2 (2001): 249-271.

6. Taulu, Samu, Matti Kajola, and Juha Simola. "Suppression of interference and Artifacts by the signal space separation method." *Brain topography* 16, no. 4 (2004): 269-275.

7. Taulu, Samu, and Juha Simola. "Spatiotemporal signal space separation method for rejecting nearby interference in MEG measurements." *Physics in Medicine & Biology* 51, no. 7 (2006): 1759.

8. Hansen, Peter, Morten Kringelbach, and Riitta Salmelin, eds. MEG: an introduction to methods. *Oxford university press*, 2010.

9. Zimmermann, R., and E. Scharein. "MEG and EEG show different sensitivity to myogenic artifacts." *Neurology & clinical neurophysiology*: NCN 2004 (2004): 78-78.

10. Claus, Steven, Demetrios Velis, Fernando H. Lopes da Silva, Max A. Viergever, and Stiliyan Kalitzin. "High frequency spectral components after secobarbital: the contribution of muscular origin—a study with MEG/EEG." *Epilepsy research* 100, no. 1-2 (2012): 132-141.

11. Muthukumaraswamy, Suresh. "High-frequency brain activity and muscle artifacts in MEG/EEG: a review and recommendations." *Frontiers in human neuroscience* 7 (2013): 138.

12. Meltzer JA, Negishi M, Mayes LC, Constable RT (2007) Individual differences in EEG theta and alpha dynamics during working memory correlate with fMRI responses across subjects. *Clin Neurophysiol* 118:2419-2436.

13. Brookes, Matthew J., et al. "Measuring functional connectivity using MEG: methodology and comparison with fcMRI." *Neuroimage* 56.3 (2011): 1082-1104.

14. Cabral, Joana, et al. "Exploring mechanisms of spontaneous functional connectivity in MEG: how delayed network interactions lead to structured amplitude envelopes of band-pass filtered scillations." *Neuroimage* 90 (2014): 423-435.

15. Colclough, Giles L., et al. "How reliable are MEG resting-state connectivity metrics?" *Neuroimage* 138 (2016): 284-293.

16. Bastos, André M., and Jan-Mathijs Schoffelen. "A tutorial review of functional connectivity analysis methods and their interpretational pitfalls." *Frontiers in systems neuroscience* 9 (2016): 175.

17. Hincapié, Ana-Sofía, et al. "The impact of MEG source reconstruction method on source-space connectivity estimation: a comparison between minimum-norm solution and beamforming." *Neuroimage* 156 (2017): 29-42.

18. Singh, K. D. (2012). Which "neural activity" do you mean? fMRI, MEG, oscillations and neurotransmitters. *Neuroimage*, 62(2).

19. Stapleton-Kotloski, Jennifer R., Robert J. Kotloski, Gautam Popli, and Dwayne W. Godwin. "Magnetoencephalography: Clinical and research practices." *Brain sciences* 8, no. 8 (2018): 157.

20. Hari, Riitta, Sylvain Baillet, Gareth Barnes, Richard Burgess, Nina Forss, Joachim Gross, Matti Hämäläinen et al. "IFCN-endorsed practical guidelines for clinical magnetoencephalography (MEG)." *Clinical Neurophysiology* 129, no. 8 (2018): 1720-1747.

21. Meltzer JA, McArdle JJ, Schafer RJ, Braun AR (2010) Neural aspects of sentence comprehension: syntactic complexity, reversibility, and reanalysis. *Cereb Cortex* 20:1853-1864.

22. Meltzer JA, Braun AR (2011) An EEG-MEG Dissociation between Online Syntactic Comprehension and Post Hoc Reanalysis. *Front Hum Neurosci* 5:10.

23. Chu RK, Braun AR, Meltzer JA (2015) MEG-based detection and localization of perilesional dysfunction in chronic stroke. *NeuroImage Clinical* 8:157-169.

24. Oshino, Satoru, Amami Kato, Akatsuki Wakayama, Masaaki Taniguchi, Masayuki Hirata, and Toshiki Yoshimine. "Magnetoencephalographic analysis of cortical oscillatory activity in patients with brain tumors: Synthetic aperture magnetometry (SAM) functional imaging of delta band activity." *Neuroimage* 34, no. 3 (2007): 957-964.

25. Chu, Ron KO, Allen R. Braun, and Jed A. Meltzer. "MEG-based detection and localization of perilesional dysfunction in chronic stroke." *NeuroImage: Clinical* 8 (2015):157-169.

26. Kielar, Aneta, Tiffany Deschamps, Ron KO Chu, Regina Jokel, Yasha B. Khatamian, Jean J. Chen, and Jed A. Meltzer. "Identifying dysfunctional cortex: dissociable effects of stroke and aging on resting state dynamics in MEG and fMRI." *Frontiers in aging neuroscience* 8 (2016): 40.

27. Huang, Ming-Xiong, Rebecca J. Theilmann, Ashley Robb, Annemarie Angeles, Sharon Nichols, Angela Drake, John D'Andrea et al. "Integrated imaging approach with MEG and DTI to detect mild traumatic brain injury in military and civilian patients." *Journal of neurotrauma* 26, no. 8 (2009): 1213-1226.

28. Shah-Basak, Priyanka P., Aneta Kielar, Tiffany Deschamps, Nicolaas Paul Verhoeff, Regina Jokel, and Jed Meltzer. "Spontaneous oscillatory markers of cognitive status in two forms of dementia." *Human brain mapping* 40, no. 5 (2019): 1594-1607.

29. Cohen, David. "Boston and the history of biomagnetism." *Neurology and Clinical Neurophysiology* 114 (2004): 1-4.

30. Cohen, David, Edgar A. Edelsack, and James E. Zimmerman. "Magnetocardiograms taken inside a shielded room with a superconducting point-contact magnetometer." *Applied Physics Letters* 16, no. 7 (1970): 278-280.

31. Cohen, David. "Magnetoencephalography: detection of the brain's electrical activity with a superconducting magnetometer." *Science* 175, no. 4022 (1972): 664-666.

32. Bardouille, Timothy, Santosh V. Krishnamurthy, Sujoy Ghosh Hajra, and Ryan CN D'Arcy. "Improved localization accuracy in magnetic source imaging using a 3-D laser scanner." *IEEE Transactions on Biomedical Engineering* 59, no. 12 (2012): 3491-3497.

33. Hironaga, Naruhito, Koichi Hagiwara, Katsuya Ogata, Mariko Hayamizu, Tomokazu Urakawa, and Shozo Tobimatsu. "Proposal for a new MEG–MRI co-registration: a 3D laser scanner system." *Clinical Neurophysiology* 125, no. 12 (2014):2404-2412

34. Troebinger, Luzia, José David López, Antoine Lutti, David Bradbury,Sven Bestmann, and Gareth Barnes. "High precision anatomy for MEG." *Neuroimage* 86 (2014): 583-591.

35. Meyer, Sofie S., James Bonaiuto, Mark Lim, Holly Rossiter, Sheena Waters, David Bradbury, Sven Bestmann et al. "Flexible head-casts for high spatial precision MEG." *Journal of Neuroscience Methods* 276 (2017): 38-45.

36. Cheour, Marie, Toshiaki Imada, Samu Taulu, Antti Ahonen, Johanna Salonen, and Patricia Kuhl. "Magnetoencephalography is feasible for infant assessment of auditory discrimination." *Experimental Neurology* 190 (2004): 44-51.

37. Ferjan Ramírez, Naja, Rey R. Ramírez, Maggie Clarke, Samu Taulu, and Patricia K. Kuhl. "Speech discrimination in 11-month-old bilingual and monolingual infants: a magnetoencephalography study." *Developmental Science* 20, no. 1 (2017):e12427.

38. Johnson, Blake W., Stephen Crain, Rosalind Thornton, Graciela Tesan, and Melanie Reid. "Measurement of brain function in pre-school children using a custom sized whole-head MEG sensor array." *Clinical neurophysiology* 121, no. 3 (2010): 340-349.

39. Okada, Yoshio, Matti Hämäläinen, Kevin Pratt, Anthony Mascarenas, Paul Miller, Menglai Han, Jose Robles et al. "BabyMEG: A whole-head pediatric magnetoencephalography system for human brain development research." *Review of Scientific Instruments* 87, no. 9 (2016): 094301.

# 4
# Functional/ Magnetic Resonance Imaging (f/MRI)

**Benjamin De Leener**
*Benjamin De Leener is an Assistant Professor in the Department of Computer and Software Engineering at Polytechnique Montreal, Canada. Dr. De Leener is also affiliated with the CHU Sainte-Justine Research Center and holds a TransMedTech Institute Chaire in Computer Engineering. His research interests pertain to the development of new technologies in pediatric neuroimaging. More particularly, my research lab focuses on developing open-source software for analyzing brain and spinal cord images acquired with magnetic resonance imaging, using advanced segmentation and registration approaches using machine learning and neurodevelopmental templates and atlases.*

## 4.1 Introduction/The Basics

Magnetic Resonance Imaging (MRI) is a powerful non-invasive imaging technique mainly used in clinics for the diagnosis of various pathologies in the central nervous system and the musculoskeletal system, including tumors, inflammations, and infections. As one of the only imaging modalities able to image soft tissues in vivo with high resolution, MRI is widely used for assessing and studying neurodegenerative diseases. Moreover, the flexibility of MRI and the fact that it uses non-ionizing radiation makes it the preferential choice for imaging metabolism, brain functions, and structure. Although this chapter will focus on the central nervous system, MRI is a very flexible imaging modality and has various other applications.

## 4.2 How It Works

MR images are created by exploiting a combination of three magnetic phenomena that affect water molecules in the body. The human body is composed largely of water, and each water molecule is composed of 2 hydrogen and one oxygen atoms. An interesting particularity of hydrogen atoms is their odd number of protons, which gives them a nuclear angular momentum (we will call these atom spins for simplicity). When placed into an external magnetic field, the spins, which would be randomly oriented under normal conditions, quickly align with the magnetic field and rotate with a specific frequency, referred to as the Larmor frequency; this varies for each type of atom. This effect is called magnetization. Under clinical conditions, the external magnetic field, called the main field or B0 field, typically ranges from 1.5T to 3.0T.[1] When spins are aligned within the main field, they can be excited using a radiofrequency magnetic pulse, called the B1 field. This phenomenon, called excitation, allows the spins magnetization vectors to rotate perpendicularly with the B0 field. Excitation requires that the spins receive a radiofrequency signal equal to the strength of the main magnetic field multiplied by the Larmor frequency of the atom. This specificity in the excitation phenomenon means that only the hydrogen atoms will be excited during MR acquisition. The duration and the strength of the B1 field is usually a small fraction of the B0 field.

After the excitation stops, the spins will return to their equilibrium state (aligned with the B0 field), through a phenomenon called relaxation. The spins are subject to two types of relaxation: the longitudinal and the transverse. Relaxation processes follow an exponential decay and are characterized respectively by the T1 and T2 time constants that vary between the different types of human tissues, along with the density of the atoms, denoted as $\rho$, within the tissues. These constants are the source of contrast in MR images, and MR parameters are optimized to increase the contrast between different body structures. During relaxation, each rotating magnetization spin emits a radiofrequency pulse that is measured by MR antennas placed around the body. Listening to the pulses is called the data acquisition phase. However, the signal received by the antennas is the summation of all the hydrogen atoms in the body and does not allow for the formation of an image. The three phenomena described above, magnetization, excitation, and relaxation, are the principles of Nuclear Magnetic Resonance (NMR), and the objective of MR imaging is to map the spatial distribution of these relaxing spins to obtain a contrast between the various structures of the body.

Assessing the spatial localization of relaxing spins can be done by applying linear-gradients during the excitation or data acquisition phases. MR scanners have three coils that generate linear-gradients in three orthogonal directions and create magnetic field variations over the whole body. The linear-gradient, generated by the coils, produces a small variation that adds up to the B0 field. Typically, applying a small linear-gradient can create a difference of 80 mT on top of the B0 field between the two extremities of the scanner. How is this used to map the spins? As the main field varies, the Larmor frequency of the spins also begins to fluctuate. When magnetic pulses at the Larmor frequency are directed over the whole body, only the spins that are located where the addition of the main field and the gradients is equal to B0 (ex: 3T) will be excited. The spins located elsewhere stay at their equilibrium state and do not contribute to the signal received by the MR antennas when entering the relaxation and acquisition phase. After all, spins are back to equilibrium, so another radiofrequency pulse is released with a slightly different frequency. This pulse will excite spins from a slightly different location. By repeating this pattern and changing the excitation frequency, we can map the whole volume inside the scanner. This process is called an MR sequence.

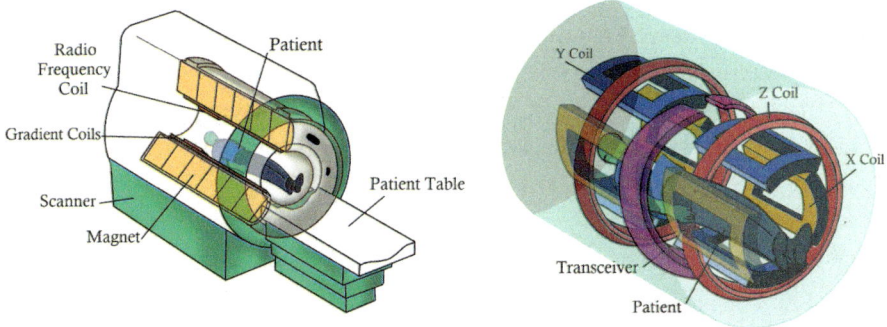

Figure 4.1 (left) schematics of an MRI scanner. (right) schematics of the gradient and transceiving antennae of an MRI scanner.

In reality, the method described above is too slow to be feasible in clinics as the image formation is much more complex, and involves elegant inverse Fourier transform techniques. Researchers and clinicians can speed up and optimize the image acquisition process to acquire a high-resolution image of the full brain within minutes. In some cases, the acquisition time can be reduced to seconds at the price of lower resolution and image quality. One fascinating aspect of MRI is that, unlike other imaging modalities, the orientation and size of the images, which can be seen as a rectangular parallelepiped in 3D space, is arbitrary. We can acquire a volume in any orientation with anisotropic voxels if desired.

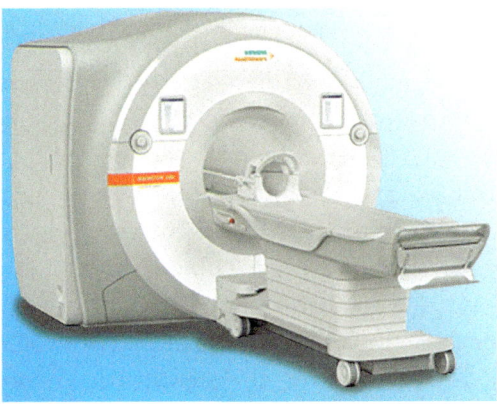

Figure 4.2 Example of a 3T MRI scanner from Siemens Healthcare Limited.

## 4.3 Typical Usage

The multiparametric aspects of MRI make it a flexible imaging modality; over the years, researchers have been very imaginative in pushing the limits of what information MRI can extract from the brain and the body. Structural MRI is the most known and most used type of MR acquisition. Usually looking at the T1 or T2 contrast of the tissues, it provides information about the anatomy of the brain (e.g., white versus gray matter), as well as the structural effect of pathologies (e.g., brain atrophy, lesions). Typically, clinicians will use structural scans to quickly assess brain conditions and calculate volumes of different brain structures.[2]her popular type of MRI acquisition is functional MRI (fMRI). As indicated by its name, fMRI is capable of measuring brain activity in real-time by detecting changes associated with blood flow and blood oxygenation.[3]

The brain structure, and particularly the organization of the neurons, can be visualized using diffusion MRI (dMRI). By encoding magnetic gradients in various directions during the acquisition phase, dMRI can measure the diffusion of the water molecules within neurons.[4] Indeed, neurons are organized into fibers that interconnect regions of the brain, and water diffuses along these fibers while blocked by the neurons' membranes. Mapping these fibers allows the measurement of the brain connectome (map of the neural connections), which is one of the main applications of dMRI. dMRI has also been used as a biomarker for the diagnosis and prognosis of neurodegenerative diseases (ex: Multiple Sclerosis, Alzheimer's Disease, Parkinson's Disease), as water diffusivity is affected by the neuron microstructure.[5]

## 4.4 History

### 4.4.1 Early Technologies - Paving The Way

Magnetic Resonance Imaging is based on Nuclear Magnetic Resonance (NMR) principles, which were discovered independently by Felix Bloch and Edward Mills Purcell in 1946, both of whom went on to win the 1952 Nobel Prize in Physics for their work.[6] Following the discovery of NMR, researchers began exploring its biomedical applications. In particular, researchers were interested in hydrogen atoms as the human body is mainly composed of water. Unfortunately, we would have to wait until the '80s to get the first images of a living human body. In 1973, Paul Lauterbur demonstrated the possible acquisition of images based on NMR using a linear magnetic gradient; later, Sir Peter Mansfield developed a rapid acquisition method to make MR imaging feasible in clinics. They were both awarded the Nobel Prize in Medicine in 2003 for their work on MRI.

### 4.4.2 First Release and Inventor(s)

The central component of an MRI scanner is the main magnet, which produces a constant and homogeneous magnetic field within the scanner. The first MRI scanner installed in clinics in the '90s produced magnetic fields ranging from 0.3 to 0.6 teslas.[7] For comparison, the earth's magnetic field ranges from 25 to 65 microteslas. The industry then began a race for the highest field strength in clinical and research scanners, to increase the image quality and resolution, despite increasing challenges due to high power deposition and severe B1 field inhomogeneities. The 1.5T and 3.0T scanners were introduced into clinics in 1985 and 1998, respectively, and are still the standard of clinical care today.[8]

### 4.4.3 Improvements Since Release

While it had been used in research for several years in various applications, the first 7.0T human MRI scanner was accepted for clinical use in North Americas in 2017, paving the way for even higher field strengths. Further development of MR hardware and fundamental work on MR physics has led to discoveries of new applications for MRI, including imaging the diffusion of water molecules within the body and imaging the functions of brain regions using blood oxygenation level-dependent (BOLD) techniques, also known as functional MRI.[9,10] Recently, new material and machine learning technologies have allowed the development of high-quality low-field MRI machines that could be used in specific clinical situations as a portable or movable device.

## 4.5 Properties

### 4.5.1 Temporal and Spatial Resolution

Because of its high in vivo spatial resolution capabilities, MRI has a significant advantage over other imaging modalities when visualizing soft tissue and brain structures. However, its low temporal resolution makes it a less effective tool for assessing brain functions.

For example, fMRI suffers from low temporal resolution and has yet to show its potential in the clinics.[11] However, fMRI has become one of the most popular functional imaging techniques in research and has been used to map brain activity evoked from sensory, motor, cognitive, and emotional tasks. It has also contributed to improving our understanding of neurobehavioral and neurodegenerative disorders such as Alzheimer's disease, Parkinson's disease, traumatic injuries, epilepsy, and multiple sclerosis.[12]

### 4.5.2 Precision and Accuracy

Most MRI acquisitions provide non-quantitative measures, which means that MR images generally do not contain numbers that represent a physical phenomenon or structure in the body.

If required, contrast agents can be used to improve the delineation of specific structures. For example, Magnetic Resonance Angiography (MRA) allows scientists to enhance the contrast between blood vessels and surrounding structures by introducing paramagnetic compounds into the blood system.[13] It should be noted that MRA can also be achieved without contrast agents, using advanced MRI techniques (e.g., phase contrast MRA, time-of-flight MRA).

A new popular research area is Quantitative MRI, which aims to generate maps of meaningful physical or chemical data that varies between tissue regions and among subjects.[14] For example, recent advances in diffusion MRI modeling provide estimations of axons' diameter, density, and myelin content.[15,16] Differences in these features could one day be utilized to directly measure neurodegeneration.[17] Unfortunately, these techniques are still very much in the development phase; scientists are working to address issues related to reproducibility and accuracy before these techniques are implemented in a clinical setting.

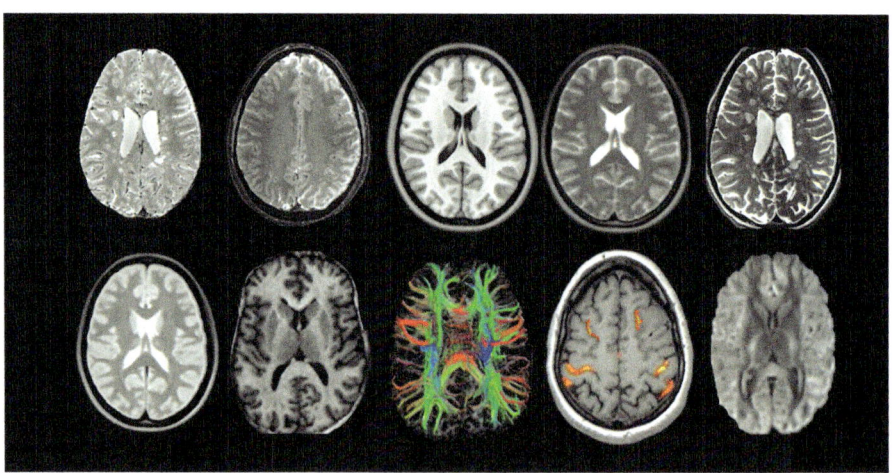

Figure 4.3 Different MRI contrasts showing various structures in the brain.

### 4.5.3 Invasiveness

MRI is a non-invasive and non-ionizing imaging modality; this means it does not require opening the body and does not use radiation that is directly harmful to human cells. As such, MRI is considered an imaging technique with low associated risk.[18,19]

### 4.5.4 Setup Requirements

MRIs are used both in research and hospital settings. Outside of the costs and risks, described below, there are certain conditions necessary for the functioning of these machines. Indeed, for an MRI scanner to operate, a strong magnetic field must be maintained at room temperature, which requires the use of advanced superconductivity and cooling technologies.

## 4.6 Logistics

### 4.6.1 Risks

An MRI machine is a high-field giant magnet that is never turned off; not surprisingly, metallic objects, including implants, can move under the MR magnet influence. Therefore, special precautions must be taken before entering the MRI room to avoid injury. The radiofrequency energy during MRI acquisition may also cause heating or malfunctions to implanted devices such as cochlear implants or pacemakers, as well as heating the body.[20] Additionally, strong oscillating currents within the internal MR coils produce loud knocking noises, which may harm hearing without adequate protection. Although there is no information to date indicating negative effects on unborn children, MRI is not recommended during the first trimester of pregnancy.[21]

### 4.6.2 Costs

Manufacturing and maintenance-related costs of an MRI scanner are high. Generally, the cost of an MRI machine is approximately $1 million USD per tesla; therefore, a 3.0T MRI scanner would cost roughly $3 million USD. It should be noted, this cost is for the MRI machine alone and does not include the installation, equipment, and maintenance costs. Depending on the location and intended purpose (i.e., research or clinical use), operating an MRI scanner for an hour costs between $500 and $2000.

### 4.6.3 Limitations

The slowness of MRI image generation means individuals must remain still in the machine for long durations of time; this can be particularly challenging for individuals with mobility issues such as people living with Parkinson's disease. MR imaging is very flexible, and MRI scanners have many acquisition parameters, which allow users to adjust sequences when imaging specific structures such as the heart and managing difficult scenarios such as imaging children. Images generated through MRI can be relatively sensitive to the parameters of the acquisition, including the MR technician that operates the machine. This limitation makes it critical for researchers and neuroradiologists to have specific expertise and exercise extreme fastidiousness when deciphering and assessing MR images.

### 4.6.4 Notable Use Cases

Over the years, MRI has been established as a powerful diagnosis tool, particularly in the field of neurology. Radiologists are now using brain MRI scans routinely to assess brain damage after traumatic injuries, and MRI is one of the most sensitive, non-invasive diagnostic and prognostic tools for Multiple Sclerosis (MS). MS is a neurodegenerative disease that affects the myelin sheath surrounding neurons; using quantitative MRI, radiologists can quantify the loss of myelin over time to estimate the progression of the disease.

Neuroscientists are constantly searching for ways to examine brain microstructures and functions non-invasively; MRI, along with other imaging modalities, has helped inform our understanding of the underlying mechanisms behind neurodegenerative diseases. For example, researchers identified the pattern of neurodegenerative progression in the brains of patients affected by Alzheimer disease at early stages using MRI. Hopefully, discoveries of this nature will help pave the way for effective treatments.

Lastly, MRI provides incredibly high spatial resolution but lacks the temporal resolution of other imaging modalities like electroencephalography (EEG) and positron emission tomography (PET). Combining MRI with functional imaging techniques offers the advantages of simultaneous high spatial structural resolution as well as high functional temporal resolution. Specifically, PET/MRI combined machines are becoming popular in clinics,[22] and manufacturers are working toward developing more MRI-compatible EEG systems.

To learn more about MRI, the following references can provide a more detailed look:

- *Principles of magnetic resonance imaging. Stanford University, 1996. By Dwight Nishimura*
- *Questions and Answers in MRI.* http://mriquestions.com/index.html

# Endnotes

1. Nishiura, D. G., A. Macovski, and J. M. Pauly. 1986. "Magnetic Resonance Angiography." *IEEE Transactions on Medical Imaging* 5 (3): 140–51.

2. Koikkalainen, Juha, Hanneke Rhodius-Meester, Antti Tolonen, Frederik Barkhof, Betty Tijms, Afina W. Lemstra, Tong Tong, et al. 2016. "Differential Diagnosis of Neurodegenerative Diseases Using Structural MRI Data." *NeuroImage*. Clinical 11 (March): 435–49.

3. Ogawa, Seiji, Tso-Ming Lee, Asha S. Nayak, and Paul Glynn. 1990. "Oxygenation-Sensitive Contrast in Magnetic Resonance Image of Rodent Brain at High Magnetic Fields." *Magnetic Resonance in Medicine: Official Journal of the Society of Magnetic Resonance in Medicine / Society of Magnetic Resonance in Medicine* 14 (1): 68–78.

4. Le Bihan, D., E. Breton, D. Lallemand, P. Grenier, E. Cabanis, and M. Laval-Jeantet. 1986. "MR Imaging of Intravoxel Incoherent Motions: Application to Diffusion and Perfusion in Neurologic Disorders." *Radiology* 161 (2): 401–7.

5. Filippi, Massimo, Nicola de Stefano, and Vincent Dousset. 2005. MR Imaging in White Matter Diseases of the Brain and Spinal Cord. Edited by Massimo Filippi, Nicola De Stefano, Vincent Dousset, and Joseph C. McGowan. *Medical Radiology Diagnostic Imaging* . Springer Science & Business Media.

6. Ai, Tao, John N. Morelli, Xuemei Hu, Dapeng Hao, Frank L. Goerner, Bryan Ager, and Val M. Runge. 2012. "A Historical Overview of Magnetic Resonance Imaging, Focusing on Technological Innovations." *Investigative Radiology* 47 (12): 725–41.

7. Edelman, Robert R. 2014. "The History of MR Imaging as Seen through the Pages of Radiology." *Radiology* 273 (2 Suppl): S181–200.

8. Ai, Tao, Morelli, Hu, Hao, Goerner, Bryan, and Runge. 2012. "A Historical Overview of Magnetic Resonance Imaging, " 47 (12): 725–41.

9. Le Bihan, Breton, Lallemand, Grenier, Cabanis, and Laval-Jeantet. 1986. "MR Imaging of Intravoxel Incoherent Motions:" 161 (2): 401–7.

10. Ogawa, Tso-Ming Lee, Nayak, and Glynn. 1990. "Oxygenation-Sensitive Contrast in Magnetic Resonance." 14 (1): 68–78.

11. Glover, Gary H. 2011. "Overview of Functional Magnetic Resonance Imaging." *Neurosurgery Clinics of North America* 22 (2): 133–39, vii.

12. Greicius, Michael. 2008. "Resting-State Functional Connectivity in Neuropsychiatric Disorders." *Current Opinion in Neurology* 21 (4): 424–30.

13. Nishimura, Dwight G., Albert Macovski, and John M. Pauly. "Magnetic resonance angiography." *IEEE transactions on medical imaging* 5, no. 3 (1986): 140-151.

14. Tofts, Paul. 2005. Quantitative MRI of the Brain: Measuring Changes Caused by Disease. John Wiley & Sons.

15. Assaf, Yaniv, Tamar Blumenfeld-Katzir, Yossi Yovel, and Peter J. Basser. 2008. "AxCaliber: A Method for Measuring Axon Diameter Distribution from Diffusion MRI." *Magnetic Resonance in Medicine: Official Journal of the Society of Magnetic Resonance in Medicine / Society of Magnetic Resonance in Medicine* 59 (6): 1347–54.

16. Zhang, Hui, Torben Schneider, Claudia A. Wheeler-Kingshott, and Daniel C. Alexander. 2012. "NODDI: Practical in Vivo Neurite Orientation Dispersion and Density Imaging of the Human Brain." *NeuroImage* 61 (4): 1000–1016.

17. Martin, Allan R., Benjamin De Leener, Julien Cohen-Adad, Sukhvinder Kalsi-Ryan, David W. Cadotte, Jefferson R. Wilson, Lindsay Tetreault, et al. 2018. "Monitoring for Myelopathic Progression with Multiparametric Quantitative MRI." *PloS One* 13 (4): e0195733.

18. Gangarosa, R. E., J. E. Minnis, J. Nobbe, D. Praschan, and R. W. Genberg. 1987. "Operational Safety Issues in MRI." *Magnetic Resonance Imaging* 5 (4): 287–92.

19. Mansouri, Mohammad, Shima Aran, Harlan B. Harvey, Khalid W. Shaqdan, and Hani H. Abujudeh. 2016. "Rates of Safety Incident Reporting in MRI in a Large Academic Medical Center." *Journal of Magnetic Resonance Imaging: JMRI* 43 (4): 998–1007.

20. Collins, C. M. 2017. "Intuitive Understanding of RF Heating Patterns in MRI." In *2017 International Conference on Electromagnetics in Advanced Applications (ICEAA)*, 1886–89.

21. Ray, Joel G., Marian J. Vermeulen, Aditya Bharatha, Walter J. Montanera, and Alison L. Park. 2016. "Association Between MRI Exposure During Pregnancy and Fetal and Childhood Outcomes." *JAMA: The Journal of the American Medical Association* 316 (9): 952–61.

22. Fraioli, Francesco, and Karar Obeed Almansory. 2019. "Clinical Applications of PET/MRI in Brain Imaging." In PET/CT in Brain Disorders, edited by Francesco Fraioli, 145–54. Cham: Springer International Publishing.

# 5
# Near-Infrared Spectroscopy (NIRS) and Functional Near-Infrared Spectroscopy (fNIRS)

**Raymundo Cassani**
*Raymundo Cassani is a Research Developer and Research Assistant at the The Neuro (Montreal Neurological Institute-Hospital), McGill University. He received the BEng degree in Communications and Electronics and the MSc degree in Microelectronics from the Instituto Politécnico Nacional, México, in 2007 and 2012 respectively. In 2018, he obtained his PhD from the Institut National de la Recherche Scientifique, as a member of the Multimodal Signal Analysis and Enhancement Lab (MuSAE Lab), where he held the positions of Postdoctoral Fellow and Research Associate. In 2021, he joined the Dynamic Neuroimaging Lab (neuroSPEED). His research includes signal processing applied to biomedical signals, such as EEG, MEG, fNIRS, ECG and EMG, all of this with applications in health diagnostics, human-machine interaction, entertainment and neurotechnologies.*

## 5.1 Introduction

Functional near-infrared spectroscopy (fNIRS) is a noninvasive optical technique used for the study of brain activity. fNIRS uses near-infrared spectroscopy (NIRS) to measure the concentration changes of deoxyhemoglobin (HHb) and oxyhemoglobin ($O_2$Hb) in the blood vessels in the cerebral cortex, thus providing insight on the metabolic demand in the cortex, which is an indirect measurement of the cortical activity.

In this chapter, a brief history of the use of optical methods for the study of biological tissues is presented, placing special interest in the study of the brain. After, the basics of NIRS are presented in detail, followed by fNIRS as the natural use of NIRS to study brain activity in real-time, its principles, characteristics, comparison with other neuroimaging modalities, and its medical and research applications.

## 5.2 History of NIRS and fNIRS

The use of optical methods for the study of human tissues dates back to the 19th century. Among the relevant discoveries of the epoch, in 1876, the German physician Karl von Vierordt developed a noninvasive and painless technique to evaluate the amount of oxygen carried in the blood. This technique was based on the observed spectral changes of red light penetrating tissue when the circulation is interrupted; unfortunately, his work remained ignored for nearly half a century.[1,2]

In the 1930s, von Vierordt's works on the use of optical methods for the study of tissue oxygenation were replicated by Ludwig Nicolai and extended by Karl Kramer and Karl Matthes, who introduced the use of two wavelengths of light, red and near-infrared (NIR), to determine the levels of deoxyhemoglobin (HHb) and oxyhemoglobin ($O_2$Hb) for human tissue. This process is possible because HHb preferentially absorbs more red than NIR light, while $O_2$Hb presents the opposite behavior. Thus, the degree of absorption of red or NIR light provides information about the concentrations of HHb and $O_2$Hb, i.e., [HHb] and [$O_2$Hb], respectively.[1,2] As such, in the 1940s, red and NIR light were used to determine the oxygen levels in muscles; this approach is known as oximetry.[3]

It was also in that decade that Glen Millikan developed the first portable human ear oximeter to study the cases of blackouts in fighter pilots at high altitudes during WWII.[3,4] In the early 1960s, Karl Norris and co-workers introduced NIR spectroscopy (NIRS) as a technique to analyze the composition of a given sample with the use of NIR light.[1] However, the main application for the work developed by Norris was the study of agricultural samples. Since then, the use of NIRS has been proven of incredible value to study the chemical composition of samples in pharmaceutical, medical and industrial applications.

The groundbreaking advance towards the use of NIRS to study the brain came in 1977 when through a series of in vivo trans-illumination experiments Frans Jöbsis demonstrated that human tissues are relatively transparent to NIR light in the 650-950 nm wavelength range. In other words, this range of wavelengths provides an "optical window" into the body.[5] In this way, his discoveries showed the possibility of continuous noninvasive monitoring of [$O_2$Hb] and [HHb] in muscles and internal organs such as the brain through skin and bone.[6] In 1985 Jöbsis and colleagues presented two works, the use of NIRS to study cerebral oxygenation in sick newborn infants[7] and during anesthesia and surgery.[8] As such, Jöbsis is considered to be the initiator of medical NIRS.[4] The use of NIRS to measure oxygenation changes in the brain cortex due to the execution of mental tasks was presented in 1993 by four different research groups.[9,10,11,12] These works are considered the starting point in functional NIRS (fNIRS) research.

The pioneer fNIRS studies used simple NIRS devices that allowed measurements in only a few cortical locations. The introduction of simultaneous measurements in multiple cortical locations led to the use of fNIRS to provide topographical information.[4] Nowadays, fNIRS is regarded as a relevant technique for the study of brain activity as fNIRS presents characteristics that complement other neuroimaging methods.

## 5.3 NIRS Overview

NIRS is a technique where a given material sample is illuminated with NIR light (wavelength 650-950 nm); then, the light that is not absorbed by the sample is quantitatively analyzed to study the composition of the sample. A thorough determination is possible as each compound (or chromophore) in the sample presents a characteristic absorption pattern for NIR light; this absorption has its origin in the molecular structure and properties of the compound.[13]

For an absorbing compound dissolved in a non-absorbing and non-scattering medium, (i.e., its optical properties: absorption and scattering coefficients are zero), the relationship between the attenuation (also known as optical density) of light with a wavelength $\lambda$ passing through the medium and the concentration of the absorbing compound is given by the Beer-Lambert law (BLL):

$$A(\lambda) = -\log_{10}\left(\frac{I_{out}(\lambda)}{I_{in}(\lambda)}\right) = \epsilon(\lambda)cd, \qquad (1)$$

where $A$ is the measured attenuation, $I_{in}$ is the intensity of the incident light, $I_{out}$ is the intensity of the transmitted light through the medium; $\epsilon$ is the wavelength-dependent molar extinction coefficient of the absorbing compound measured in M⁻¹cm⁻¹; $c$ is the molar concentration of the absorbing compound in the solution measured in M, and $d$ is optical pathlength, the distance between the points where the light enters and leaves the medium measured in cm. For non-scattering media $\epsilon = \alpha\log_{10}(e)$, with $\alpha$ as the molar absorption coefficient. The product $n\alpha c$ corresponds to the absorption coefficient (or factor) $\mu_a$ measured in cm⁻¹. In the case of more than one compound, the total attenuation is the summation of the attenuation for each compound.

Among the main characteristics that render NIRS a powerful technique for the study of human tissues we find:

1. Human tissues are relatively transparent to light in the NIR spectrum (650-950 nm).
2. The incident NIR light is either absorbed by chromophores such as fats, proteins, melanin, and hemoglobin, among others, or scattered in the tissues.
3. The quantity of light that is absorbed depends on two variables: the concentration of the compounds and their absorption coefficient for a given wavelength. In this sense, a compound with a fixed concentration will present an

absorption spectrum that indicates how the light is absorbed for different wavelengths. Figure 5.1 shows the absorption spectra of important compounds present in human tissues.

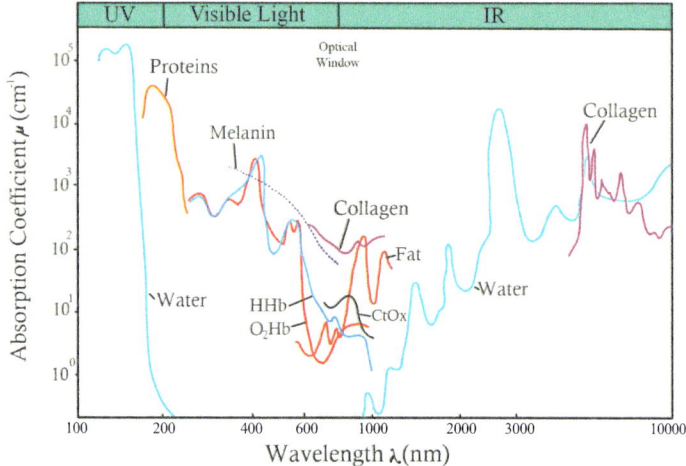

Figure 5.1. Absorption spectra for different chromophores present in human tissues, Adapted From Scholkmann, Felix, Stefan Kleiser, Andreas Jaakko Metz, Raphael Zimmermann, Juan Mata Pavia, Ursula Wolf, and Martin Wolf. "A review on continuous wave functional near-infrared spectroscopy and imaging instrumentation and methodology." *Neuroimage* 85 (2014): 6-27.

4. Various compounds present high absorption coefficients in the NIR range, but they are present in relatively low concentrations relative to hemoglobin, making hemoglobin the main absorbing compound. Hemoglobin absorption spectrum depends on its oxygenation status; as such, two compounds of special interest for clinical purposes are deoxyhemoglobin (HHb) and oxyhemoglobin ($O_2$Hb). As HHb and $O_2$Hb possess different absorption spectra, it is possible to estimate the concentration of these compounds and thus derive information on blood oxygenation. The absorption spectra inside the "optical window" for HHb, $O_2$Hb, and water are presented in figure 5.2. Note that the major absorption of NIR light in the tissues is due to the hemoglobin located in small vessels (capillary).

5. Due to the composition of human tissues, the scattering of NIR light is 100 times more probable than its absorption; this is to say, NIR light can be transmitted through many centimeters of tissue. Moreover, because of the complex light scattering in different tissues, the optical pathlength (distance traveled by the light) is longer than the physical distance between the entry and the exit of the NIR light.

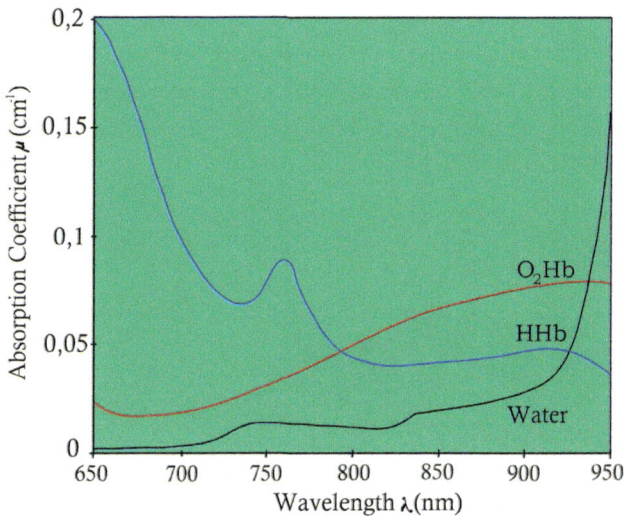

**Figure 5.2.** Absorption spectra for HHb, O$_2$Hb and water in the NIRS optical window (650 - 950nm), Adapted from Bozkurt, Alper, and Banu Onaral. "Safety assessment of near infrared light emitting diodes for diffuse optical measurements." *Biomedical engineering online* 3, no. 1 (2004): 1-10.

The BLL formulation presented in Eq. (1) assumes a non-scattering medium (scattering coefficient $\mu_s$ equal to zero), and this is not the case for human tissues. Thus, to account for scattering media, diverse methods have been developed. Of these methods, the modified Beer-Lamber law (MBLL)[14] is the most used method. The MBLL allows the conversion of the measured attenuation of the NIR light into concentrations of compounds.

$$A(\lambda) = -\log_{10}\left(\frac{I_{out}}{I_{in}}\right) = \sum_i \epsilon_i(\lambda) c_i DPF(\lambda) d + G(\lambda) \qquad (2)$$

Where index $i$ indicates the compounds under study, commonly HHb and O$_2$Hb; *DPF* is a differential pathlength factor that compensates for the increased distance the light travels as $\mu_s$ is different from zero; finally, $G$ is a time-invariant unknown geometry-dependent factor. Finally, by knowing [HHb] and [O$_2$Hb], it is possible to infer the level of oxygenation of the studied tissue.

To study the oxygenation levels of the brain a source of NIR light and a detector are placed on the scalp. The distance between source and detector is defined by the desired penetration depth of NIR light, and the penetration depth is approximately half of the distance between the source and the detector.

NIR light is emitted by the source (two wavelengths are used). In its travel from source to detector, NIR light is mainly absorbed by HHb and O$_2$Hb by the time it reaches the detector. Thus, the measured attenuation of the NIR light corresponds to the concentrations of HHb and O$_2$Hb in the tissue below and between the source and the detector. Additionally, NIR light is diffused (scattered) in all directions inside the head tissues (scalp, skull, and subarachnoid space filled with cerebrospinal fluid); as a result, the spatial distribution of NIR light through the layers is a banana-shaped region. This region is illustrated in figure 5.3.

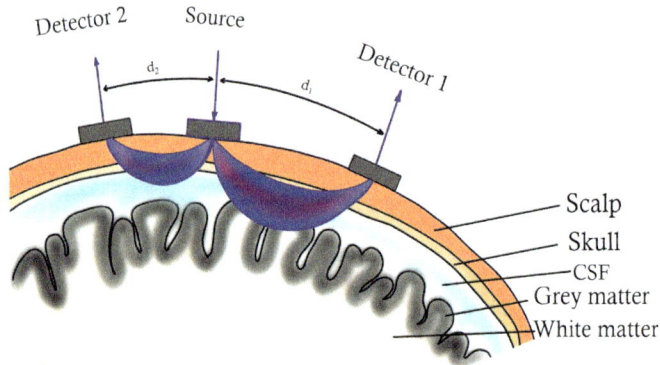

Figure 5.3. Path followed by NIR light through the different layers of the head. Depth is proportional to the distance between source and detector. From Pinti, Paola, Ilias Tachtsidis, Antonia Hamilton, Joy Hirsch, Clarisse Aichelburg, Sam Gilbert, and Paul W. Burgess. "The present and future use of functional near-infrared spectroscopy (fNIRS) for cognitive neuroscience." *Annals of the New York Academy of Sciences* 1464, no. 1 (2020): 5.

Interestingly, in the brain, the level of oxygenation depends on blood flow, which, in turn, is dependent on neuronal activity. In this sense, with the use of NIRS, it is possible to measure changes in oxygenation in the brain; and from these variations, to infer levels of neural activity by its demand for oxygen. This approach is known as functional NIRS (fNIRS).

## 5.4  fNIRS Overview

Functional near-infrared spectroscopy (fNIRS) is a noninvasive neuroimaging technique that uses NIRS to analyze oxygenation due to functional activation in the brain. fNIRS is often referred to by other names such as optical topography or near-infrared imaging (NIRI).

When in a specific region of the brain, there is an increment of neural activity, the consumption of oxygen and glucose increases to keep with that demand, and local blood vessels dilate, resulting in an increment of blood flow in that region. As the increment of oxygen transported to the region typically exceeds the local neuronal rate of oxygen utilization, there is an overabundance of cerebral blood oxygenation (increase in $[O_2Hb]$, and a decrease in $[HHb]$) in the active areas between 3-6 s after the neural activity.[15]

This relationship between the local increment of oxygenated blood flow and brain activity is known as neurovascular coupling, or hemodynamic response, and is depicted in figure 5.4. By using NIRS, fNIRS exploits the neurovascular coupling phenomenon to infer changes in the neural activity in a given region by analyzing the local changes in blood oxygenation.[4,16] This measurement of brain activity with indirect variables is similar to the approach used in functional magnetic resonance imagery (fMRI) presented in chapter 4, where the blood-oxygen-level-dependent (BOLD) signal is an indicator of neural activity.

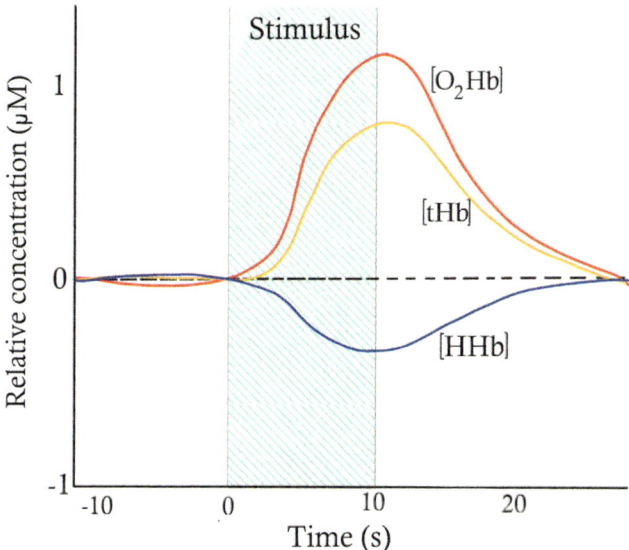

**Figure 5.4.** Typical neuronal hemodynamic response, from Scholkmann, Felix, Stefan Kleiser, Andreas Jaakko Metz, Raphael Zimmermann, Juan Mata Pavia, Ursula Wolf, and Martin Wolf. "A review on continuous wave functional near-infrared spectroscopy and imaging instrumentation and methodology." *Neuroimage* 85 (2014): 6-27.

With the use of Eq(2), it is possible to infer the temporal changes in [HHb] and [$O_2$Hb]. Thus, for an interval $\Delta t = t_1 - t_0$, the relationship between the temporal changes in the [HHb] and [$O_2$Hb] and the changes in the measured attenuation are given as:

$$\Delta A(\Delta t, \lambda) = -\log_{10}\left(\frac{I_{out}(t_1, \lambda)}{I_{out}(t_0, \lambda)}\right) = \sum_i \epsilon_i(\lambda) \Delta c_i DPF(\lambda) d, \quad (3)$$

where $\Delta c_i = c_i(t_1) - c_i(t_0)$ represents the temporal changes in the compound's concentrations. Typical values for ε and *DPF* can be found in the fNIRS literature.

As fNIRS allows the characterization of brain hemodynamics in a noninvasive, portable, comfortable, and potentially wearable way, it has become a useful tool to study either physiological or pathological conditions. Its attributes are reflected in the steady growth that fNIRS research has enjoyed in the last two decades, with the number of related publications doubling every 3.5 years.[17] A general overview of fNIRS devices is provided below, followed by a comparison of fNIRS with other neuroimaging techniques and its current uses.

### 5.4.1 Devices

The miniaturization and affordability of sensors and circuitry have led to great advances in fNIRS technology, from the single-channel fNIRS devices used in the early 1990s to current fNIRS devices that can simultaneously measure +200 channels providing detailed topographic maps of the ongoing brain activity. Moreover, depending on their main application, fNIRS devices can be portable and wearable, opening the door for the acquisition of fNIRS signals in places other than typical clinical environments. Despite the great diversity of fNIRS devices, some relevant characteristics to consider for selection include the illumination method, light wavelengths used, technologies used to emit and detect light, and the number of channels.

#### 5.4.1.1 Illumination type

According to the type of illumination used in fNIRS devices, these can be divided into three categories: continuous-wave (CW), time-domain (TD), and frequency-domain (FD).

CW (or continuous intensity) fNIRS devices are the simplest and most used fNIRS systems. As the name indicates, these devices continuously emit NIR light, typically at two or more wavelengths. Backscattered light is detected, and light attenuation is measured. From the changes in the light attenuation, changes in [HHb] and [O$_2$Hb] are registered using a value control of zero at the start of recording. Absolute baseline concentrations cannot be resolved, as CW fNIRS devices are not able to separate and quantify the contribution of absorption and scattering. However, in experiments where the functional activity is evaluated relative to a baseline, the absolute concentrations are not needed. The absolute concentrations of [HHb] and [O$_2$Hb] can be obtained with TD and FD fNIRS devices.[2,18]

In TD (also known as time-resolved) fNIRS devices, a short duration (~100 ps) light pulse is emitted, and the temporal point spread function (impulse response) of the light after it has passed through the tissue is analyzed. The scattering process broadens the duration of the pulse while the absorption modifies its intensity. As such the optical properties ($\mu_a$ and $\mu_s$) of the tissue can be estimated.[1,16]

The FD (or phase modulation) fNIRS devices follow an approach similar to TD devices, but in the frequency domain. Light is modulated in intensity (amplitude modulation) at radio frequencies, after passing through the tissue, amplitude, and phase shift of the emerging wave are measured. With these parameters, it is possible to determine the optical properties of the tissue, as the phase contains information about the time of travel and the amplitude of the absorption.[1,19]

Figure 5.5 presents the main three types of illumination used in fNIRS devices. Regardless of the illumination technique, NIR light is emitted and received by sources and detectors, respectively. Collectively, sources and detectors are referred to as optodes.

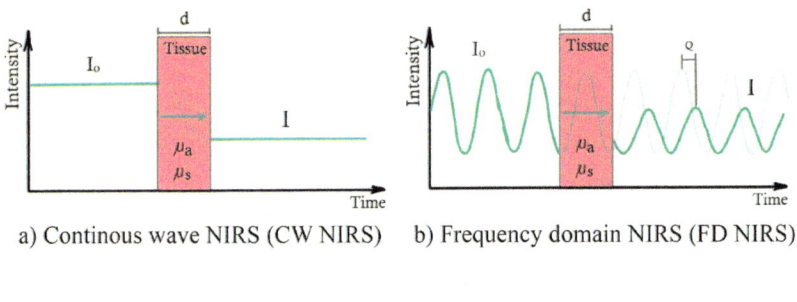

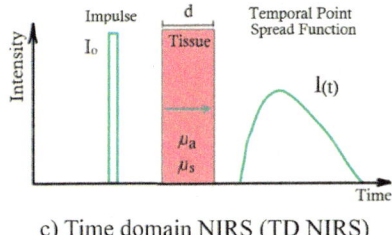

**Figure 5.5.** Type of illumination: CW, FD, and TD. From Scholkmann, Felix, Stefan Kleiser, Andreas Jaakko Metz, Raphael Zimmermann, Juan Mata Pavia, Ursula Wolf, and Martin Wolf. "A review on continuous wave functional near-infrared spectroscopy and imaging instrumentation and methodology." *Neuroimage* 85 (2014): 6-27.

### 5.4.1.2 Optodes: sources and detectors

Two types of NIR light sources are used in fNIRS devices: laser diodes and light-emitting diodes (LEDs). Both diodes are made of semiconductors and use the electroluminescence phenomenon. Laser diodes have some advantages over LEDs, as LEDs provide incoherent light with a broad bandwidth up to 50 nm, while laser diodes emit coherent light with narrower bandwidths. On the other hand, LEDs allow more flexibility in the wavelength selection, are smaller and less expensive; for these reasons, LEDs are commonly used as an alternative to laser diodes.[2]

Regardless of the source of NIR light, the emission component has to be carefully designed to avoid fluctuations in the intensity and wavelength of the radiated light, as these fluctuations introduce measurement errors. The transduction from light to an electric signal is based on the photoelectric effect. The most common semiconductor devices used as detectors in fNIRS devices are the photodiode, avalanche photodiode, and photomultiplier tube. There are two options to transfer the light from the sources to the scalp, and from the scalp to the detectors: either the optodes are placed directly on the scalp, or the light is channelized between the scalp and the optodes by optic fibers. The first approach presents the advantage of being more robust to movements from the subject.

### 5.4.1.3 Number of channels

A fNIRS channel is defined as the combination of a source and a detector. Thus, a fNIRS channel measures the oxygenation levels of the area below and between its source and its detector. fNIRS devices have drastically evolved from single-channel measurements in the 1990s to current devices with more than 200 channels. The theoretical maximum of channels is the product of the number of sources and the number of detectors. However, in practice the number of channels is lower as due to their placement over the scalp, not all detectors can receive light from all the sources. Nowadays, there is no agreement on the placement of the optodes on the scalp, as general practice locations are borrowed from the international 10-20 system used in EEG (chapter 2).

Moreover, the selection of source-detector distance depends on the properties of the NIR light used (intensity and wavelength), as well as the age of the subject and the head region measured. Longer source-detector distances allow us to explore deeper regions of the brain but lead to a low signal-to-noise ratio (SNR). Typical values for source–detector distances are 3-3.5 cm for adult studies and 2-2.5 cm for infants.[4,18]

### 5.4.1.4 Cost

Most fNIRS devices in the market are CW-based, and their cost is linked to the number of channels, optodes technology, and portability. These devices can cost from US$10,000 to US$100,000. In general, TD- and FD-based devices are more expensive than CW devices as they require sophisticated equipment. A list of the main manufactures of fNIRS devices can be found in: https://fnirs.org/resources/instruments/. Moreover, open documentation and design files for a portable CW NIRS device can be found in http://www.opennirs.org/.

## 5.4.2 Signal processing

The changes in [HHb] and [O$_2$Hb] are obtained by evaluating Eq(3) for two different wavelengths, and solving:

$$\begin{bmatrix} \Delta [\text{HHb}] \\ \Delta [\text{O}_2\text{Hb}] \end{bmatrix} = (d)^{-1} \begin{bmatrix} \epsilon_{\text{HHb}}(\lambda_1) & \epsilon_{\text{O}_2\text{Hb}}(\lambda_2) \\ \epsilon_{\text{HHb}}(\lambda_2) & \epsilon_{\text{O}_2\text{Hb}}(\lambda_1) \end{bmatrix}^{-1} \begin{bmatrix} \Delta A(\Delta t, \lambda_1)/DPF(\lambda_1) \\ \Delta A(\Delta t, \lambda_2)/DPF(\lambda_2) \end{bmatrix} \quad (4)$$

The raw fNIRS signals (i.e., the intensities recorded by the detectors ($\Delta A(\Delta t, \lambda_1)$ and $\Delta A(\Delta t, \lambda_2)$), are often corrupted by artifacts. Due to its nature, raw fNIRS signals are distorted by activity in cardiac pulsation, respiration, and Mayer waves (cyclic changes in arterial blood pressure). Movements of the head and face also have negative effects on the quality of the signals, as they may cause movement on the optodes. Lastly, ambient light may also be present in the signals as noise. All these artifacts can lead to inaccurate quantification of [O$_2$Hb] and [HHb] temporal dynamics, thus must be removed or rejected.[2,20]

Currently, there are no standardized signal processing pipelines for fNIRS signals. However, common processing pipelines found in the fNIRS literature comprehend the following steps:

1. Raw fNIRS signals are visually inspected to identify large artifacts due to optode movement. In this step, the presence of heart-beat oscillations is a good sign, as it indicates the good optical coupling between the optodes and the scalp.
2. Raw fNIRS signals are converted to changes in [O$_2$Hb] and [HHb] concentrations by solving Eq.(4).
3. The physiological artifacts in the concentration signals can be easily removed using the band-pass digital filters.
4. Finally, $\Delta$[HHb]($t$) and $\Delta$[O$_2$Hb]($t$) signals are used to perform statistical analysis and/or feature computation.[21]

Interestingly, some fNIRS works report the use of digital filtering on raw fNIRS signals before the computation of the concentration signals. Moreover, given the similarities between the fNIRS signals and the BOLD signal, diverse methods to analyze the latter have been used in fNIRS research. An extensive review in current methods for processing fNIRS signals can be found in Pinti et al, (2019) "Current status and issues regarding pre-processing of fNIRS neuroimaging data: investigation of diverse signal filtering methods within a general linear model framework."[22]

### 5.4.3 Risks

In general, high-intensity NIR light sources are desirable as they maximize the amount of light that reaches the detector, improving the SNR. Moreover, high intensities allow longer source-detector distances, which in turn enable the study of deeper structures. However, high light intensity can lead to tissue heating due to the irradiation and conductive heat transport from the source. This potential reaction may not only distort the measurements but may endanger or at least cause discomfort to the subject.[2,23]

### 5.4.4 fNIRS Compared with Other Neuroimaging Modalities

Similar to other neuroimaging modalities such as fMRI (chapter 4) and PET (chapter 6), fNIRS provides an indirect measurement of brain activity, which is inferred from the metabolic footprints of neural activity. As such, there is an inherent delay between the onset of neuronal activation and the changes in the fNIRS signals. This delay is not present in methods that directly measure the electrical activity of the brain, such as EEG (chapter 2) and MEG (chapter 3). Regarding spatial and temporal resolution, fNIRS falls in the middle of the range obtained by other modalities. Due to its optical nature, fNIRS does not produce, nor is affected by, electromagnetic interference. As such, it can be used in parallel with other modalities (e.g., EEG and fMRI) to have a more detailed characterization of brain activity. Table 5.1 presents a comparison in different characteristics for fNIRS, fMRI, EEG, MEG, and PET.[18]

Despite being present for over two decades, there is a lack of standardization of instrumentation, methods for signal processing, statistical analysis, feature computations, and more in fNIRS research. This situation is expected to change with a growing adaption of fNIRS and the existence of organizations such as the Society for functional Near-Infrared Spectroscopy (SfNIRS).

### 5.4.5 fNIRS Uses

As a result of its characteristics, fNIRS is regarded as a flexible tool that has proven to be suitable for the study of brain development, cognitive and affective states, and physiological and pathological conditions.

In the field of neurodevelopment, fNIRS stands out among other neuroimaging modalities because it is suitable for the study of brain activity in infant participants (often neonatal), as they are not required to be still as in fMRI and MEG recording sessions. Also, no radioactive tracers are needed as in PET, and brain activity can be acquired with higher spatial resolution than EEG.

Table 5.1 Comparison of fNIRS with other neuroimaging modalities.

| | fNIRS | fMRI | EEG | MEG | PET |
|---|---|---|---|---|---|
| Neural activity measurement | Indirect | Indirect | Direct | Direct | Indirect |
| Signal | Hemodynamic response (HHB, $O_2$Hb) | Hemodynamic response (BOLD) | Electric potentials on scalp | Magnetic fields in the head | Brain metabolism |
| Spatial resolution | ~ 1 cm | ≥0.5 mm voxels | 5-9 cm | ~1 cm | 3-4 mm |
| Penetration depth | Brain cortex | Whole head | Brain cortex | Deep structures | Whole head |
| Sampling rate | Low ≤ 25 Hz | Low ≤ 3 Hz | High > 1000 Hz | High > 1000 Hz | Low < 0.1 Hz |
| Robustness to motion | Yes | No | Yes | No | No |
| Participants | Everyone | Limited | Everyone | Limited | Limited |
| Outside Lab conditions | Yes | No | Yes | No | No |
| Wearable? | Yes | No | Yes | No | No |
| Long term monitoring | Yes | No | Yes | No | No |
| Cost | Low | High | Low | High | High |

Pioneering in the field aimed to detect the neuronal response evoked by stimulus in the visual and auditory cortices. More recent applications include the study of object processing, social communication, motion processing, action observation, the regulation of emotions, and face processing.[17,24] In the study of the adult brain, fNIRS has been used to find correlates between cortical activation, and cognitive and affective states. Some of the states explored with fNIRS include cognitive workload, attention, perception, working memory, valence, and arousal. These states have also been studied with other modalities such as EEG. The comparison between fNIRS and EEG does not show a clear advantage of one modality over the other. However, it suggests that by combining them, it is possible to exploit their capabilities to achieve better outcomes.

Most of the work on fNIRS and mental states is performed offline. However, online research is carried out to provide a passive brain-computer interface (BCI); this is to say, a system that monitors the cognitive (or affective) state of the user and adapts itself accordingly to enrich the interaction between the user and the system. The simultaneous use of fNIRS and other modalities opens the door for the use of hybrid BCIs (chapter 12), that aim to improve their performance by combining modalities.[17,25,26] Moreover, fNIRS has been used to study and reach a better understanding of different psychiatric disorders, such as schizophrenic illnesses, affective disorders, and developmental syndromes such as attention-deficit hyperactivity disorder and autism. Lastly, fNIRS has also been used to study normal and pathological aging, neurodegeneration, epilepsy, cerebrovascular disease, and more.[17,18]

### 5.4.6 Future

Technological advances in fNIRS hardware will lead to the widespread use of fNIRS not only in research but in clinical applications. Moreover, TD and FD fNIRS devices are expected to be more affordable, allowing the measurement of the optical properties in the tissues. Current advances in signal processing and machine learning will have an enormous impact on the development of fNIRS-based systems to diagnose diseases and disorders and on human-machine interfaces. An important challenge is defining guidelines and standards for the acquisition, processing, and analysis of fNIRS signals. This uniformity will allow a direct comparison between works from different research groups, and consequently, better and refined methods to extract valuable information from the fNIRS recordings.

### 5.4.7 Conclusion

With its origins in the discovery of the optical window that human tissues offer to NIR light, fNIRS has been used for over 20 years as an interesting tool for the study of brain activity. Compared to other neuroimaging modalities, fNIRS characteristics such as cost, portability, and time resolution give fNIRS an advantage over modalities such as fMRI and PET. On the other hand, fNIRS presents advantages over EEG and MEG, such as spatial resolution and robustness to electromagnetic interference. As such, it has attracted the attention of researchers and is expected to be used as a valuable clinical tool.

# Endnotes

1. Ferrari, Marco, and Valentina Quaresima. "Near infrared brain and muscle oximetry: from the discovery to current applications." *Journal of Near Infrared Spectroscopy* 20, no. 1 (2012): 1-14.

2. Scholkmann, Felix, Stefan Kleiser, Andreas Jaakko Metz, Raphael Zimmermann, Juan Mata Pavia, Ursula Wolf, and Martin Wolf. "A review on continuous wave functional near-infrared spectroscopy and imaging instrumentation and methodology." *Neuroimage* 85 (2014): 6-27.

3. Severinghaus, John W. "Takuo Aoyagi: discovery of pulse oximetry." *Anesthesia & Analgesia* 105, no. 6 (2007): S1-S4.

4. Ferrari, Marco, and Valentina Quaresima. "A brief review on the history of human functional near-infrared spectroscopy (fNIRS) development and fields of application." *Neuroimage* 63, no. 2 (2012): 921-935.

5. Jobsis, Frans F. "Noninvasive, infrared monitoring of cerebral and myocardial oxygen sufficiency and circulatory parameters." *Science* 198, no. 4323 (1977): 1264-1267.

6. Piantadosi, Claude A. "Early development of near-infrared spectroscopy at Duke University." *Journal of biomedical optics* 12, no. 6 (2007): 062102.

7. Brazy, Jane E., Darrell V. Lewis, Michael H. Mitnick, and Frans F. Jöbsis vander Vliet. "Noninvasive monitoring of cerebral oxygenation in preterm infants: preliminary observations." *Pediatrics* 75, no. 2 (1985): 217-225.

8. Fox, Elisabeth, Frans F. Jöbsis-Vander Vliet, and Michael H. Mitnick. "Monitoring cerebral oxygen sufficiency in anesthesia and surgery." In *Oxygen Transport to Tissue VII*, pp. 849-854. Springer, Boston, MA, 1985.

9. Kato, Toshinori, Atsushi Kamei, Sachio Takashima, and Takeo Ozaki. "Human visual cortical function during photic stimulation monitoring by means of near-infrared spectroscopy." *Journal of Cerebral Blood Flow & Metabolism* 13, no. 3 (1993): 516-520.

10. Chance, B., Z. Zhuang, Chu UnAh, C. Alter, and L. Lipton. "Cognition-activated low-frequency modulation of light absorption in human brain." *Proceedings of the National Academy of Sciences* 90, no. 8 (1993): 3770-3774.

11. Hoshi, Yoko, and Mamoru Tamura. "Detection of dynamic changes in cerebral oxygenation coupled to neuronal function during mental work in man." *Neuroscience letters* 150, no. 1 (1993): 5-8.

12. Villringer, Arno, J. Planck, C. Hock, L. Schleinkofer, and U. Dirnagl. "Near infrared spectroscopy (NIRS): a new tool to study hemodynamic changes during activation of brain function in human adults." *Neuroscience letters* 154, no. 1-2 (1993): 101-104.

13. Davies, A. M. C. "An introduction to near infrared spectroscopy." *NIR news* 16, no. 7 (2005): 9-11.

14. Delpy, David T., Mark Cope, Pieter van der Zee, Simon Arridge, Susan Wray, and J. S. Wyatt. "Estimation of optical pathlength through tissue from direct time of flight measurement." *Physics in Medicine & Biology* 33, no. 12 (1988): 1433.

15. Sitaram, Ranganatha, Andrea Caria, and Niels Birbaumer. "Hemodynamic brain–computer interfaces for communication and rehabilitation." *Neural networks* 22, no. 9 (2009): 1320-1328.

16. Quaresima, Valentina, and Marco Ferrari. "Medical near infrared spectroscopy: a prestigious history and a bright future." *NIR news* 27, no. 1 (2016): 10-13.

17. Boas, David A., Clare E. Elwell, Marco Ferrari, and Gentaro Taga. "Twenty years of functional near-infrared spectroscopy: introduction for the special issue." (2014): 1-5.

18. Pinti, Paola, Ilias Tachtsidis, Antonia Hamilton, Joy Hirsch, Clarisse Aichelburg, Sam Gilbert, and Paul W. Burgess. "The present and future use of functional near-infrared spectroscopy (fNIRS) for cognitive neuroscience." *Annals of the New York Academy of Sciences* 1464, no. 1 (2020): 5.

19. Delpy, D. T., and M. Cope. "Quantification in tissue near–infrared spectroscopy." *Philosophical Transactions of the Royal Society of London. Series B: Biological Sciences* 352, no. 1354 (1997): 649-659.

20. Girouard, Audrey, Erin Treacy Solovey, Leanne M. Hirshfield, Evan M. Peck, Krysta Chauncey, Angelo Sassaroli, Sergio Fantini, and Robert JK Jacob. "From brain signals to adaptive interfaces: using fNIRS in HCI." In *Brain-Computer Interfaces*, pp. 221-237. Springer, London, 2010.

21. Tak, Sungho, and Jong Chul Ye. "Statistical analysis of fNIRS data: a comprehensive review." *Neuroimage* 85 (2014): 72-91.

22. Pinti, Paola, Felix Scholkmann, Antonia Hamilton, Paul Burgess, and Ilias Tachtsidis. "Current status and issues regarding pre-processing of fNIRS neuroimaging data: investigation of diverse signal filtering methods within a general linear model framework." *Frontiers in human neuroscience* 12 (2019): 505.

23. Bozkurt, Alper, and Banu Onaral. "Safety assessment of near infrared light emitting diodes for diffuse optical measurements." *biomedical engineering online* 3, no. 1 (2004): 1-10.

24. Lloyd-Fox, Sarah, Anna Blasi, and C. E. Elwell. "Illuminating the developing brain: the past, present and future of functional near infrared spectroscopy." *Neuroscience & Biobehavioral Reviews* 34, no. 3 (2010): 269-284.

25. Strait, Megan, and Matthias Scheutz. "What we can and cannot (yet) do with functional near infrared spectroscopy." *Frontiers in neuroscience* 8 (2014): 117.

26. Bunce, Scott C., Kurtulus Izzetoglu, Hasan Ayaz, Patricia Shewokis, Meltem Izzetoglu, Kambiz Pourrezaei, and Banu Onaral. "Implementation of fNIRS for monitoring levels of expertise and mental workload." In *International Conference on Foundations of Augmented Cognition*, pp. 13-22. Springer, Berlin, Heidelberg, 2011.

# 6
# Positron Emission Tomography (PET)

**Thomas Funck**
*Dr. Thomas Funck completed his PhD in Neuroscience on neurotransmitter receptor mapping with PET at McGill University with Alan C. Evans and Alexander Thiel. He is a post-doctoral research felllow at Forschungszentrum Jülich in the lab of Nicola Palomero-Gallagher. His research focuses on using image processing and AI techniques to create high resolution 3D brain atlases from 2D autoradiographic and histological sections.*

## 6.1   Introduction

Positron Emission Tomography (PET) uses a radioactive tracer to quantify different aspects of brain biology and physiology. While magnetic resonance imaging (MRI) generally provides better spatial resolution and electroencephalography (EEG) better temporal resolution, PET has two important advantages. What makes PET truly unique is the variety of biological phenomena that can be measured and that it provides absolute quantitative and semi-quantitative measures. The specific, quantitative nature of PET measurement combined with its inherent flexibility makes PET an essential brain imaging modality for mapping the human brain.

To get a sense of the diversity of the use cases for PET, consider the following examples. Three of the classic applications of PET are the measurement of glucose metabolism, oxygen consumption, and cerebral blood flow. Researchers also developed PET techniques to image the serotonin, dopamine, and GABA neurotransmitter receptors. PET can also measure neuroinflammation. More recently, PET has been used to study the biological hallmarks of Alzheimer's disease, amyloid plaques, and tau neurofibrillary tangles.[1,2] The natural question that arises from this long, but hardly exhaustive, enumeration: how can a single imaging technique measure so many different things?

PET is based on the injection of a radioactive tracer (i.e., radiotracer) and the monitoring of dynamic spread of the radiotracer within the body as a whole or within a specific organ (e.g., the brain). Most radiotracers are composed of two parts: a radioactive positron-emitting isotope (radionuclide) and a ligand that binds to some molecular structure or receptor in the body. Once the radiotracer is injected into the body, the ligand tends to bind to a target receptor and accumulates. Regions with a higher density of the target receptor will accumulate more of the ligand and, consequently, emit a greater amount of radioactive energy. The scanner can indirectly detect the radioactive energy emitted by the radiotracer. However, note that some radiotracers, such as 0-15, are composed of a radionuclide with no corresponding ligand. These radiotracers are used to measure blood flow or volume.

PET is, therefore, a particularly flexible imaging modality because radiotracers can be designed to bind to many different molecular targets. The particular targets that can be measured with PET are limited in part by which ligands can attach to a suitable radionuclide without altering its binding properties. Radiotracers used for brain PET must also pass the blood-brain barrier that filters solutes flowing from the bloodstream to the brain.

The quantitative and semi-quantitative measurements acquired with PET are inherently informative and make comparisons between different PET scans obvious. By using modeling techniques to control for the amount of radiotracer present in the bloodstream or present in regions without the target receptor, it is possible to estimate, in a more precise manner, how much radiotracer is bound to the molecular target. This insight provides an objective assessment of radiotracer binding that, depending on the radiotracer, can be converted into a biologically meaningful measurement. Moreover, PET is exceptionally sensitive and can produce an accurate quantification of receptors with very low concentrations ($\sim 10^{-9}$-$10^{-12}$ mol/L).[3]

While PET has advantages in terms of flexibility, specificity, and quantification, it is also expensive, potentially invasive, has mediocre spatial resolution, and limited temporal resolution.

## 6.2 How Does it Work?

Imaging with PET is based on the radioactive decay of a radioisotope injected into a living human or non-human animal. The nucleus of a radioisotope contains a greater number of protons versus neutrons. This ratio of protons to neutrons is unstable and, by progressively converting protons to neutrons, tends to a more stable configuration. The conversion causes the emission of a positron and a neutrino from the nucleus.

The positron follows a random trajectory over which its energy gradually decreases. The positron eventually collides with an electron for a very brief period of time, approximately $10^{-10}$s. The combined positron and electron annihilate and emit two photons with an energy of 511-KeV along paths at approximately 180°

and may be detected by the scanner. Detected annihilation events are referred to as counts. Thus, while PET is named after positron emission, it is the photon produced by the annihilation event that is detected by the scanner.

In a vacuum, the photons travel along a straight path from the point of annihilation. In a dense medium like the brain, it is possible for the trajectory of the rays to be altered through interactions with surrounding atoms, which can result in the photon being absorbed (i.e., photon attenuation) or scattered. The attenuation and scattering of photons lead to an erroneous number of counts detected by the scanner, which depends heavily on the anatomy of the object being scanned. Sophisticated correction techniques have been developed to account for these phenomena and produce quantitatively accurate PET images.

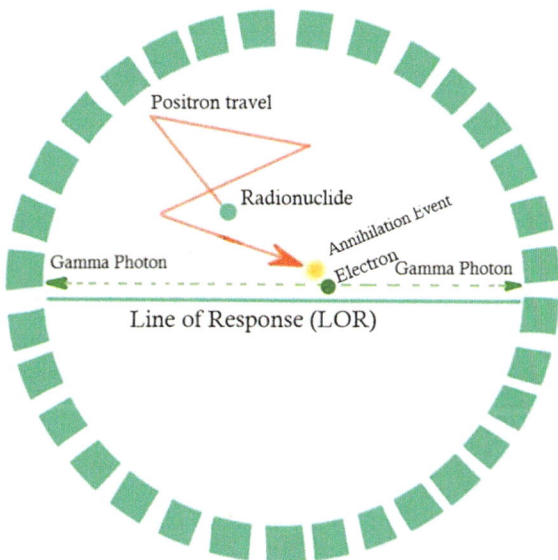

Figure 6.1 Schema of PET physics. A positron is emitted by a radionuclide and travels in a random direction until it encounters an electron. The positron and electron annihilate, producing two photons that travel in opposite directions. The photons are detected by two detectors that record that an annihilation event has occurred somewhere on the LOR between the detectors.

The photons are recorded by a pair of scintillation detectors. The location of the annihilation is assumed to have occurred on the line of response (LOR) between the two detectors. The detected pair of photons are referred to as a count.

PET detectors are made of scintillation crystals that transform the photons into light waves.[4,5] The light waves are then converted to an electrical signal by photomultiplier tubes attached to the detectors.[4] The combination of the scintillation detector that converts the photon to light energy and the photomultiplier tube that converts the light to an electrical signal is referred to as the PET camera.

The detectors are arranged around the scanner's field of view, usually in a circle or octagonal geometry.[6] The PET system uses a short "coincidence" time window to distinguish between genuine and random coincidences between two detectors.[7] Pairs of detectors identify photons within a coincidence time window and are assumed to have been produced by the same annihilation event.[8] This method is imperfect and can introduce noise when photons from different annihilation events (i.e., single photons) are detected within the coincidence window.

The raw PET count data is stored in a special format called a sinogram. The sinogram stores the raw count data based on the angle of the LOR between the detector pairs and the offset of the LOR from the center of the scanner. This representation of the detected counts does not readily provide an image that can be visually interpreted. The sinogram must be reconstructed into an image using complex computational techniques.

Once the image has been reconstructed from the raw sinogram, subsequent computational modeling is necessary to transform the PET image from an image of radioactivity concentration to an image quantifying some aspect of the brain's physiology or biology. This type of modeling is called "tracer kinetic analysis" because it attempts to quantify the binding kinetics of the radiotracer to arrive at an estimate of a parameter of interest to the researcher (e.g., glucose metabolism or receptor density).

Many different tracer kinetic models exist for quantifying radiotracer dynamics and differ based on the type of radiotracer and the physiological or biological parameter in which the researcher is interested.

The physiological models used for tracer kinetic analysis generally assume a fixed set of physiological states, called "compartments," between which the radiotracer can pass. For example, the radiotracer can be freely available or bound in either arterial blood or brain tissue.[9]

An important concept in tracer kinetic analysis is that the radiotracer can bind to the target of interest, referred to as "specific" binding or to off-target sites referred to as "non-specific binding." The purpose of tracer kinetic analysis is to control for free and spuriously, non-specifically bound radiotracer to arrive at an estimate of how much radiotracer is actually bound to the target of interest.

Ideally, quantitative PET requires the measurement of the arterial concentration of the radiotracer. Doing so allows researchers to distinguish between how much of the measured radioactivity in the brain comes from the cerebral vasculature and how much is actually located in the brain tissue. Distinguishing between the arterial and brain radioactivity concentration allows for a more accurate estimate of the distribution of radioactivity that accumulates in the brain tissue.

## 6.3 History

The development of PET has been the product of parallel developments in nuclear physics and medicine over many decades. As new insights into nuclear physics and radioactivity were uncovered, they were quickly translated into medical applications in the emerging field of nuclear medicine. Indeed, the story of PET begins in the late 19th and early 20th-centuries with the discovery of radioactive energy.[10,11,12,13] These early discoveries in radioactive molecules were translated into medical research with the injection of radioactive substances in humans.[14,15]

The concept of the radiotracer was pioneered by George Charles von Hevesy[16] — who later won the 1943 Nobel Prize in Chemistry for this work — He first used radiotracers in plants and shortly after that in humans to, initially, study the effects of lead on the metabolism of a living subject.[17] Meanwhile, as early as 1924, a technique called autoradiography was created that could produce images of the distribution of a radionuclide in an animal.[18]

The invention of the cyclotron in 1932 permitted the synthesization of radionuclides.[19] The cyclotron allowed medical researchers to produce iodine radionuclides used to study thyroid diseases in animals and humans.[20,21]

An essential step for the eventual invention of PET was the creation of the PET camera. In 1947, Robert Hofstadter, who was awarded the Nobel Prize in Physics in 1961, demonstrated that a paired scintillation crystal and photomultiplier tube could be used as a photon detector.[22]

In 1953, Gordon Brownell and William Sweet developed the first instrument to measure the coincidence of radioactive particles in vivo.[23] This simple device consisted of two detectors placed opposite one another and on each side of a patient's head. They mapped detected coincidences at different positions along the patient's skull onto a two-dimensional drawing of the patient's head. Within ten years, James Robertson and Lucas Yamamoto at Brookhaven National Laboratory created a PET scanner with paired arrays of coincidence detectors.[24]

The development of techniques to measure physiology using radionuclides led researchers in the 1940s to begin developing tracer kinetic models to quantify physiological parameters based on radioactivity concentration.[25] These techniques were not initially developed for PET but served as the basis for tracer-kinetic modeling techniques developed later.

While there had been important improvements in PET instrumentation through the 1950-1960s, there was still a fundamental problem: how to create an image from recordings of paired detectors. The creation of computational techniques for the reconstruction of images from paired detectors was a pivotal development.[26] Ter-Pogossian, Hoffman, and Phelps used this functional application to develop the first modern PET scanner and developed a reconstruction algorithm based on computed tomography.[27,28] They termed the technique positron-emission transaxial tomography (PETT).

The 1970-80s saw many important improvements in PET technology and the first commercially available PET scanners. Notably, techniques were developed to correct for physical artifacts in the PET scanner(e.g., photon attenuation or scatter.[29] A seminal series of papers were published by Hoffman, Phelps, and Mazzioatta et al. that studied the precise conditions under which PET could be used to acquire quantitatively accurate measurements of radioactivity within the brain.[30,31,32,33,34]

Another important PET innovation that occurred in the 1980s and eventually bore fruit in the following decade was the development of time-of-flight (TOF) PET.[27] With standard PET imaging, it is impossible to determine where an annihilation event has occurred between two detector pairs. TOF PET attempts to estimate the position of the radioactive decay by using the difference in the time at which the photons arrive at their respective detectors and hence estimate their "time of flight." Localizing the position of the annihilation event allows for significant improvements in the spatial resolution of PET images. In the 1980s, the available scintillation detectors were too slow to implement this effectively. However, improvements in the material used for the detectors made the calculation of TOF feasible and eventually widely used in commercial PET scanners.[27,35]

Early PET systems were only designed to acquire a series of 2D images along the axial plane (i.e., perpendicular) to the patient in the scanner. Scientists at Hammersmith Hospital created the first PET scanner compatible with full 3D image acquisition.[36] Detectors in a 3D PET system can detect photons from paired detectors within the same axial plane and with detectors in other axial planes. This ability increases the angle from which the detectors can identify paired photons, dramatically increasing the number of radioactive decay events that the scanner is likely to record.

Through the 1990 and 2000s, a major avenue for research was integrating PET with structural imaging modalities. Integration was first accomplished with the development of combined PET and computed tomography (CT) systems, the first of which was developed in 1998.[37] Although CT is very useful for performing attenuation correction with PET, it exposes patients to additional radioactivity and has limited contrast for soft tissue (e.g., gray and white matter).

Combined PET and MRI scanners were developed in part to address the limitations of PET/CT. The combined PET/MRI scanner poses considerable technical challenges because the MRI's magnetic field disrupts the electronics used by the PET system (i.e., the photomultiplier tubes). The advantage of PET/MRI is not only that it allows a joint PET and sMRI image but also performs studies that combine PET with fMRI.

# 6.4 Properties

Two physical limitations prevent perfect localization of the decaying radionuclide and constitute intrinsic limits on the spatial resolution of PET.

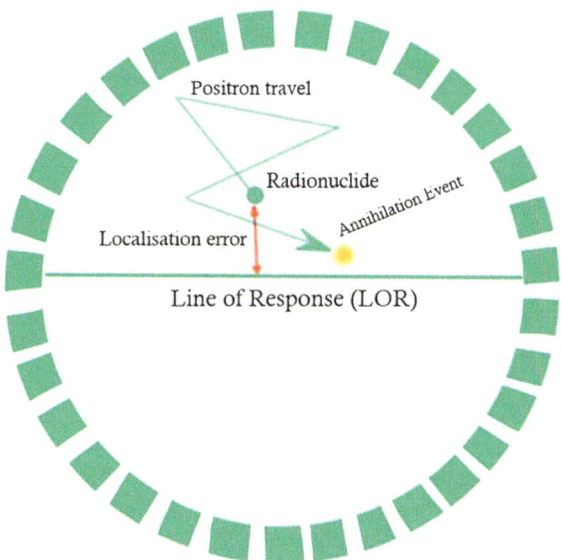

Figure 6.2 The positron travels along a random path before annihilating. This means the LOR is likely not to cover the exact location of the positron emission.

The first factor is that the path traveled by the positron is inherently random. It is impossible to determine the exact location from which the position was emitted based on the annihilation event. The distance that the positron travels between emission and annihilation is a function of the maximum energy of the radionuclide in question (Figure 6.2).

Photon non-collinearity is a second constraint on the maximum resolution obtainable with PET imaging. When a positron combines with an electron, there is often a small amount of remaining momentum that causes the photons to be emitted at an angle that is not exactly 180° but varies around this average following a normal distribution (see Figure 6.3).[38] In practice, the trajectories of two annihilation photons will not be a straight line. Photon non-collinearity is Gaussian distributed with a FWHM (Full width at half maximum) of approximately 0.5°.[39] The effect of photon non-collinearity on the FWHM of the PET image is proportional to the distance of the annihilation event to the photon detectors. Photon detectors may be either discrete or continuous. In the case of discrete detectors, their spatial resolution is proportional to their surface area and, thus, impose a technical limit on PET resolution.

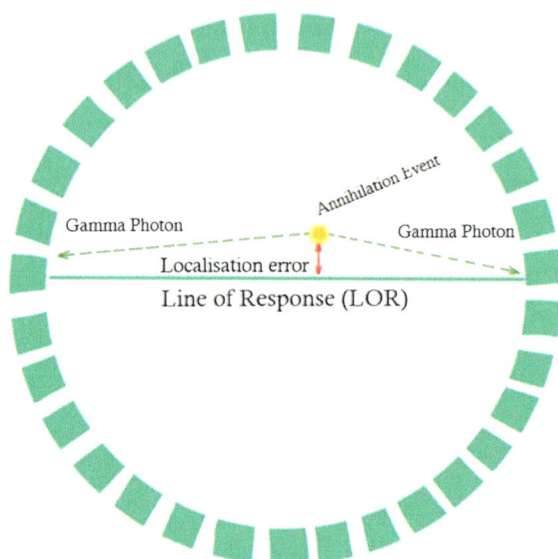

Figure 6.3 Photon non-collinearity reduces PET resolution by causing a count to be detected on the wrong LOR.

## 6.4.1 Precision and Accuracy

Precision and accuracy depend on the corrections applied to the raw count data, the properties of the PET scanner, and the type of quantification conducted.

One way to assess the precision of a brain imaging modality is to perform a "test-retest" study where the same participant is scanned twice. PET has been shown to produce highly correlated results in test-retest studies[40,41] even across different scanners (~0.98%),[42] but may be lower in regions with lower receptor density.[43]

A common way to evaluate the accuracy of PET is using "phantom" scans. In a phantom scan, a glass object is filled with a known concentration of radioactive solution and scanned. The radioactivity measured in the image can then be compared to the known radioactivity in the phantom object to evaluate the accuracy of the image. If the measured region is larger than approximately twice the FWHM resolution of the scanner, then the PET image will correctly represent the true radioactivity concentration in the phantom object.[44]

The biological accuracy of PET can be tested against another brain imaging modality called autoradiography. Autoradiography is the gold-standard modality for receptor mapping but is extremely expensive and can only be performed post-mortem. A study comparing PET versus autoradiography for the same receptor in the same human patients found a significant correlation in receptor density measured with both modalities.[45]

## 6.4.2 Invasiveness

A major limitation of PET is that it requires procedures that are invasive to the subject. First, it is necessary to inject the patient with a dose of the radiotracer, either in a single bolus or as a constant injection. Although the injection is a safe and routine procedure, it can add to participant discomfort, especially for those with a fear of needles. The most accurate form of tracer kinetic analysis is through the use of arterial blood sampling. However, this requires drawing blood from the patient during the scan, which adds technical complications to the scanning procedure and can increase patient discomfort. Thus, PET involves significant invasiveness, especially compared to other 3D brain imaging modalities like MRI.

## 6.4.3 Set Up Requirements

The setup requirements for establishing a PET center are considerable. While some radiotracers may be commercially available in some locations, this is limited to radiotracers that are frequently used in the clinic, specifically [18-F] — fluorodeoxyglucose (FDG). Full PET research centers often require a cyclotron that can be used to attach radioisotopes to the biological ligand. In addition to the costs associated with setting up and running a cyclotron, a PET center will also require a dedicated radiochemistry laboratory to synthesize the radiotracer and perform quality control on batches of radiotracers before injection into participants. All of this is before the actual purchase, use, and maintenance of the PET scanner itself. PET is, therefore, one of the most complex and expensive in vivo brain imaging modalities to operate.

## 6.4.4 Risks

PET uses radioactive isotopes and, therefore, poses risks related to exposure to radioactivity. However, these risks are limited when PET is used according to the safety guidelines of the International Commission on Radiological Protection (ICRP). The impact of radioactivity on a body is in Sieverts (Sv) measured in the number of Joules per kilogram, weighted by the type of radioactive energy.[46] According to these standards, the average individual can be safely exposed to 1mSvy of radiation per year.[46] A typical clinical PET scan exposes the participant to 2-10mSv of radioactivity, comparable to the radiation exposure from computed tomography (CT).[47]

The reason that PET requires relatively small amounts of radioactivity is due to the high specificity of radiotracers for their target binding sites and because of the high sensitivity of the PET system. These mutually beneficial characteristics allow a relatively small amount of radiotracer to produce high-quality images without exposing the participant to excessive radioactivity.

Despite the relatively low radioactivity exposure from a single PET scan, certain populations are still at greater risk including, children, fetuses in pregnant women, and lactating women. Fetuses and children are problematic because their rapidly reproducing cells mean they are more likely to develop cancerous growth from radiation exposure. Therefore, these groups are only scanned in the clinic when the potential benefits of medical treatment outweigh the risks associated with radiation exposure.

The greater risk associated with PET radioactivity is not for the patient but for the nurses and technicians that routinely conduct PET scans.[48] They encounter radioactive participants daily and must be protected against excessive exposure to radioactive particles. Specific safety protocols must, therefore, be put in place to protect healthcare workers from daily radiation exposure.

### 6.4.5 Costs

Based on the set up requirements described above, it is clear that PET is an expensive imaging modality. Not only is it necessary to have a cyclotron, a radiochemistry laboratory, and a PET scanner, but it is also essential to employ the necessary technicians and scientists to set up, run, and maintain these instruments and facilities. The result is that the cost of a typical PET scan costs several thousand dollars. The setup costs can potentially be reduced by outsourcing the production of the radiotracer to commercial producers. However, this limits the PET center to using commercially available radiotracers such a [18-F]-FDG.

### 6.4.6 Limitations

The cost and safety limitations outlined above pose significant practical limitations. The spatial resolution of PET also limits its quantitative accuracy.

Safety restrictions prevent the use of PET for research purposes in potentially vulnerable populations, such as children, and restrict the number of scans a single individual can have within a given time period. The result of this is that PET cannot be used to study child brain development in humans. The limit on the number of scans also means that PET cannot be used to repeatedly scan the same participant more than a couple of times within a year, making it difficult to track subtle changes over time.

The high cost of PET means that not all groups have access to it as more affordable modalities, such as EEG, and that it is hard to acquire large datasets with hundreds of scans. The smaller sample sizes of PET studies is particularly problematic because it makes it difficult to detect small but significant differences between population groups.

Finally, while PET is, in principle, very accurate when measuring within a large region, in practice, researchers frequently wish to measure from anatomic regions that fall within the resolution of the scanner, such as the cortical grey matter. The result is that these data must be carefully corrected for potential resolution artifacts, and the results must be interpreted with caution.

### 6.4.7 Notable Uses

The most successful application of PET has certainly been the use of [18-F]-FDG to measure glucose metabolism. FDG was used for human brain mapping and has proven extremely successful in the clinic.[49,50] [18-F]-FDG is regularly used in breast, pancreatic, lymphatic, colorectal cancers, to name only a few.[51,52]

## Endnotes

1. Landau, S. M., B. A. Thomas, L. Thurfjell, M. Schmidt, R. Margolin, M. Mintun, M. Pontecorvo, S. L. Baker, W. J. Jagust, and Alzheimer's Disease Neuroimaging Initiative. "Amyloid PET imaging in Alzheimer's disease: a comparison of three radiotracers." *European journal of nuclear medicine and molecular imaging* 41, no. 7 (2014): 1398-1407.

2. Leuzy, Antoine, Kerstin Heurling, and Michael Schöll. "PET Biomarkers for Tau Pathology." In *Radiopharmaceuticals*, pp. 227-234. Springer, Cham, 2020.

3. Budinger, Thomas F., and T. Jones. "History of Nuclear Medicine and Molecular Imaging." (2014): 1-37.

4. Kubetsky, L. A. "Multiple amplifier." *Proceedings of the Institute of Radio Engineers* 25, no. 4 (1937): 421-433.

5. Hofstadter, Robert. "Thallium halide crystal counter." *Physical Review* 72, no. 11 (1947): 1120.

6. Ter-Pogossian, Michel M., Michael E. Phelps, Edward J. Hoffman, and Nizar A. Mullani. "A positron-emission transaxial tomograph for nuclear imaging (PETT)." *Radiology* 114, no. 1 (1975): 89-98.

7. Baba, T., S. Harada, H. Asano, K. Sugimoto, N. Takenaka, and K. Mochiki. "Nuclear Instruments and Methods in Physics Research A." *Nuclear Instruments and Methods in Physics Research A* 605 (2009): 209-214.

8. Shukla, Arvind K., and Utham Kumar. "Positron emission tomography: An overview." *Journal of medical physics/Association of Medical Physicists of India* 31, no. 1 (2006): 13.

9. Pike, Victor W. "PET radiotracers: crossing the blood–brain barrier and surviving metabolism." *Trends in pharmacological sciences* 30, no. 8 (2009): 431-440.

10. Becquerel, Henri. "Sur les radiations émises par phosphorescent." *Comptes Rendus* 122 (1896): 420-421.

11. Curie P., Curie M, Bemont G. "Sur une nouvelle substance fortement radio-active contenue dans la pechblende." *Comptes rendus de l'Académie des Sciences*. 1898. 127:1215–1218.

12. Thomson, J. J. "Cathode rays." *Philosophical Magazine* 90, no. S1 (2010): 25-29.

13. Rutherford, Ernest, and Frederick Soddy. "XLI. The cause and nature of radioactivity. Part I." *The London, Edinburgh, and Dublin Philosophical Magazine and Journal of Science* 4, no. 21 (1902): 370-396.

14. Proescher, Frederick. "The intravenous injection of soluble radium salts in man." *Radium* 1 (1913): 9-10.

15. Seil, Harvey A., C. H. Viol, and M. A. Gordon. "The elimination of soluble radium salts taken intravenously and per os." *NY Med J* 101 (1915): 896-898.

16. Hevesy, George. "The Absorption and Translocation of Lead by Plants: A Contribution to the Application of the Method of Radioactive Indicators in the Investigation of the Change of Substance in Plants." *Biochemical Journal* 17, no. 4-5 (1923): 439-445.

17. Blumgart, Herrmann L., and Otto C. Yens. "Studies on the velocity of blood flow: I. The method utilized." *The Journal of clinical investigation* 4, no. 1 (1927): 1-13.

18. 18. 18. Lacassagne, Antoine, and J. S. Lattes. "Méthode autohisto-radiographique pour la detection dans les organes du polonium injecté." *Comptes rendus de l'Académie des sciences* 178 (1924): 488-491.

19. Lawrence, Ernest O., and M. Stanley Livingston. "The production of high speed light ions without the use of high voltages." *Physical Review* 40, no. 1 (1932): 19.

20. Livingood, J. J., and G. T. Seaborg. "Radioactive isotopes of iodine." *Physical review* 54, no. 10 (1938): 775.

21. Hertz, Saul, A. Roberts, and Robley D. Evans. "Radioactive iodine as an indicator in the study of thyroid physiology." *Proceedings of the Society for Experimental Biology and Medicine* 38, no. 4 (1938): 510-513.

22. Hofstadter, Robert. "Thallium halide crystal counter." *Physical Review* 72, no. 11 (1947): 1120.

23. Sweet, William H., and Gordon L. Brownell. "The use of radioactive isotopes in the detection and localization of brain tumors." *Radioisotopes in Medicine: A Course Given September*, 1953 125 (1956): 211.

24. Ketchum, Linda E. "Brookhaven, Origin of TC-99M and F-18 FDG, Opens New Frontiers for Nuclear Medicine." *Journal of Nuclear Medicine* 27, no. 10 (1986): 1507-1515.

25. Kety, Seymour S., and Carl F. Schmidt. "The determination of cerebral blood flow in man by the use of nitrous oxide in low concentrations." *American Journal of Physiology-Legacy Content* 143, no. 1 (1945): 53-66.

26. Hounsfield, Godfrey N. "Computerized transverse axial scanning (tomography): Part 1. Description of system." *The British journal of radiology* 46, no. 552 (1973): 1016-1022.

27. Ter-Pogossian, M. M., Nizar A. Mullani, David C. Ficke, Joanne Markham, and Donald L. Snyder. "Photon time-of-flight-assisted positron emission tomography." *Journal of computer assisted tomography* 5, no. 2 (1981): 227-239.

28. Phelps, M. E., S. C. Huang, E. J. Hoffman, C. Selin, L. Sokoloff, and D. E. Kuhl. "Tomographic measurement of local cerebral glucose metabolic rate in humans with (F-18) 2-fluoro-2-deoxy-D-glucose: validation of method." *Annals of Neurology: Official Journal of the American Neurological Association and the Child Neurology Society* 6, no. 5 (1979): 371-388.

29. Chang, Lee-Tzuu. "A method for attenuation correction in radionuclide computed tomography." *IEEE Transactions on Nuclear Science* 25, no. 1 (1978): 638-643.

30. Hoffman, Edward J., Sung-Cheng Huang, Michael E. Phelps, and David E. Kuhl. "Quantitation in positron emission computed tomography: 4. Effect of accidental coincidences." *Journal of computer assisted tomography* 5, no. 3 (1981): 391-400.

31. Huang, S-C., R. E. Carson, E. J. Hoffman, J. Carson, N. MacDonald, J. R. Barrio, and M. E. Phelps. "Quantitative measurement of local cerebral blood flow in humans by positron computed tomography and 15O-water." *Journal of Cerebral Blood Flow & Metabolism* 3, no. 2 (1983): 141-153.

32. Hoffman, Edward J., Sung-Cheng Huang, David Plummer, and Michael E. Phelps. "Quantitation in positron emission computed tomography: 6. effect of nonuniform resolution." *Journal of computer assisted tomography* 6, no. 5 (1982): 987-999.

33. Hoffman, Edward J., Sung-Cheng Huang, Michael E. Phelps, and David E. Kuhl. "Quantitation in positron emission computed tomography: 4. Effect of accidental coincidences." *Journal of computer assisted tomography* 5, no. 3 (1981): 391-400.

34. Mazziotta, John C., Michael E. Phelps, David Plummer, and David E. Kuhl. "Quantitation in positron emission computed tomography: 5. Physical--anatomical effects." *Journal of Computer Assisted Tomography* 5, no. 5 (1981): 734-743.

35. Wagner Jr, Henry N. "A brief history of positron emission tomography (PET)." In *Seminars in nuclear medicine*, vol. 28, no. 3, pp. 213-220. WB Saunders, 1998.

36. Townsend, D. W., T. Sprinks, T. Jones, A. Geissbuhler, M. Defrise, M. C. Gilardi, and J. Heather. "Three dimensional reconstruction of PET data from a multi-ring camera." *IEEE Transactions on Nuclear Science* 36, no. 1 (1989): 1056-1065.

37. Beyer, Thomas, David W. Townsend, Tony Brun, Paul E. Kinahan, Martin Charron, Raymond Roddy, Jeff Jerin, John Young, Larry Byars, and Ronald Nutt. "A combined PET/CT scanner for clinical oncology." *Journal of nuclear medicine* 41, no. 8 (2000): 1369-1379.

38. Gerhart, J. B., B. C. Carlson, and R. Sherr. "Annihilation of positrons in flight." *Physical Review* 94, no. 4 (1954): 917.

39. Colombino, P., B. Fiscella, and L. Trossi. "Study of positronium in water and ice from 22 to -144 C by annihilation quanta measurements." *Il Nuovo Cimento (1955-1965)* 38, no. 2 (1965): 707-723.

40. Devous, Michael D., Abhinay D. Joshi, Michael Navitsky, Sudeepti Southekal, Michael J. Pontecorvo, Haiqing Shen, Ming Lu et al. "Test–retest reproducibility for the tau PET imaging agent flortaucipir F 18." *Journal of Nuclear Medicine* 59, no. 6 (2018): 937-943.

41. Lodge, Martin A. "Repeatability of SUV in oncologic 18F-FDG PET." *Journal of Nuclear Medicine* 58, no. 4 (2017): 523-532.

42. Van Velden, Floris HP, Reina W. Kloet, Bart NM Van Berckel, Fred L. Buijs, Gert Luurtsema, Adriaan A. Lammertsma, and Ronald Boellaard. "HRRT versus HR+ human brain PET studies: an interscanner test–retest study." *Journal of Nuclear Medicine* 50, no. 5 (2009): 693-702.

43. Egerton, Alice, Arsime Demjaha, Philip McGuire, Mitul A. Mehta, and Oliver D. Howes. "The test–retest reliability of 18F-DOPA PET in assessing striatal and extrastriatal presynaptic dopaminergic function." *Neuroimage* 50, no. 2 (2010): 524-531.

44. Hoffman, E. J., P. D. Cutler, W. M. Digby, and J. C. Mazziotta. "3-D phantom to simulate cerebral blood flow and metabolic images for PET." *IEEE Transactions on Nuclear Science* 37, no. 2 (1990): 616-620.

45. Koepp, Matthias J., Kieran SP Hand, Clarie Labbé, Mark P. Richardson, Wim Van Paesschen, Virginia H. Baird, Vincent J. Cunningham, Norman G. Bowery, David J. Brooks, and John S. Duncan. "In vivo [11C] flumazenil-PET correlates with ex vivo [3H] flumazenil autoradiography in hippocampal sclerosis." *Annals of Neurology: Official Journal of the American Neurological Association and the Child Neurology Society* 43, no. 5 (1998): 618-626.

46. Wrixon, A. D. "New recommendations from the International Commission on Radiological Protection—a review." *Physics in Medicine & Biology* 53, no. 8 (2008): R41.

47. Vallabhajosula, Shankar. *Molecular imaging: radiopharmaceuticals for PET and SPECT.* Springer Science & Business Media, 2009.

48. Covens, Peter, D. Berus, N. Buls, P. Clerinx, and Filip Vanhavere. "Personal dose monitoring in hospitals: global assessment, critical applications and future needs." *Radiation protection dosimetry* 124, no. 3 (2007): 250-259.

49. Riedl, Valentin, Katarzyna Bienkowska, Carola Strobel, Masoud Tahmasian, Timo Grimmer, Stefan Förster, Karl J. Friston, Christian Sorg, and Alexander Drzezga. "Local activity determines functional connectivity in the resting human brain: a simultaneous FDG-PET/fMRI study." *Journal of neuroscience* 34, no. 18 (2014): 6260-6266.

50. Di, Xin, and Bharat B. Biswal, and Alzheimer's Disease Neuroimaging Initiative. "Metabolic brain covariant networks as revealed by FDG-PET with reference to resting-state fMRI networks." *Brain connectivity* 2, no. 5 (2012): 275-283.

51. Delbeke, Dominique. "Oncological applications of FDG PET imaging." *Journal of Nuclear Medicine* 40, no. 10 (1999): 1706-1715.

52. Fletcher, James W., Benjamin Djulbegovic, Heloisa P. Soares, Barry A. Siegel, Val J. Lowe, Gary H. Lyman, R. Edward Coleman et al. "Recommendations on the use of 18F-FDG PET in oncology." *Journal of Nuclear Medicine* 49, no. 3 (2008): 480-508.

# 7 Intracranial electroencephalography (iEEG)

## Chaim N. Katz
Chaim Katz is a Ph.D. candidate at the Institute of Biomedical Engineering, University of Toronto. He completed his undergraduate degree in Electrical and Computer Engineering and Masters degree in Clinical Engineering. His Ph.D., supported by NSERC Vanier Canada Graduate Scholarship, focuses on pursuing novel deep brain stimulation technologies for modulating memory function. He is fortunate to work with individuals with epilepsy on the epilepsy monitoring unit, where he collects and analyzes intracranial electroencephalography.

## Dr. Jose Zariffa
Dr. José Zariffa is a Senior Scientist at the Kite Research Institute, Toronto Rehab, University Health Network, and an Associate Professor at the Institute of Biomedical Engineering, University of Toronto. His research interests focus on neuroprosthetics and technology for upper limb neurorehabilitation, encompassing work in neural interfaces, wearable sensors, electrophysiology, and machine learning.

## Dr. Taufik A. Valiante
Dr. Valiante is a Neurosurgeon (Epilepsy, Tumour, and Spine) and Surgeon Scientist at University Health Network and Department of Surgery, University of Toronto. He is cross-appointed to the Institute of Biomedical Engineering and Electrical and Computer Engineering at the University of Toronto. He is interested in understanding the building blocks of the human brain (neurons) and the ultimate manifestation of their collective activity (oscillations to cognition – depending on the scale of investigation). His research interests include work on memory, eye movements, epilepsy, biophysical properties of neurons, computational modelling, mathematical modelling, neuromodulation (electrical, music, optical), development of physical tools (optical, electrical), and brain-machine interfaces. These multi-scale endeavours are in pursuit of a personal desire to realize the title of a very formative book introducing him to the field of experimental neuroscience, entitled "From Neuron to Brain" – which he has adopted as his lab's name.

## 7.1 Introduction

Intracranial electroencephalography (iEEG) requires the surgical implantation of electrodes within the cranium (skull) to record electrical signals from the cerebral cortex (the brain's outer layer) and stimulate the brain. iEEG instrumentation provides a powerful, bidirectional interface to the brain, allowing the recording of electrical signals associated with physiological processes and pathology and stimulating it (neuromodulation) to provide clinical benefit and explore research questions. iEEG has provided us with an important window into brain function.

## 7.2 Historical aspects

Many present-day technologies enable the investigation of the brain from both structural and functional perspectives. Structural imaging modalities include magnetic resonance imaging (MRI) and computed tomography (CT). In contrast, functional measures of brain activity include positron emission tomography (PET), scalp electroencephalography (EEG), magnetoencephalography (MEG), and iEEG.

Early work highlighting the importance of iEEG recordings found unique electrical signals associated with brain tumors that gave rise to seizures.[1] In fact, to this day, iEEG is primarily used for clinical purposes in epilepsy patients to localize their seizure foci (the site in the brain from which the seizure is thought to originate). Such recordings were first performed intraoperatively in 1939 at the Montreal Neurological Institute by Wilder Penfield, demonstrating the ability to identify where an epilepsy patient's seizures arise.[2,3] Recordings were performed using electrodes placed on the pial surface (the innermost envelope of the brain) of the brain without penetration into deeper structures — hence why these recordings have also been referred to as electrocorticography (ECoG). The practice of stereoencephalography (sEEG) emerged in the 1940s when scientists and clinicians began implanting fine wire electrodes in the human brain in order to target deep brain structures.[4,5] These electrodes, unlike the intraoperatively performed surface recordings, allowed for more prolonged monitoring and thus the opportunity to record seizure activity to localize the area from which the seizures arose so that this structure might be removed. Subsequently, the chronic form of ECoG, where strips and grids of electrodes were implanted on the pial surface for extended periods of time, became the North American mainstay for extraoperative iEEG recordings. Meanwhile, sEEG was the most commonly utilized form of iEEG in Europe. Recently, however, sEEG has increasingly become the primary form of iEEG recordings around the world.

iEEG remains an important diagnostic tool for those individuals with epilepsy that fail to respond to medical therapy alone. In such cases, sometimes, non-invasive recording techniques also provide conflicting localizing information. However, the patient appears to have a focal and potentially operable form of epilepsy. Therefore, iEEG provides a technique to solve this localizing issue. For example, temporal lobe epilepsy is the most common drug-resistant epilepsy in adults, and many individuals require iEEG recordings to determine from which temporal lobe the seizures are arising. Their seizures can appear to have bitemporal foci in scalp EEG recordings. In such patients, electrodes are often implanted within the hippocampi, structures in the temporal lobe that are critical for memory and learning. Such implantation provides a unique clinical opportunity that facilitates the study of the electrophysiology of memory and other cognitive functions at an unparalleled spatiotemporal resolution.[6]

## 7.3 iEEG Properties

### 7.3.1 Indications and sources of electrical signals

In humans, iEEG is clinically used to determine the location of the onset of seizures, also known as the seizure focus. iEEG is also performed entirely for research purposes in a myriad of animal species. iEEG electrodes come in two major categories: 1) Subdural electrodes are essentially sheets of electrodes arranged in strips or grids and are placed via a craniotomy (removal and replacement of part of the skull) or burr holes in areas suspected to be generating seizures; 2) sEEG electrodes, on the other hand, are needle-like in form, with contacts placed along their length, to record from both superficial and deep structures (Figure 7.1).

The implanted electrodes act as electrical sensors that record changes in electrical potential between the electrode and a reference electrode that is typically placed far away outside of the skull and under the skin. Hence, what is recorded is the relative changes in electrical potential with units of volts (V).

How electrical potentials are generated in the brain is important to understand. The curious reader is referred to an excellent review, "The origin of extracellular fields and currents — EEG, ECoG, LFP and spikes" (Buzsáki, György, Costas A. Anastassiou, and Christof Koch, 2012) with greater details of what iEEG electrodes actually record.[7] Briefly, the origin of the recorded potentials occurs at the cellular level where positive and negatively charged ions travel in and out of the cell bodies, including both excitatory cells (predominantly neurons) and inhibitory cells (predominantly interneurons). Ions move down their electrochemical gradients, which are actively maintained (the brain is the most metabolically active organ in the brain requiring 1/3 of the heart's output) so that when a channel opens, ions flow either in or out.

Depending on the neurotransmitter released by each neuron, these potentials can be excitatory (i.e., depolarizing) or inhibitory (i.e., hyperpolarizing).

The potentials result from a flow of ions across the neuronal cell membrane. Such ionic flow results in a transient net accumulation of charge near the recording electrode, relative to the reference electrode, generating a potential difference that can then be amplified and recorded as a voltage. Charge accumulation also causes the generation of electrical fields that can be detected with the implanted electrodes. Such electrical fields decay at a rate inversely proportionally to the squared distance. Therefore, iEEG recordings largely reflect activity produced by populations of relatively local excitatory and inhibitory neurons, and primarily the postsynaptic potentials generated by neurotransmitter release.

Electrical signals from the brain can be recorded at different physical scales based on the electrode and its placement on the outer layer of the brain (Figure 7.1A). Whereas scalp EEG primarily records synchronous cortical activity from large brain regions (possibly from 100 million to 1 billion neurons), iEEG permits recording from a smaller neuronal population (10's to 100's of thousands of neurons) either from the cortical surface or from deeper subcortical areas using sEEG.[8] Microelectrodes can even permit recording single neuron firing activity.

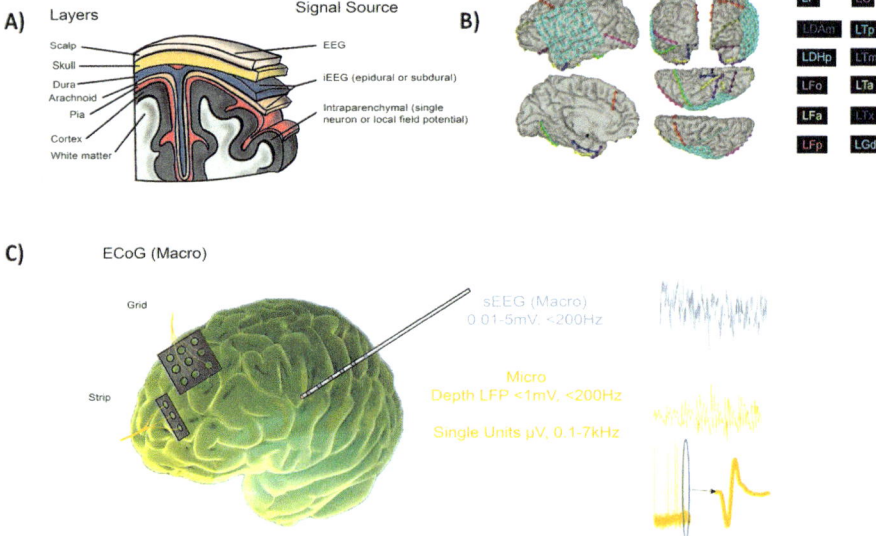

**Figure 7.1** Types of electrical recordings that can be obtained from the brain. A is adapted from [9] and brain reconstruction created using iElvis toolbox.[10]

Figure 7.1B demonstrates an example reconstruction of electrode placements in a clinical setting using a craniotomy procedure with grid, strips and depth electrodes and corresponding anatomical acronyms, obtained using MRI, CT, and iElvis toolbox.[10] The value of such data is often unrealized as many laboratories lack tools for localizing electrodes relative to the anatomy. To remedy this, a MATLAB toolbox has been developed for intracranial electrode localization and visualization, iELVis. iELVis uses existing tools (BioImage Suite, FSL, and FreeSurfer) to reconstruct since iEEG can be recorded using different placements (Figure 7.1C). Electrodes can be placed in a craniotomy using grid, depth, and strip electrodes and in sEEG using an electrode drilled from the outside.

Additionally, the macro recordings from either the sEEG or ECoG have examples of voltages and frequencies available for that recording. Micro electrodes enable recording of more localized signal even single neuron activity (after signal processing). Such contacts can be embedded in different ways on different types of electrodes.

## 7.3.2 Decomposing iEEG signals

The iEEG voltage signal from any single electrode is an amalgamation of signals from different spatial sources and different frequencies. Given that electrical fields travel in space and superimpose upon one another, a voltage signal at a single electrode is likely generated from multiple sources both nearby and far away. A number of very sophisticated techniques exist for trying to compute the different sources that contribute to a signal recorded at one point in space by trying to solve the so-called inverse problem.[8]

Local field potentials (LFPs) measure the electrical activity of neurons in the surrounding area. For a full review of perceived cellular contributions to LFPs, see Buzsáki.[7] Briefly, there is no single contribution to the electrically recorded activity. First and foremost, as mentioned, recorded cellular activity decreases in magnitude inversely proportional to the square of the distance from the source. Through iEEG, one can localize activity to investigate memory and cognitive functions and their possible dependence on the precise temporal pattern of activity in neural assemblies.[11] It is believed that inhibitory and excitatory neurons interact to create oscillatory behavior/rhythms within the brain, and these synchronized activities are grouped by frequency bands.[8] For example, the first oscillation, termed "alpha" waves by Berger, appears as a visually discernable oscillation in the EEG that is more pronounced when the subject closes their eyes.[12] This seminal work leads to the idea that brain waves are modulated with behavior and thus might provide some mechanistic insight into the brain. Since that time, several different frequencies of waves have been described that appear to be modulated with behavior and accompany pathology (table 7.1).

Table 7.1 Breakdown of different oscillations

| Frequency Band (Hz) | Oscillation | Possible Correlated Function |
|---|---|---|
| <4 | Delta | Sleep |
| 4-7 | Theta | Memory/attention |
| 8-15 | Alpha | Internal processing states/sensory gating |
| 16-30 | Beta | Motor activity |
| 30-100 | Low Gamma | Memory, attention, feedforward information |
| >100 | Gamma | "Activated cortex"[13] |
| 140-220 | Ripples | Memory Consolidation |

Brain activity can be decomposed into different frequency bands. Some dominant bands are generally accepted to be involved in different tasks. However, it would be an oversimplification to say that each band is only involved in one task. For example, these bands of activity can all be involved in memory-related tasks.[14] Indeed, much of contemporary neuroscientific research is devoted to describing how different oscillations are modulated by behavior.[15] Additionally, oscillations are likely to play crucial roles in communication between different brain areas,[16] and are an important substrate for communication between various brain networks.[17] In this light, decomposing brain signals into a sum of individual oscillations of different frequencies quite naturally follows from the observed electrophysiology. Fortunately, Fourier's theory provides a convenient and physiologically relevant framework to decompose brain signals. This theory states that any time-series can be decomposed into an infinite sum of sine and cosine waves (oscillations) of different frequencies, amplitudes, and phases.

In figure 7.2, four sinusoids are contributing to the overall signal. It presents a conceptual example of how a sum of sinusoids composes an iEEG signal due to naturally occurring biophysical processes in the brain. Each sinusoid has a frequency, power, and phase depending on the time of the signal (Figure 7.2A). The bottom panel in A is the sum of all the other previous sinusoids, and one can notice different oscillatory contributions, but the strongest is the contribution of the 50Hz signal. Thus, each component contributes to the overall signal, which is obtained as the summation of these sinusoids. To extract this information, one can visualize the signal's power across frequencies or oscillations (Figure 7.2B). The spectral density is a commonly used tool in various disciplines, including working with iEEG. Spectral density decomposes the signal (bottom panel of A in this case) to the various contributions of oscillations and the respective power over that time window. In this case, since signals are pure sinusoids, there are four clear peaks in frequency, with the largest contribution being 50Hz.

# Intracranial electroencephalography (iEEG)

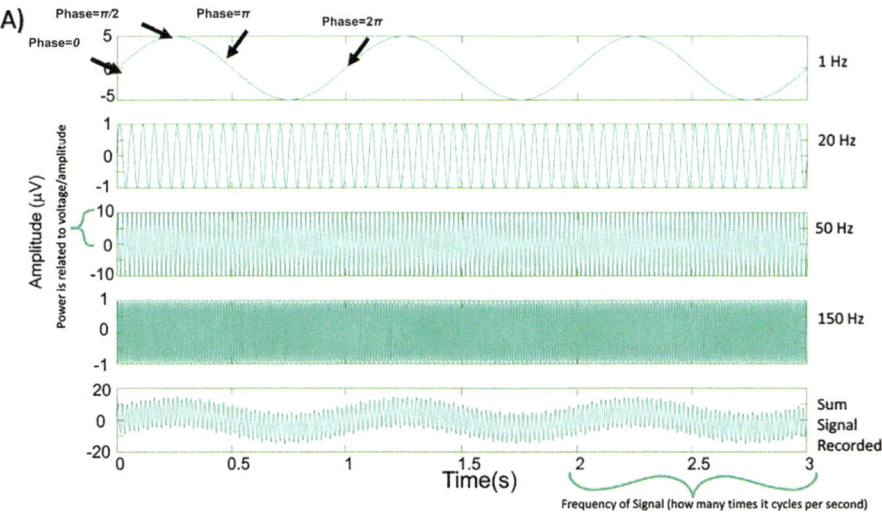

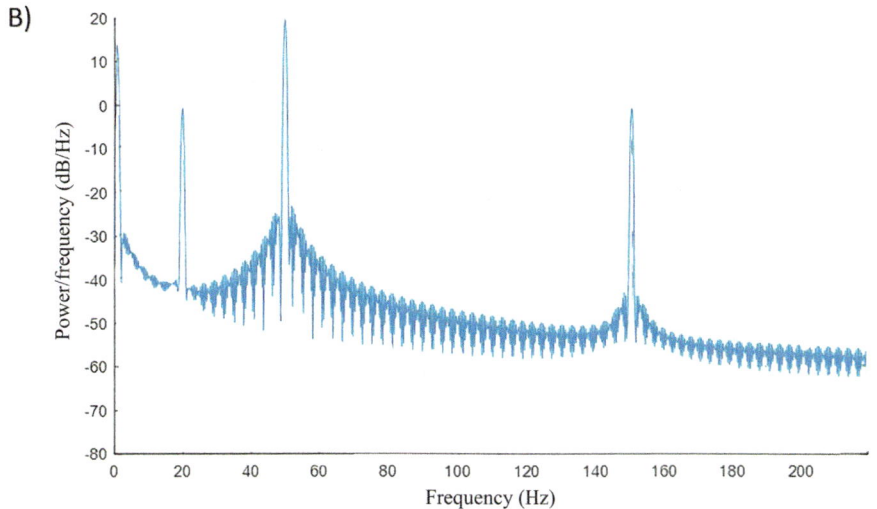

Figure 7.2 Fourier theory

Using iEEG, one can investigate properties of specific oscillations such as their frequency, power, or synchrony using their phase alignment during relevant events (See figure 7.3).

Three aspects of an ongoing signal and the physiological meanings are visualized in figure 7.3. Neurons can fire at specific phases of frequency, evidenced above by the arrow indication of neuron firing timing occurring closer to the trough of the ongoing oscillation of various frequencies. The coupling of activation between different frequencies of activity can also be recorded where firing/

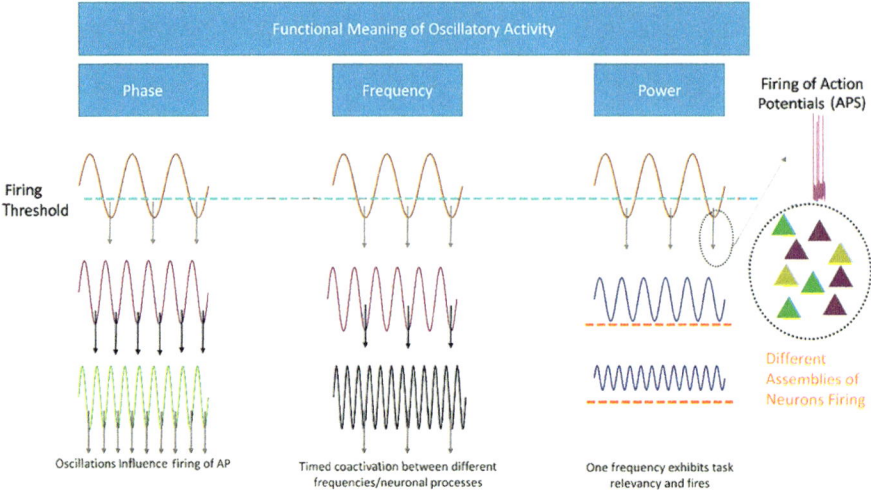

Figure 7.3 Physiological Relevance of Brain Oscillations, inspiration from Klimesch et al.[18]

activation occurs at similar times and phases across different assemblies. Finally, the relevance of an oscillation power to a specific task can be recorded whereby one oscillation may have increased power and firing while other frequencies may not be engaged. Different frequencies of oscillation can be associated with different tasks or functional activities, as seen in table 7.1. Each color in the assembly on the right reflects a different firing of neurons or activation that could be involved in the recorded oscillation.

### 7.3.3 Spatial and Temporal Resolution

One of the key advantages of using iEEG is its excellent spatial and temporal resolution. Brain activity is almost instantaneous in the sense that neurons fire action potentials and these fields propagate very rapidly. Other imaging modalities, such as fMRI, can image the entire brain and its related structures, but they can only resolve dynamic changes over several seconds. The recording technology used in iEEG allows dynamic sampling of brain activity at a much faster rate. In addition to this rapid sampling, the proximity of iEEG electrodes to the actual brain tissue allows for a high spatial resolution, which allows targeted recordings of the structures of interest.

The brain regions where iEEG electrodes are implanted depend on the clinical applications for the patient. For example, some patients may receive four electrodes within a single structure of the brain but no electrodes elsewhere. Furthermore, different types of iEEG electrodes may be utilized in different scenarios. For instance, grid electrodes used for ECoG provide greater spatial resolution compared to scalp EEG, but they can only record activity from a restricted brain region. These relationships are most clearly demonstrated when comparing the temporal and spatial resolutions across different techniques to investigate the brain (Figure 7.4). Electrode sizes provide one of the clearest indications of the physiological activity and resolution of activity recorded using iEEG. For example, a scalp EEG, which uses electrodes with a diameter of ~10mm, measures integrated activity from over 10cm$^2$ or more of the cortex. Alternatively, ECoG electrodes have a typical diameter of 2mm and record from a cortical surface area of ~4mm$^2$, capturing a diverse population of activity of ~500,000 neurons. sEEG can record similar types of activity and is cylindrical in nature with a contact length of ~2mm, a diameter of ~1mm, and a surface area of 10mm.[19] Smaller electrodes and greater proximity to the brain area of interest enable a higher signal-to-noise ratio. Such a higher spatial resolution of the recording also suggests the recording of more direct activity. This spatial resolution is greatest when using microelectrodes, which can record activity from single neurons in addition to the changes in ongoing local field potential.

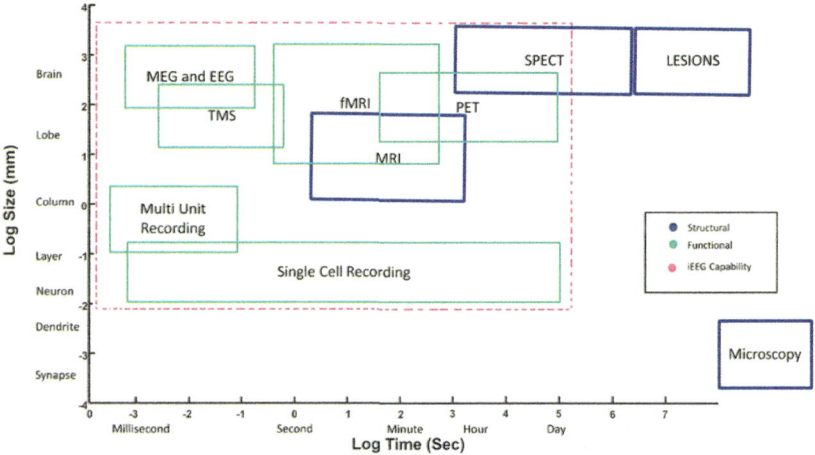

Time and Spatial Resolutions of Different Technologies To Investigate The Brain

**Figure 7.4** Approximate Temporal and Spatial Resolutions of Different Techniques to Investigate the Brain.

As evidenced in figure 7.4, with 24/7 iEEG, one can record with a temporal resolution of milliseconds of activity and observe changes across days. Spatially, using microwires, one can record as small as single units across different areas of the brain.

## 7.4 Signal processing to infer functionality

All iEEG signals need to be processed to remove artifacts and noise. Then specific features are extracted from the signal to make inferences about how different spectral features change with behavior or pathological activity.

There are many computational tools available in common programming languages to extract information from iEEG signals, and some excellent resources on the topic.[20] However, before any signal processing steps, it is imperative to look at the raw voltage signals to make sure it all makes sense. This step can save many hours of processing, given that the art and science of data analysis is truly about "garbage in, garbage out." Some common processing tools are briefly described below.

### 7.4.1 Referencing

Given that voltage is a relative signal, choosing the reference for the electrodes can make a significant difference in the results. Despite this, there is no "standard" way to reference the signals. Initial (raw) iEEG recordings are typically monopolar, where a reference electrode is placed far away from the recording sites. For iEEG signals, the reference electrode is typically a four-contact subgaleal electrode placed at the time of surgery or needle electrodes placed by the EEG technicians at the mastoid or vertex. These locations are chosen such that they are unlikely to pick up any muscle or movement artifacts (which is typically identified as broadband activity that is particularly visible when the patient chews or talks[21]). Once acquired, these monopolar signals can then be re-referenced. Such re-referencing helps to visualize activity in different "montages" and remove common signals that contaminate all the electrodes, possibly from a noisy reference electrode. For example, bipolar referencing is where signals in adjacent electrodes are subtracted from one another. This process is a simple and powerful way to remove many artifacts. Another commonly used approach is to remove the signal that is common to all the electrodes. This "common average" referencing is performed by averaging the signal from all electrodes and then removing that average from each channel.

### 7.4.2 Trial Averaging for Event-Related Potentials (ERPs)

One of the original forms of analyzing data using iEEG is to align the data to the beginning of a specific set of stimuli (trials), for example, the onset of an image or a sound. Subsequently, the voltage signals from these trials aligned to the stimulus onset are averaged to yield an event-related potential (ERP). Averaging results in a reduction of the background noise level since noise is not aligned to the response onset and thus gets averaged out. ERPs are straightforward and easy to compute, and one can compare the changes between ERPs in the same brain region across multiple conditions. One of this approach's limitations is that some brain responses are not specifically time-locked to the stimulus. Such "induced" responses, as opposed to "evoked responses," occur at variable times and are averaged out of the response. In these situations, other spectral approaches (see below) can identify these induced responses.

### 7.4.3 Time-Frequency Analysis

Oscillations are a ubiquitous phenomenon in the brain. Although there remains debate as to whether they may be epiphenomena, they continue to be intensely studied given that they are so heavily modulated by behavior and clearly affect neural processing.[15,22–24] Using various signal processing approaches, termed "time-frequency analyses," the amplitude and phase of different oscillations of different frequencies can be extracted as a function of time. There are three common ways to implement time-frequency analyses, all of which seek to reveal similar information, and some have argued provide similar results.[25] These include the Fourier Transform (FT), Wavelet Transform, or Hilbert Transform.

This section will focus on the Fourier Transform and the idea of a dynamic changing signal over time. Fourier Transform assumes that the signal statistics do not change over time. This assumption is obviously not the case when dealing with an iEEG signal, as brain activity is constantly changing. Therefore, the idea of how this time-frequency transform works is visualized in figure 7.5. Since the data is changing over time, the first step is to segment the data into small time windows that better adhere to the Fourier Transform's stationarity requirements. This segment of the signal is then decomposed into its Fourier components (consisting of varying frequencies and their respective phases and power). These components are acquired by calculating a metric of similarity between the extracted signal with varying oscillations of sinusoids. As evidenced by figures 7.2B and 7.5B, one can obtain a power associated with each frequency of the signal in that time window.

Once the frequency characteristics of that segment are extracted, one time slice is obtained for the spectrogram (figure 7.5C). To complete the rest of the spectrogram, one must simply slide the time window along the full length of the signal. Such sliding extracts frequency characteristics of the signal over time for this one recording.

An important note of this section is that extensive literature exists around signal processing of the retrieved signal and different ways to optimize the features of interest. One must decide on the specific resolutions and features of the signal required to effectively answer a given research question.

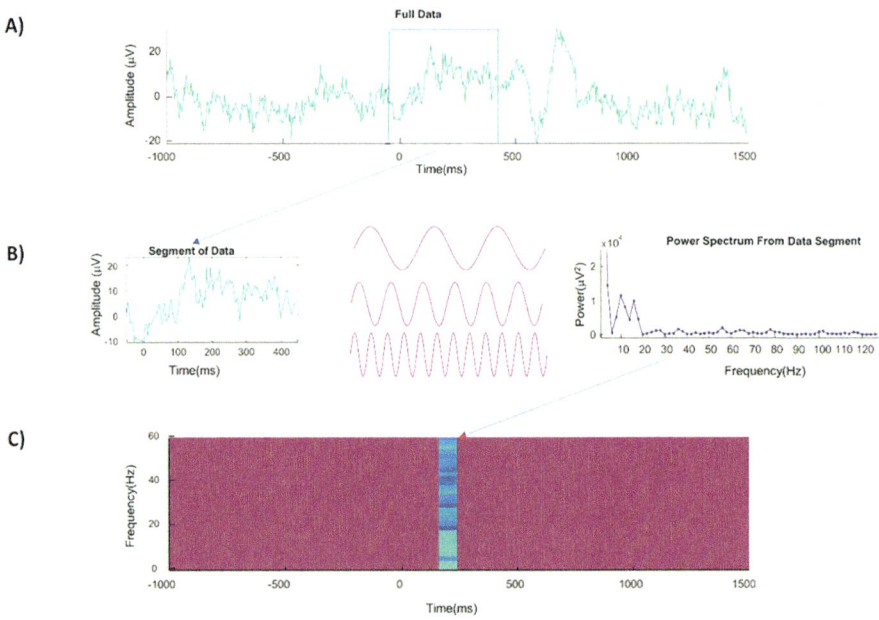

Figure 7.5 Transforming into Frequency Domain, inspired by Mike X Cohen.[20]

Figure 7.5 shows a clear example of how one would transform the voltage signal to the frequency domain. A) Example: iEEG voltage signal aligned to a certain event at time t=0. A time segment is taken in the window shown here by the dotted line. B) This window of activity is then compared to sinusoids or signals of varying frequency. Based on this signal's similarity to these varying frequencies, the power across frequencies can be extracted. C) Power of this time window is then visualized as the power across frequencies in the center of this time window. This example is considered one slice of the spectrogram since only a one-time segment has been computed.

### 7.4.4 Connectivity

The brain functions as a highly interconnected set of regions regardless of the physical scale at which one observes its function. It thus remains a key neuroscientific interest to characterize the strength of the connections between different brain regions as a proxy for communication between these brain regions.[17,26] Such connectivity is conceptualized to fall under three major categories: structural, functional, and effective.[27]

iEEG can estimate the functional connectivity between brain regions by analyzing the statistical similarity between the recordings obtained from these regions. The more statistically related two signals are in two different brain regions, the more functionally connected they are thought to be, and this is used to infer how strongly they communicate with one another. There are many types of functional connectivity measures that one can compute between two voltage time series; the simplest is the Pearson Correlation Coefficient of the signals. More complex approaches involve time-frequency decomposition (discussed above) to estimate the phase relationship between different brain regions, termed phase-synchrony.[28]

Another measure is coherence, which describes both the phase and amplitude relationship between two signals in the frequency domain. In figure 7.3, under the section of frequency, a proposed mechanism of communication is visualized. Different assemblies may have firing tuned to different oscillation frequencies, and these oscillations are synchronous in their firing. Such synchrony can happen at different frequencies within the same electrode channel across time and events. This connectivity metric can also occur between sites within the same frequency bands or different frequency bands. Such coherence can be measured in power, phase, and even between single units and the ongoing oscillation. One can also look at the direction of connectivity if recording activity between two electrodes. A causality metric is needed for this type of measurement. Granger causality is a typically used measurement to determine the direction of this connectivity by evaluating to what extent one signal can be used to "predict" the activity of the other signal.

### 7.4.5 Single Unit Analysis

Microelectrode recordings are used to record the extracellular signatures of action potentials fired by individual neurons — single-unit recordings. The unit refers to the action potential waveform generated by a nearby neuron. Such recordings were the technological undergird for the discoveries that lead to an understanding of how space is represented in the mouse brain and motivated the 2014 Nobel Prize for winners Dr. John M. O'Keefe, Dr. May-Britt Moser, and Dr. Edvard I. Moser in Physiology or Medicine. Microelectrodes can be used in humans as well, most commonly by supplementing standard clinical sEEG recordings with microwires that protrude from the tips of existing clinical macroelectrodes.[29] Such recordings do not pose any additional risk to the patients and provide an unprecedented opportunity to study the human brain with single-cell resolution.[29]

Spike sorting is required to differentiate individual units/neurons from one another since a single microwire can detect the activity of multiple units. Spike sorting utilizes various spike features (i.e., half-width, peak-to-trough amplitude, etc.) to cluster waveforms into different units[30] — a technique that still is somewhat both an art and a science. Such recordings have provided a key understanding of human brain "computations," particularly in memory regions of the brain where these sEEG electrodes are commonly deployed.

## 7.5 Usability

### 7.5.1 Risks

The two major risks associated with this surgery are infection and hemorrhages, with rates about 2-3% and <1%, respectively. Some may think that inserting electrodes into the brain would damage the underlying neural tissue; however, direct brain injury due to implanting depth electrodes has not been demonstrated. Other major risks are those common to any surgery.

### 7.5.2 Limitations

iEEG provides excellent temporal and spatial resolution when compared against other techniques for functionally characterizing the brain. However, there are some drawbacks to its use described below.

#### 7.5.2.1 Noise and artifacts

The signals typically recorded by iEEG are on the order of micro-volts requiring amplification to be digitized and stored on a computer for further analysis. In the clinical setting, there are many potential sources of noise (medical equipment, patient bed, alarm system, etc.). However, the necessity of signal amplification makes it so any small change in noise level (e.g., phone charging) may introduce a large amount of artifact into the signal.

Reducing this noise may involve removing devices around a patient connected to power and trying to find an optimal reference. Sometimes the reference may be damaged, leading to higher amplitude signals or multiple large slow frequency artifacts. A reference change may be required in software or physically plugging in a different clinical reference. If the reference used during recording is of good quality, re-referencing afterward is not a problem, but using a bad reference during the recording could lead to unusable data. Also, because iEEG recordings are often from brains predisposed to seizure activity, one needs to consider spikes and activity that may be recorded due to epilepsy or motor artifacts. In fact, even eye movements can introduce an artifact in intracranial structures[31,32]

#### 7.5.2.2 Filtering and signal changes

A filter works by focusing the signal on specific frequency bands of interest. By comparing segments of the signal to a given frequency of oscillation, such filtering can introduce unwanted oscillations into a signal that are not physiologically present. Additionally, since a signal is filtered in a window based on weighted averages of the signal, it can even smear the signal reducing the temporal resolution.

Therefore, choices of filtering and signal processing can significantly impact the signal and its qualities. Therefore, any time one is trying to answer a question or use the feature to predict an outcome, care must be taken with the signal processing and pipeline used to analyze the data. A detailed discussion of filter choices can be found in Widmann et al.[33]

### 7.5.2.3 Clinical placements

The biggest factor of iEEG is that electrodes are placed based on the clinical need for seizure localization. One needs to be skilled in designing research questions to align with typical implants in their brain. Therefore, if one wants a specific question answered, but the structure in the brain to investigate does not have electrodes implanted in it, there is no solution. It is important to use appropriate study designs to answer questions across different patients. Also, these study designs need to consider that not many people perform this kind of procedure. Therefore, it is not easy to control for age, gender, education, and other factors. Even withstanding the variety in the data collected, it is considered gold. Also, groups have started to collaborate and do cross-site studies to increase the numbers of iEEG data sets with specific tasks to better understand regions of the brain and how activity differs across the larger population.

## 7.5.3 Use Case and Future Perspectives

### 7.5.3.1 Brain-Machine Interfaces

Brain-machine interfaces (BMI) are defined as an artificial process that allows the brain to exchange information directly with an external device.[34] To enable the brain to communicate requires the extraction of a signal. Such a signal can be recorded using scalp EEG or iEEG. The major difference with iEEG is that more localized activity and single units can control the technology. A neuroprosthetic version of a BMI can assist, augment, or repair cognitive or sensorimotor symptoms. For example, one of the major clinical uses for this BMI technology is in people with locked-in syndrome. They are paralyzed but can use a BMI to interact with the world around them by using a cursor to spell or indicate certain questions to their caregiver. Such a process has been used in everything from moving a cursor on a screen to controlling a robotic arm. iEEG signals can be acquired and utilized to work with BMIs in two distinct ways. First, in 1970 Humphrey et al. showed that even recording the frequency of a group of cells firing could predict displacement, as in the velocity of force provided by a monkey in a grasping task.[35]

At a similar time in 1969, Fetz showed that animals could modulate their own firing rate of activity to obtain a reward.[36] Therefore, one can use the ongoing activity to decode a task or ask a subject to regulate their activity in a feedback manner. Hence, one can control a device using the brain or regulate brain activity using a feedback device. Such feedback can even be used in memory-related structures[37]. The iEEG signal acquired for use in a BMI can be investigated for how information is encoded and decoded in the brain, how activity might impact the brain's plasticity during a task, and how such activity is altered in pathological conditions. All of this is only possible with iEEG.

### 7.5.3.2 Future Perspectives

The future is bright for iEEG with the unparalleled temporal and spatial resolution to deeper brain structures involved in very complex activity. With advances in technology using high-density microelectrode recordings, one can investigate neuronal circuit architecture in humans. Additionally, with progress in wireless electrodes and implant capacities, this technology can venture into the real world. Finally, iEEG is a fundamental tool being used in the world for neuromodulation. Neuromodulation — as defined by the newly established Toronto Center for Advancing Neurotechnological Innovation ([CRANIA](https://crania.ca/)) –(https://crania.ca/) "changes brain, spinal cord or nerve function using advanced device(s) that interface with specific areas of the central or peripheral nervous system to reduce symptoms and address underlying disorder(s)." Such technology can be used in clinical and research settings. Using iEEG will help to better understand the neural activity that leads to such symptoms or disorders mechanistically. One can then use extracted features from the iEEG signal to inform technologies to assist and improve these conditions. Historically, iEEG started almost 100 years ago, but researchers are only scratching the surface of this exciting signal and the world of innovations before us.

## 7.6  Conclusion

This chapter gave a very high-level overview of the nature of iEEG, where it came from, and how it can and will be used in the future. There are always limitations to any technology, but there are many insights to be gained from using iEEG for exploratory scientific research and clinical application. Some people may be fortunate enough to work out of a lab with a strong infrastructure to get real data and pose new questions. However, if that is not possible, the research world has transitioned to creating open repositories of iEEG data and using computational modeling to simulate data and different pathologies. Using this technology is part of an exciting field, and it is the authors' hope that this brief chapter will inspire you to read more, learn more, and use some of these principles to answer your questions about the brain.

# Endnotes

1. Foerster, O. & Altenburger, H. Elektrobiologische Vorgänge an der menschlichen Hirnrinde. *Dtsch. Z. Nervenheilkd.* **135**, 277–288 (1935).

2. Almeida, A. N., Martinez, V. & Feindel, W. The first case of invasive EEG monitoring for the surgical treatment of epilepsy: Historical significance and context. *Epilepsia* **46**, 1082–1085 (2005).

3. Penfield, W. THE EPILEPSIES: WITH A NOTE ON RADICAL THERAPY. *N. Engl. J. Med.* **221**, 209–218 (1939).

4. Hayne, R., Russell, M. & Knott, J. CHARACTERISTICS OF ELECTRICAL OF HUMAN CORPUS STRIATUM AND NEIGHBORING STRUCTURES. *J. Neurophysiol.* **12**, 185–195 (1949).

5. Talairach, J. & Bancaud, J. Lesion, 'irritative' zone and epileptogenic focus. *Confin. Neurol.* (1966). doi:10.1159/000103937

6. Johnson, E. L. & Knight, R. T. Intracranial recordings and human memory. *Curr. Opin. Neurobiol.* **31**, 18–25 (2015).

7. Buzsáki, G., Anastassiou, C. a. & Koch, C. The origin of extracellular fields and currents — EEG, ECoG, LFP and spikes. *Nat. Rev. Neurosci.* **13**, 407–420 (2012).

8. Nunez, P. *Electrical Fields of the Brain: The Neurophysics of EEG.* (Oxford University Press, 1981).

9. Schalk, G. & Leuthardt, E. C. Brain-computer interfaces using electrocorticographic signals. *IEEE Rev. Biomed. Eng.* (2011). doi:10.1109/RBME.2011.2172408

10. Groppe, D. M. *et al.* iELVis: An open source MATLAB toolbox for localizing and visualizing human intracranial electrode data. *J. Neurosci. Methods* **281**, 40–48 (2017).

11. Axmacher, N., Mormann, F., Fernández, G., Elger, C. E. & Fell, J. Memory formation by neuronal synchronization. *Brain Res. Rev.* **52**, 170–182 (2006).

12. Berger, H. Das Elektrenkephalogramm des Menschen. *Naturwissenschaften* **23**, 121–124 (1935).

13. Miller, K. J. *Broadband spectral change: Evidence for a macroscale correlate of population firing rate? Journal of Neuroscience* **30**, 6477–6479 (2010).

14. Hanslmayr, S. & Staudigl, T. How brain oscillations form memories--a processing based perspective on oscillatory subsequent memory effects. *Neuroimage* **85 Pt 2**, 648–55 (2014).

15. Buzsáki, G. *Rhythms of the Brain.* (Oxford University Press, 2006).

16. Fries, P. Rhythms for Cognition: Communication through Coherence. *Neuron* **88**, 220–235 (2015).

17. Varela, F., Lachaux, J. P., Rodriguez, E. & Martinerie, J. The brainweb: Phase synchronization and large-scale integration. *Nat. Rev. Neurosci.* **2**, 229–239 (2001).

18. Klimesch, W., Freunberger, R., Sauseng, P. & Gruber, W. A short review of slow phase synchronization and memory: Evidence for control processes in different memory systems? *Brain Res.* **1235**, 31–44 (2008).

19. Parvizi, J. & Kastner, S. Promises and limitations of human intracranial electroencephalography. *Nat. Neurosci.* **21**, 474–483 (2018).

20. Cohen, M. X. Analyzing Neural Time Series Data: Theory and Practice. *MIT Press* 600 (2014). doi:10.1017/CBO9781107415324.004

21. Goncharova, I. I., McFarland, D. J., Vaughan, T. M. & Wolpaw, J. R. EMG contamination of EEG: Spectral and topographical characteristics. *Clin. Neurophysiol.* (2003). doi:10.1016/S1388-2457(03)00093-2

22. Sohal, V. S., Zhang, F., Yizhar, O. & Deisseroth, K. Parvalbumin neurons and gamma rhythms enhance cortical circuit performance. *Nature* (2009). doi:10.1038/nature07991

23. Anastassiou, C. A., Perin, R., Markram, H. & Koch, C. Ephaptic coupling of cortical neurons. in *Nature Neuroscience* **14**, 217–224 (Nature Publishing Group, 2011).

24. Womelsdorf, T., Valiante, T. A., Sahin, N. T., Miller, K. J. & Tiesinga, P. Dynamic circuit motifs underlying rhythmic gain control, gating and integration. *Nat. Neurosci.* **17**, 1031–1039 (2014).

25. Bruns, A. Fourier-, Hilbert- and wavelet-based signal analysis: Are they really different approaches? *J. Neurosci. Methods* **137**, 321–332 (2004).

26. Fries, P. A mechanism for cognitive dynamics: neuronal communication through neuronal coherence. *Trends Cogn. Sci.* **9**, 474–80 (2005).

27. Friston, K. J. Functional and Effective Connectivity: A Review. *Brain Connect.* (2011). doi:10.1089/brain.2011.0008

28. Lachaux, J. P., Rodriguez, E., Martinerie, J. & Varela, F. J. Measuring phase synchrony in brain signals. *Hum. Brain Mapp.* **8**, 194–208 (1999).

29. Rutishauser, U., Cerf, M. & Kreiman G. *Single Neuron Studies of the Human Brain*. *Single Neuron Studies of the Human Brain* (2015). doi:10.7551/mitpress/9780262027205.001.0001

30. Mahallati, S., Bezdek, J. C., Popovic, M. R. & Valiante, T. A. Cluster tendency assessment in neuronal spike data. *PLoS One* (2019). doi:10.1371/journal.pone.0224547

31. Katz, C. N. *et al.* Differential Generation of Saccade, Fixation, and Image-Onset Event-Related Potentials in the Human Mesial Temporal Lobe. *Cereb. Cortex* https://doi.org/10.1101/442855 (2020). doi:10.1093/cercor/bhaa132

32. Kovach, C. K. *et al.* Manifestation of ocular-muscle EMG contamination in human intracranial recordings. *Neuroimage* **54**, 213–233 (2011).

33. Widmann, A., Schröger, E. & Maess, B. Digital filter design for electrophysiological data - a practical approach. *J. Neurosci. Methods* **250**, 34–46 (2015).

34. Moxon, K. A. & Foffani, G. Brain-machine interfaces beyond neuroprosthetics. *Neuron* **86**, 55–67 (2015).

35. Humphrey, D. R., Schmidt, E. M. & Thompson, W. D. Predicting measures of motor performance from multiple cortical spike trains. *Science (80-. ).* (1970). doi:10.1126/science.170.3959.758

36. Fetz, E. E. Operant conditioning of cortical unit activity. *Science (80-. ).* (1969). doi:10.1126/science.163.3870.955

37. Patel, K., Katz, C. N., Kalia, S. K., Popovic, M. R. & Valiante, T. Volitional Control of Individual Neurons in the Human Brain. *bioRxiv* (2020). doi:10.1101/2020.05.05.079038

# Neuroimaging Devices Comparison Chart

# Comparison Chart

| Device | EEG | MEG | fMRI | fNIRS | PET | ECoG |
|---|---|---|---|---|---|---|
| Modality | Electrical Activity | Magnetic Field Measurements | Hemodynamic Changes | Hemodynamic Changes | Positron Radio-tracer Tracking | Intracranial EEG |
| Temporal Resolution | High (~1 ms)[1] | High (~1 ms)[2] | Medium (~5 s)[3] | High (~1 ms)[4] | Low (sec – min)[5] | High (<1 ms)[6] |
| Spatial Resolution | Low (7–10 cm)[7] | High (2–3 mm)[7] | High (3–4 mm)[3] | Medium (10–20 mm)[3] | High (5–10 mm)[3] | High (<1 mm)[6] |
| Penetration Depth | Dependent upon frequency* | Centimeters[8] | Limitless[9] | Centimeters[10] | Limitless[9] | Dependent upon frequency |
| Equipment Cost | <$1,000[11] | $2,500,000[12] | ~$1,000,000[13] | >$10,000[14] | ~$2,000,000[15] | ~$10,000[16] |
| Average Clinical Cost in U.S. | ~$450[17] | $600[12] | ~$2,600[3] | ~$150[18] Kim | ~$6,000[19] (CostHelperHealth n.d.) | ~$10,000[16] |
| Invasive? | No | No | No | No | Yes | Yes |
| Portable? | Yes | No | No | Yes | No | Yes |

*Generally, EEG measures activity from the superficial neocortex. This varies based on EEG frequency and specification. ECoG is more precise, and generally measures from the cerebral cortex on which it rests. EEG equipment costs depend on specifications. Most simple EEGs cost less than $1,000.

# Endnotes

1. Burle, Boris, Laure Spieser, Clémence Roger, Laurence Casini, Thierry Hasbroucq, and Franck Vidal. "Spatial and temporal resolutions of EEG: Is it really black and white? A scalp current density view." *International Journal of Psychophysiology* 97, no. 3 (2015): 210-220.

2. Proudfoot, Malcolm, Mark W. Woolrich, Anna C. Nobre, and Martin R. Turner. "Magnetoencephalography." *Practical neurology* 14, no. 5 (2014): 336-343.

3. Glover, Gary H. "Overview of functional magnetic resonance imaging." *Neurosurgery Clinics* 22, no. 2 (2011): 133-139.

4. Wilcox, Teresa, and Marisa Biondi. "fNIRS in the developmental sciences." *Wiley Interdisciplinary Reviews: Cognitive Science* 6, no. 3 (2015): 263-283.

5. Sarraf, Saman, and Jian Sun. "Functional brain imaging: A comprehensive survey." arXiv preprint arXiv:1602.02225 (2016).

6. Hill, N. Jeremy, Disha Gupta, Peter Brunner, Aysegul Gunduz, Matthew A. Adamo, Anthony Ritaccio, and Gerwin Schalk. "Recording human electrocorticographic (ECoG) signals for neuroscientific research and real-time functional cortical mapping." *JoVE (Journal of Visualized Experiments)* 64 (2012): e3993.

7. Singh, Sanjay P. "Magnetoencephalography: basic principles." *Annals of Indian Academy of Neurology* 17, no. Suppl 1 (2014): S107.

8. Braeutigam, Sven. "Magnetoencephalography: fundamentals and established and emerging clinical applications in radiology." *International Scholarly Research Notices* 2013 (2013).

9. Lu, Feng-Mei, and Zhen Yuan. "PET/SPECT molecular imaging in clinical neuroscience: recent advances in the investigation of CNS diseases." *Quantitative imaging in medicine and surgery* 5, no. 3 (2015): 433.

10. Johnson, A., M. Roskosky, B. Freedman, and M. S. Shuler. "Depth penetration of near infrared spectroscopy in the obese." *J Trauma Treat* 4, no. 263 (2015): 2167-1222.

11. Peyton, R. "Selecting an EEG device." Human NIR Vision Project, Science for the Masses, April 11, 2014, https://scienceforthemasses.org/2014/04/11/selecting-an-eeg-device/

12. Schwindt, Peter, D. "A Cryogen-Free, Low-Cost Atomic Magnetometer Array for Magnetoencephalography." Grantome. NIH. June 1, 2014. http://grantome.com/grant/NIH/R01-EB013302-03.

13. LBN Medical, "How Much Does an MRI Machine Cost (Updated 2019)." April 17, 2019. https://lbnmedical.com/how-much-does-an-mri-machine-cost/

14. Artinis Medical Systems. "NIRS device specification overview." October 11, 2018, https://www.artinis.com/blogpost-all/2018/10/11/artinis-nirs-devices-specs

15. Lee, Jaimy. "Average Price Paid for PET/CT Systems Drops 27%." Modern Healthcare. August 16, 2013, https://www.modernhealthcare.com/article/20130816/NEWS/308169951/average-price-paid-for-pet-ct-systems-drops-27

16. Kuzniecky, Ruben, Carmen Baez, Guzmán Aranda, Eveline Teresa Hidalgo, Ameeta Grover, Cordelia Orillac, Yvonne Zelenka, and Howard L. Weiner. "Epilepsy surgery in Panama: Establishment of a successful hybrid program as a model for small middle-income countries." *Epilepsia* 59, no. 11 (2018): 2137-2144.

17. CostHelper. "How Much Does an EEG Cost? - Accessed July 4, 2019. https://health.costhelper.com/eeg.html.

18. Kim, Hak Yeong, Kain Seo, Hong Jin Jeon, Unjoo Lee, and Hyosang Lee. "Application of functional near-infrared spectroscopy to the study of brain function in humans and animal models." *Molecules and cells* 40, no. 8 (2017): 523.

19. CostHelper. "How Much Does a PET Scan Cost? Accessed July 4, 2019. https://health.costhelper.com/pet-scans.html.

# 8
# Transcranial Electrical Stimulation (tES)

### Niranjan Khadka
Dr. Niranjan Khadka is a post-doctoral research fellow at the Harvard Medical School and Massachusetts General Hospital. His main areas of research include computational neuroscience, medical devices for neuropsychiatric disorders, safety and efficacy of medical devices, non-invasive and invasive modalities of brain and spinal cord electrical. Dr. Khadka has 10+ years of experience in benchtop electrode and device testing, in vitro invasive brain stimulation studies (SCS and DBS), human and small animal tDCS experiments, and computational modeling of brain and spinal cord stimulation. Moreover, Dr. Khadka reviews for >10 peer reviewed journals and is a review editor of Frontiers in Augmented and Synthetic Neuroergonomics.

### Marom Bikson
Dr. Marom Bikson is a Cattell Professor of Biomedical Engineering at the City College of New York (CCNY) of the City University of New York (CUNY) and codirector of the Neural Engineering Group at the New York Center for Biomedical Engineering. Bikson has published over 200 papers and book chapters and is inventor on over 30 patent applications. He is known for his work on brain targeting with electrical stimulation, cellular physiology of electric effects, and electrical safety. Bikson coinvented High-Definition transcranial Direct Current Stimulation (HD-tDCS), the first noninvasive, targeted, and low-intensity neuromodulation technology. He consults for medical technology companies and regulatory agencies on the design, validation, and certification of medical instrumentation. Bikson is cofounder of Soterix Medical Inc. and WiPOX LLC. Marom Bikson received a Ph.D. in biomedical engineering from Case Western Reserve University, in Cleveland, and a B.S. in biomedical engineering from Johns Hopkins University, Baltimore.

## 8.1   Introduction

Transcranial electrical stimulation (tES) devices apply electrical waveforms through electrodes placed on the scalp to modulate brain function.[1] Various types of tES devices are used for a wide range of indications spanning neurological and psychiatric disorders,[2,3] blood-brain barrier polarization[4] neurorehabilitation after injury, and altering cognition in healthy adults.[5] All tES devices share certain common features, including a waveform generator (typically a current controlled source), electrodes that are either fully disposable or include a disposable electrolyte, and an adhesive to position the electrodes on the scalp (Figure 8.1). Various tES subclasses are named based on dose. For example, electroconvulsive therapy (ECT) is a special class of tES applying high stimulation intensity. A tES "dose" is defined by the size and position of electrodes, and waveform including the pattern, duration, and intensity of the current.[6]

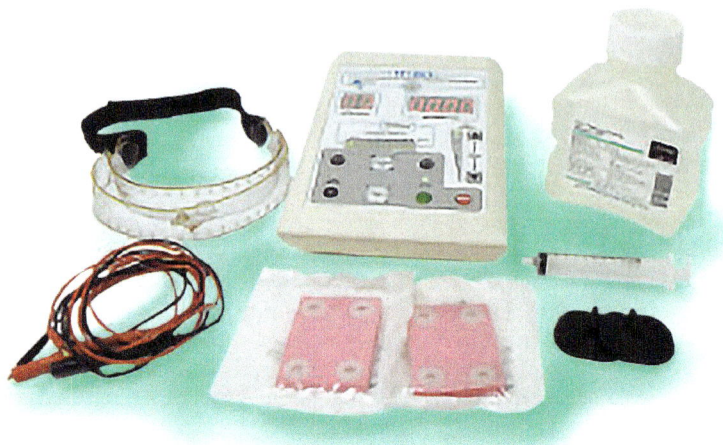

Figure 8.1 Example of a tES device, headgear, snap electrode, and lead wire used to connect electrodes to the stimulator. Generally, conventional sponge-electrodes are soaked with a controlled volume of saline using a syringe. Rubber electrodes are placed inside the sponge pockets. Sponge electrodes are then secured on the scalp using a headgear. The rubber electrodes are energized using corresponding anode and cathode wires connected to the stimulator.

This chapter is largely focused on low-intensity tES, which includes transcranial Direct Current Stimulation (tDCS), transcranial Alternating Current Stimulation (tACS), and transcranial Pulsed Current Stimulation (tPCS).[7] tES electrode types are 1) electrolyte-soaked sponge; 2) adhesive hydrogel;[7] 3) High-Definition (HD);[8] 4) hand-held solid metal; 5) free paste on electrode; and 6) dry.[9] Computational current flow models support device design.[10] Consensus on the tolerability of tES is protocol specific, but medical grade devices minimize risk.

## 8.2 Historical development of tES devices

The history of electrical stimulation dates back to the discovery of electrical phenomena, and static voltage sources are among the earliest examples of electrical technology,[11] though with unclear relation to the modern tDCS dose. There is a continuous history of transcranial electrical stimulation technology development and testing, much of it on non-DC waveforms such as pulsed stimulation (Figure 8.3).[12] Human trials investigating tDCS for neuropsychiatric disorders continued through the middle of the 20th century, typically with lower current intensities and longer durations than modern tDCS.[13] The importance of canonical trials circa 2000 (showing a polarity-specific modulation of brain excitability by tDCS) is evidenced by these trials establishing the modern tDCS dose: 1 mA applied over tens of minutes with relatively large electrodes.[14] Subsequent pilot trials instituted a 2 mA intensity for therapeutic interventions[15] maintained for almost all subsequent clinical evaluation.[16] These developments established the contemporary tDCS dose and thus the specification of modern tDCS devices (Figure 8.2). Iontophoresis (transdermal drug delivery using potential gradient) devices were adopted for some tDCS trials as an off-label medical device, though they may not provide a steady output.[17]

Ongoing refinements in dose (e.g., use of 1.5 mA in cognitive neuroscience),[18] electrodes (e.g., HD-tDCS), integration with imaging (e.g., fMRI), and home-use (e.g., remote supervised) are reflected in specific tDCS device features. Usability device features such as enhanced programming (microcontroller), control systems (e.g., response to impedance changes), rechargeable batteries, disposable electrodes, enhanced headgear materials, wireless connectivity, and the integration of monitoring technology[19] reflect general progress in available technologies while maintaining the tDCS dose (Figure 8.2).

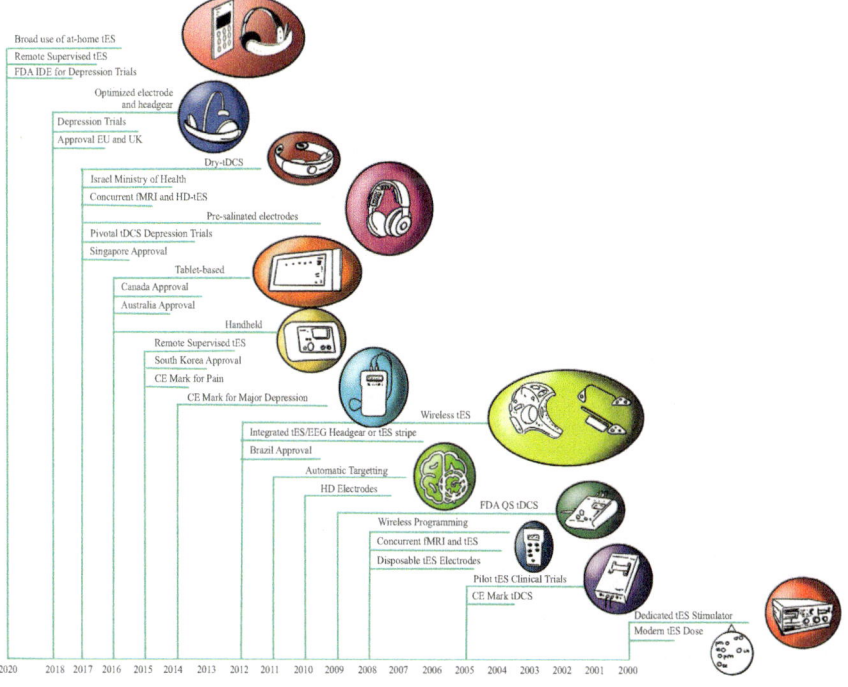

**Figure 8.2** Timeline of tDCS Innovations: Technology and Regulatory Milestones. tDCS: transcranial Direct Current Stimulation. CE mark: Conformité Européenne Marking. fMRI: functional Magnetic Resonance Imaging. FDA QS: Food and Drug Administration Quality Systems. HD: High Definition/Density. EEG: Electroencephalography.

## 8.3 Basics of tES devices and dose

The tES device is essentially a current source connected to electrodes on the subject's scalp. A tES dose is defined as the current waveform applied to the body and the number, shape, and location of electrodes placed on the scalp. The electrodes guide the waveform into the head and serve as the interface between the device and the body. A tES device should be designed to reliably deliver the target dose, including any operator controls, safety features, and instructions for use. Electrode montage collectively refers to the electrode number, shape, and location. There is a minimum of two electrodes. The waveform is produced by a powered device that can be directly attached to the electrodes using connector lead wires (Figure 8.1). A headgear is used to hold the electrodes in the desired positions, or the electrodes can be adhesive. If the device is small, it may be attached to the headgear, but, more typically, it is a hand-held or benchtop device. Electrode design (e.g., materials) is reported separately from montage and waveform, but a central theme here is that because of reproducibility, usability, and tolerability factors, electrode design critically informs both possible dose and device form (usability) factors.

Sub-classes of tES are defined by a specific dose and intended use. For example, a form of tES that delivers high intense stimulation (~1000 mA) to produce a seizure in an anesthetized patient is called Electroconvulsive Therapy (ECT).[20] This chapter is largely focused on low-intensity approaches that are well below the intensity needed to produce seizures, typically only 1-4 mA.[21] These low-intensity approaches do not cause discomfort when applied to alert individuals who may be engaged in different activities (training, performing tasks) during stimulation. In fact, low-intensity tES typically does not provide an overt response related to brain stimulation — with any changes in brain function subtle — but can produce an overt sensation such as tingling that are not related to direct brain modulation. In most cases, stimulation is applied for several minutes (for example, 10 min) using two electrodes (typically a few $cm^2$) on the head. Therefore, often the distinguishing feature of different sub-classes of tES is the waveform shape and electrode montage rather than the peak intensity or period of use.[22]

tES devices that deliver low-intensity stimulation, such as tDCS, tACS, and tPCS, are typically battery-powered. tES devices used for ECT and devices that apply brief high-intensity stimulation for neurophysiological evaluation (e.g., a single 1000 mA pulse) are wall powered. In addition to waveform, electrode number and shape determine dose in some cases further inform the sub-class of tES classification. For example, the use of small electrode arrays is classified as High-Definition (e.g., High-Definition tDCS,[8] High-Definition tACS [23]).

The current enters through the anode electrode into the body and exits the body through the cathode. At any instant of stimulation, there must be at least one active anode and one active cathode. For tES devices where the waveform polarity is fixed, such as tDCS and monophasic tPCS, each electrode has a fixed assignment of either anode or cathode (Figure 8.3). For tES devices where the waveform is biphasic, such as tACS and biphasic tPCS, each electrode alternates between functioning as an anode or cathode (Figure 8.3). When there are two electrodes, the current at one electrode is always the opposite of the other (1 mA at a single anode, indicates -1 mA at a single cathode). When there are more than two electrodes, the summed current across anode electrodes must equal to the summed current across the cathode electrodes[24] — because of the conservation of current where the total current entering the body must equal to the total current exiting the body.

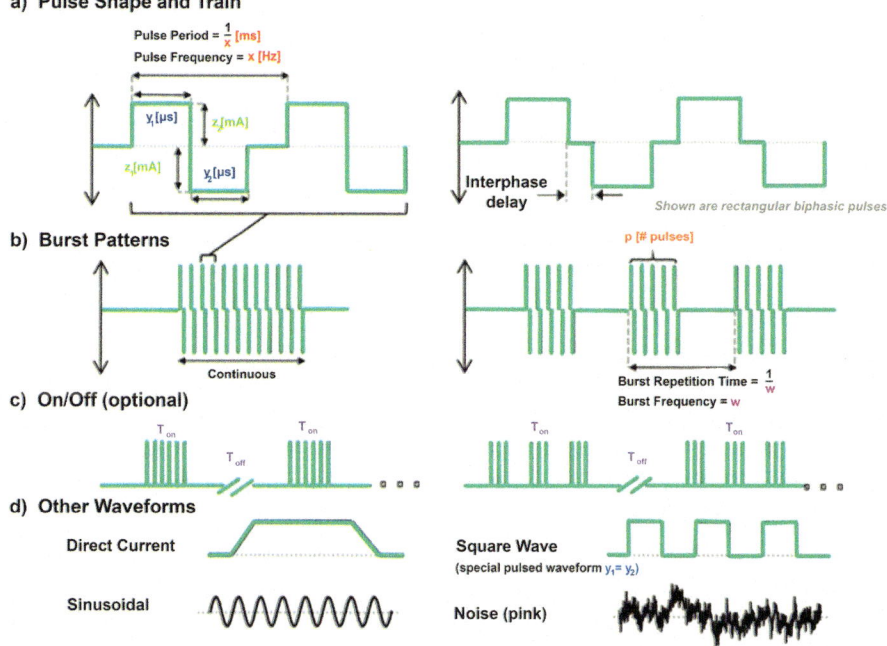

**Figure 8.3** Different types of waveforms used in tES and their parameters. (A) represents rectangular biphasic pulses with frequency "x (Hz)", period " (s)", amplitude "Z1=Z2 (mA)", and pulse width "y1=y2 (s)". (B) represent burst patterns of pulses (continuous or discrete) where "P" is number of pulses, "w" is the burst frequency and "" is burst repetition time. (C) shows monophasic burst on (Ton) and burst off (Toff). Other waveforms such as direct current (DC), square wave, sinusoidal, and pink noise are shown in D.

## 8.4 Design aspects of tES electrodes

The key technical contributors to the broad adaption of tES are the portability and ease of use, along with the tolerability profile of most tES techniques. For limited-intensity tES techniques, adverse events are largely limited to effects that occur at the skin such as transient skin sensations (e.g., perception of warmth, itching, and tingling) and redness[25,26] that might be related to skin current flow.[27] Because adverse events are limited to the skin, the design and preparation of tES electrodes are considered central to tolerability.[9] Electrode design, in turn, can govern which waveforms will be tolerated. When established electrode protocols are not followed or poor electrode design is used, tES produces significant skin irritation and burns.[28] Electrode design also ensures reliable dose delivery. In addition, the electrode design should also address the ease and robustness of use (e.g., the potential for home use). For clinical trials, since sensations also determine effective blinding, tES electrodes impact blinding reliability.[21] Finally, to the extent that tES electrodes design shapes current flow through the brain, electrode selection and preparation are critical for reproducibility and efficacy.

The typical tES device uses just two electrodes of comparable size, positioned on the head.[6] However, strategies with asymmetric electrode size,[29] an electrode at or below the neck,[30] or an increasing number of electrodes (using High-Definition electrodes) can alter tES spatial focality.[8]

Electrodes can be positioned based anatomical landmarks on the head. These can be modestly sophisticated requiring a trained operator and tape measure, for example, using the EEG 10/10 system (e.g., anode on C3). Other more simplistic placement techniques are based on gross anatomical landmarks (e.g., over the eyebrow). When head gear is used, it is either designed to support the determination of specific electrode positions (e.g., a cap or marked straps[31]) or generic mechanical support (e.g., rubber bands[32]) so independent measurements can be used to measure the position of electrodes first (Figure 8.4). More sophisticated placement techniques include neuronavigated,[33] functional,[34] specialized head-straps,[35] or image-based approaches (e.g., EEG reciprocity[19,36]).

tES electrodes include two essential components: 1) a conductive rubber or metal separated from the skin by 2) a saline-soaked sponge, gel, or paste — which are collectively called the electrolyte.[6] Additional components of the electrode are often intended to provide mechanical support to the conductive rubber/metal or electrolyte, or otherwise facilitate electrode use (e.g., adhesion). In electrochemistry terms, the conductive rubber or plate would be the electrode, while the saline, gel or paste would be the electrolyte.[24] However, in tES literature, the entire assembly is called the electrode.[22]

Here we refer to the "electrochemical electrode" as metal or conductive rubber which is defined at the interface between the metal/rubber and the electrolytes. This interface is where electrochemical reactions (e.g., pH changes) occur.

# Transcranial Electrical Stimulation (tES)

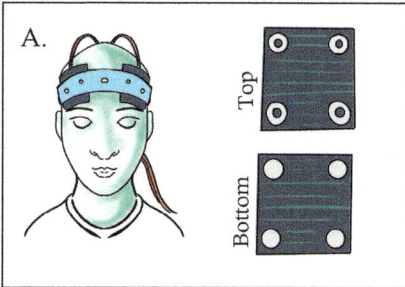
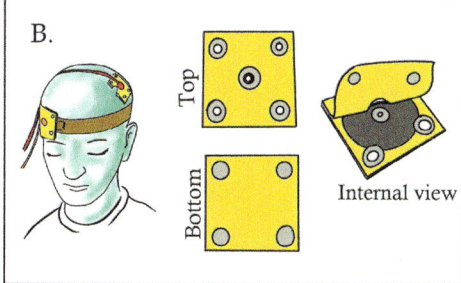

**Figure 8.4** Architecture of sponge-electrode and its variations. (A, B) Examples of electrodes positioned on the scalp with the intention to stimulate the brain transcranially. Variations in sponge electrode design can make a significant difference in usage (both 5x5 cm2). In both cases, a conductive rubber electrode is placed between saline soaked sponges, but in one case, a metal snap is attached to the conducive rubber electrode. (A) For sponges without the metal rivet, a wire needs to be inserted inside the sponges to connect to the conductive rubber electrodes. A rubber band is then used to hold the electrodes to the scalp. (B) For sponges with a metal rivet, a lead with a snap connector may be used. In this case, the snap connector can be integrated into a head gear. This example is intended to show how seemingly small changes in electrode deign can have significant impact on overall usability.

In tES when electrode size is described, (e.g., 5 x 5 cm$^2$) it is the interface (surface) between the skin and the electrolyte, not the electrochemical electrode surface. None-the-less, the configuration of all electrolyte and electrochemical-electrode dimensions and materials are important to control and document as this affects tolerability. [28,37,38]

The thickness of the sponge or paste essentially controls the minimum distance between the conductible rubber/metal and the skin. Contact of conductive rubber or metal with the skin during tES is always avoided as this compromises tolerability and introduces the risk of significant skin irritation. This risk is the main reason why the more involved an electrode preparation technique is, the more prone it is to set-up error (e.g., insufficient electrolyte thickness in a free-paste electrode), and the less deployable it is. Electrodes intended for wide or deployed use should require minimum preparation (e.g., adhesive electrodes, pre-saturated sponge electrodes).

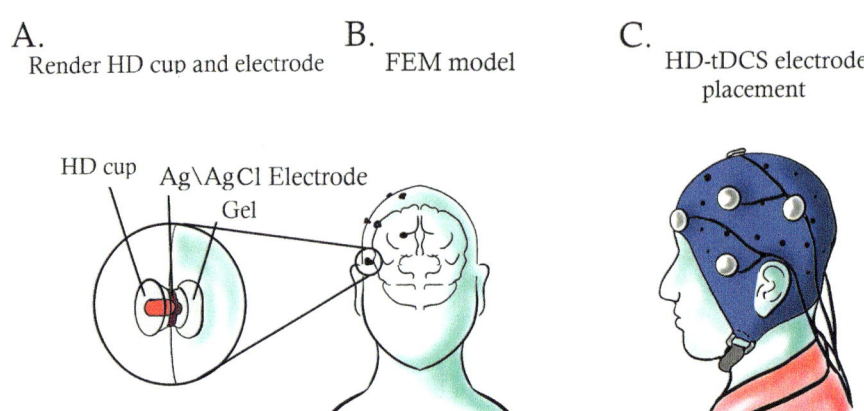

Figure 8.5 High definition (HD) tES device and electrodes. In contrast to other types of tES electrode, HD electrode are relatively small. A HD-cup placed on the skin contain the metal electrodes (Ag/AgCl) and the electrolyte gel. Shown is the 4x1-ring configuration of electrode placement where four electrodes of matched polarity are positioned around a central electrode of opposite polarity. Electrodes are secured in a 4x1 configuration using a specialized head cap.

There are two essential functions of the electrolyte, and by extension, the materials used to support the electrolyte shape such as sponge, hydrogel polymer, and other support materials that contain a viscous electrolyte (such as the HD case (Figure 8.5)). Both functions of the electrolyte relate to preventing direct contact between metal/conductive rubber electrode and skin. The first aforementioned function relates to electrochemical products, including changes in pH that occur only at the metal/rubber and electrolyte interface[24] such that a "thick" electrolyte (e.g., realized by a thick sponge, gel, or holder) minimizes these reactions from reaching the skin and causing irritation. The second function relates to normalizing current flow patterns through the skin; related to this, the saline, conductive paste, or conductive gel is used to maintain good contact quality at the skin.[37,39] If, as result of poor electrode design (e.g., conductive metal/rubber not fully protected from the skin) or preparation (e.g., a metal/rubber electrode pushed through paste), the metal/rubber contacts the skin, these electrochemical changes or poor current density patterns can adversely impact the skin and aggravated skin irritation is likely.

The overall cardinal functions of electrodes used in tES are to 1) support reliable delivery of the desired dose; and 2) protect the skin from electrochemical reactions occurring at the surface of the metal/rubber, including normalizing current density across the skin (e.g., minimize hotspot) and preventing any electrochemical reactions (occurring at the electrochemical electrode) from impacting the skin. Because electrochemical reactions are key concerns, all electrodes designed for tES include some mechanism to separate the metal/rubber from the skin. The electrolyte, being the conductive element contacting the skin, takes on importance in general performance. As expanded upon in the following sections, the design of the electrolyte (and by extension all support materials used around it) is central to the classification of electrode types:

1) *Sponge-electrode*: A sponge saturated with the fluid electrolyte, typically saline, with a metal/rubber inside the sponge (sponge pocket design) or on the sponge surface opposite the skin (Figure 8.4). The sponge sets the electrolyte shape and conductive path.

2) *Self-adhesive integrated electrode*: A hydrogel electrolyte with sufficient rigidity not to flow or spread, and with the gel or material around the gel including an adhesive component.

3) *HD electrode*: A stiff mechanical support (short tube/cup) material that contains the electrolyte, typically gel and also controls the position of the metal (Figure 8.5). Used for smaller electrodes and so suitable for arrays.

4) *Free electrolyte on hand-held conductor*: "Free" indicates application by the operator without strict thickness control by the electrode assembly. Re-used solid metal electrode, covered per-use with a thin electrolyte layer, and an operator handles to press down. Used in some forms of ECT and not considered further here.

5) *Free paste on conductive rubber electrode*: The paste may also provide adhesion. Used in some investigational forms of tDCS/tACS and not considered in detail here.

6) *Dry electrodes*: Novel designs that are not adhesive and leave no residue (not liquid or paste). Experiments are not discussed in detail here.

These general design approaches create restrictions on 1) the size of the electrode (e.g., small HD vs. large sponge) that can impact the ability to leverage electrode arrays for targeting; 2) how much preparation is required and the need for headgear; 3) if the electrodes can be applied to the hair regions of the scalp.

## 8.5 Indications for tES use

The tES spans many clinical and behavioral interventions, and as noted, many sub-techniques,[22] such as tDCS, tACS, and tPCS. What relates these different techniques is that they apply a current through electrodes on the scalp to stimulate the brain directly, rather than the periphery.[6] Research that uses tES thus focuses on direct cortical modulation as an explanation for changes in behavior, cognition, neurophysiology, and imaging studies.[40]

From the perspective of the device, the dose is designed and selected to achieve specific changes in brain function and thus clinical or cognitive outcomes. While this is a large parameter space, it can be reduced to parameters of the electrode montage (e.g., how many, what size, where) and features of the waveform (e.g., intensity, frequency). The electrode montage is generally considered to determine *which* brain regions are influenced, and waveform determines *how* they are influenced — though, in practice, montage and waveform will integrate to determine where and how the brain is influenced.

For example, tDCS is applied as a possible treatment for major depressive disorder (MDD). A brain region of interest in MDD research is the dorsolateral prefrontal cortex (DLPFC), which is targeted with tDCS by placing electrodes bilaterally on the forehead.[3] tES clinical trials intending to treat pain disorders (e.g., migraine, fibromyalgia, craniofacial pain) often target the motor cortex (M1) with an "active" electrode, while the "return" electrode is placed on the contralateral forehead (called the "supra-orbital" or SO position) (Figure 8.4C).[14]

## 8.6 Current Flow Modeling Informs Electrode/Device Design and Set-up

Computational models predict the resulting current flow (electric field distribution) in the brain for a given dose and anatomy (Figure 8.6). Computational models have been developed[41–43] and validated[44] over a decade. It is important not to conflate established montage-specific effects (e.g., "shaping" the outcomes of stimulation) with a demonstration of focality (e.g., current delivery to one region of interest). Rather, models of conventional tDCS[45] and HD-tDCS[8] support testing hypothesis that links brain regions to neurophysiologic or behavioral changes.[10] This includes registering results from computational current flow models with the imaging data.[46]

Computational models are ancillary software used to inform the design,[26] set-up, and programming of tES devices. Device specifications limit the dose range that can be explored by a model, while conversely, models can encourage the creation of new device technology.[42] For example, a home-based system relying on adhesive electrodes would restrict the positional electrode location to explore with computational models to position them below the hairline,[47] which in turn, simulates the development of simple-to-use electrodes that can go over the hairline.[31] The potential for focal transcranial stimulation was suggested first by computational models,[45] but it was not until practical HD electrodes were developed[48] that approaches to optimize transcranial stimulation using HD arrays could be tested.

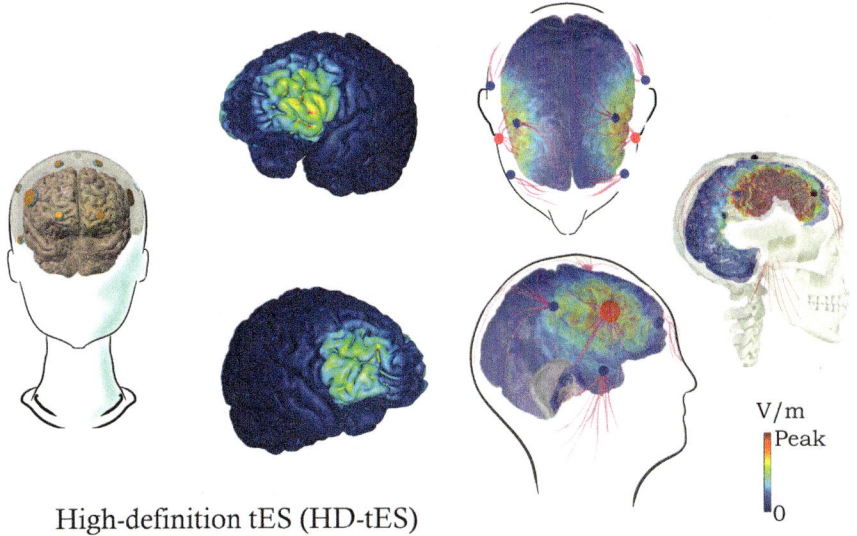

High-definition tES (HD-tES)

**Figure 8.6** Computational FEM head models and predicted electric field magnitude of dual-hemisphere HD-tES montage. (Left) 3D image of a segmented brain generated from an MRI scan of a healthy adult and electrode placement over the cortex. (Middle) electric field magnitude and current density stream inside the head's tissue layers during HD-tES. (Right) Dissected view of skull with activated brain region by HD-tES.

## 8.7 Safety and Tolerability of tDCS Devices

The tolerability of any intervention depends not simply on the device and dose but the protocol, including the subject's demographic and clinical characteristics (i.e., inclusion/exclusion criteria (e.g., age, preexisting condition), operator training and certification, ongoing monitoring, and parallel interventions). Therefore, the scientific consensus that tDCS is safe and tolerated is explicitly limited to those protocols tested. Human trials of tDCS in the USA are almost always considered Non-Significant-Risk (risk comparable to daily activities). However, this risk designation — whether made by the Food and Drug Administration (FDA) or by an Institutional Review Board (IRB) — must be made on a protocol-specific basis. Recommendations on safety and tolerability cannot be made on a blanket level to any device but must also specify the method of use.

The tES device design may be considered to minimize risk to the extent that the device can reliably control the dose and allow consistent electrode setup when used within the limits of established protocols. Medical grade tES devices and accessories designed and manufactured to internationally recognized medical standards — regardless of region-specific approval for treatment – provide the highest standard of control with respect to reliability.

Tingling is a common adverse effect reported in low-intensity tES studies.[7] For low-intensity techniques like tDCS, the severity of adverse events is low across all conditions (Figure 8.7). As discussed above, electrode size and salinity of sponge-electrodes may influence sensation.[28] In principle, electrode design must be optimized to reduce the frequency and intensity of tingling and related sensations in clinical trials, enhancing blinding effectiveness. For this same reason, studies that focus on the efficacy of the tES (tDCS) blinding technique but provide little attention to the electrode design and preparation techniques (including document operator training) are of limited generalized value. There is a dissociation between erythema and tingling — tingling being higher under thin sponge stimulation than thick electrodes.[25] A potential reason may be that the thick sponge produces a more uniform current density at the skin surface, resulting in evenly diffused erythema distribution and lower tingling sensation.

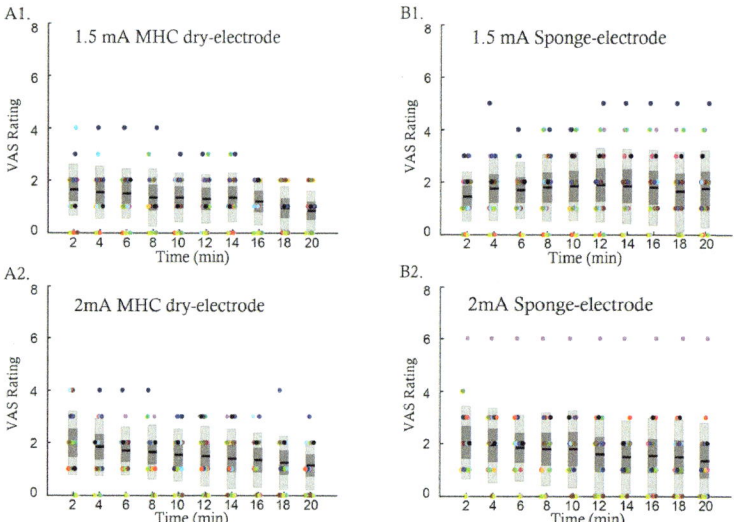

**Figure 8.7** Visual Analogue Scale (VAS) pain score at different stimulation intensities (1.5 mA and 2 mA tDCS) for a conventional sponge and MHC dry electrode. Participants were color-coded as the cumulative adverse events and relationship to tDCS data, and the VAS pain score (1-10 scale; 1: no pain, 10: unbearable pain) was collected every 2 minutes during each stimulation session. There was no significant difference ($P < 0.05$) in the VAS rating across all four stimulation sessions. Adapted from Khadka et al., 2018.[9]

## 8.8 Home-based tDCS Devices

The advantage of tES (including tDCS) is deployability. Factors like cost, portability, safety, and ease-of-use allow tES (tDCS) to be used in a wide range of clinical environments and at home.[49] However, devices designed for use by certified operators at research or clinical centers may not be suitable across deployed conditions. Standards for remote-supervised tDCS have been developed and validated[50] to address this concern. The principle of remote-supervised tDCS is, under continuous medical or research supervision, to control compliance, proper dose control, and risk. Features of suitable device include mechanisms to limit dose (e.g., one 2 mA 20-minute session per day) and simple and robust method to prepare and apply electrodes (e.g., single-use pre-saturated snap electrodes and single position headgear). While the ethics and merits of self-administered tDCS (outside of medical or research supervision) are discussed, and specifications for tDCS devices that minimize risk have been developed.

## 8.9 Conclusion

The tES device is a current source connected to electrodes on the subject's scalp. tES dose is defined as the current waveform applied to the body and the number, shape, and location of electrodes placed on the scalp that guide the waveform into the head. Approaches using low-intensity tES, limited to a few milliamperes, include tDCS and tACS. A practical tES device is equipped to reliably deliver the dose, including any operator controls, safety features, and instructions for use. The waveform is produced by a powered device and may be hand-held or benchtop and connected, or the device may be integrated into a headgear that includes an electrode. Other than the waveform, device features such as shape, weight, power supply, and user interface are not explicitly part of dose but can be critical for usability (e.g., ability to apply correctly, acceptability and compliance). The applications of tES are diverse and expanding, spanning treatment of neurological and psychiatric disorders, neurorehabilitation, and mental health and performance. The level of evidence for the efficacy of different tES doses across different applications varies.

## Endnotes

1. Nitsche MA, Cohen LG, Wassermann EM, et al. Transcranial direct current stimulation: State of the art 2008. *Brain Stimulat*. 2008;1(3):206-223. doi:10.1016/j.brs.2008.06.004

2. Edemann-Callesen H, Habelt B, Wieske F, et al. Non-invasive modulation reduces repetitive behavior in a rat model through the sensorimotor cortico-striatal circuit. *Transl Psychiatry*. 2018;8(1):11. doi:10.1038/s41398-017-0059-5

3. Leite J, Gonçalves ÓF, Pereira P, et al. The differential effects of unihemispheric and bihemispheric tDCS over the inferior frontal gyrus on proactive control. *Neurosci Res*. 2018; 130:39-46. doi:10.1016/j.neures.2017.08.005

4. Shin DW, Fan J, Luu E, et al. In Vivo Modulation of the Blood-Brain Barrier Permeability by Transcranial Direct Current Stimulation (tDCS). *Ann Biomed Eng*. 2020;48(4):1256-1270. doi:10.1007/s10439-020-02447-7

5. Adair D, Truong D, Esmaeilpour Z, et al. Electrical stimulation of cranial nerves in cognition and disease. *Brain Stimulat*. 2020;13(3):717-750. doi:10.1016/j.brs.2020.02.019

6. Woods AJ, Antal A, Bikson M, et al. A technical guide to tDCS, and related non-invasive brain stimulation tools. *Clin Neurophysiol Off J Int Fed Clin Neurophysiol*. 2016;127(2):1031-1048. doi:10.1016/j.clinph. 2015.11.012

7. Paneri B, Adair D, Thomas C, et al. Tolerability of Repeated Application of Transcranial Electrical Stimulation with Limited Outputs to Healthy Subjects. *Brain Stimulat*. 2016;9(5):740-754. doi:10.1016/j.brs.2016.05.008

8. Alam M, Truong DQ, Khadka N, Bikson M. Spatial and polarity precision of concentric high-definition transcranial direct current stimulation (HD-tDCS). *Phys Med Biol*. 2016;61(12):4506. doi:10.1088/0031-9155/61/12/4506

9. Khadka N, Borges H, Zannou AL, et al. Dry tDCS: Tolerability of a novel multilayer hydrogel composite non-adhesive electrode for transcranial direct current stimulation. *Brain Stimulat*. 2018;11(5):1044-1053. doi:10.1016/j.brs.2018.07.049

10. Bikson M, Truong DQ, Mourdoukoutas AP, et al. Modeling sequence and quasi-uniform assumption in computational neurostimulation. *Prog Brain Res*. 2015;222:1-23. doi:10.1016/bs.pbr.2015.08.005

11. Paulus W, Opitz A. Ohm's law and tDCS over the centuries. *Clin Neurophysiol Off J Int Fed Clin Neurophysiol*. 2013;124(3):429-430. doi:10.1016/j.clinph.2012.08.019

12. Guleyupoglu B, Schestatsky P, Edwards D, Fregni F, Bikson M. Classification of methods in transcranial electrical stimulation (tES) and evolving strategy from historical approaches to contemporary innovations. *J Neurosci Methods*. 2013;219(2):297-311. doi:10.1016/j.jneumeth.2013.07.016

13. Esmaeilpour Z, Schestatsky P, Bikson M, et al. Notes on Human Trials of Transcranial Direct Current Stimulation between 1960 and 1998. *Front Hum Neurosci*. 2017;11:71. doi:10.3389/fnhum.2017.00071

14. Nitsche MA, Paulus W. Excitability changes induced in the human motor cortex by weak transcranial direct current stimulation. *J Physiol*. 2000;527(3):633-639. doi:10.1111/j.1469-7793.2000.t01-1-00633.x

15. Fregni F, Boggio PS, Mansur CG, et al. Transcranial direct current stimulation of the unaffected hemisphere in stroke patients. *Neuroreport*. 2005;16(14):1551-1555. doi:10.1097/01.wnr.0000177010.44602.5e

16. Brunoni AR, Moffa AH, Sampaio-Junior B, et al. Trial of Electrical Direct-Current Therapy versus Escitalopram for Depression. *N Engl J Med*. 2017;376(26):2523-2533. doi:10.1056/NEJMoa1612999

17. Chhatbar PY, Sawers JR, Feng W. The Proof is in the Pudding: Does tDCS Actually Deliver DC Stimulation? *Brain Stimulat*. 2016;9(4):625-626. doi:10.1016/j.brs.2016.05.002

18. Turkeltaub PE, Benson J, Hamilton RH, Datta A, Bikson M, Coslett HB. Left lateralizing transcranial direct current stimulation improves reading efficiency. *Brain Stimulat*. 2012;5(3):201-207. doi:10.1016/j.brs.2011.04.002

19. Leite J, Morales-Quezada L, Carvalho S, et al. Surface EEG-Transcranial Direct Current Stimulation (tDCS) Closed-Loop System. *Int J Neural Syst*. 2017;27(6):1750026. doi:10.1142/S0129065717500265

20. George MS, Nahas Z, Li X, et al. Novel treatments of mood disorders based on brain circuitry (ECT, MST, TMS, VNS, DBS). *Semin Clin Neuropsychiatry*. 2002;7(4):293-304.

21. Khadka N, Borges H, Paneri B, et al. Adaptive current tDCS up to 4 mA. *Brain Stimulat*. Published online August 5, 2019. doi:10.1016/j.brs.2019.07.027

22. Bikson M, Esmaeilpour Z, Adair D, et al. Transcranial electrical stimulation nomenclature. *Brain Stimulat*. 2019;12(6):1349-1366. doi:10.1016/j.brs.2019.07.010

23. Reinhart RMG, Nguyen JA. Working memory revived in older adults by synchronizing rhythmic brain circuits. *Nat Neurosci*. 2019;22(5):820-827. doi:10.1038/s41593-019-0371-x

24. Merrill DR, Bikson M, Jefferys JGR. Electrical stimulation of excitable tissue: design of efficacious and safe protocols. *J Neurosci Methods*. 2005;141(2):171-198. doi:10.1016/j.jneumeth.2004.10.020

25. Ezquerro F, Moffa AH, Bikson M, et al. The Influence of Skin Redness on Blinding in Transcranial Direct Current Stimulation Studies: A Crossover Trial. *Neuromodulation Technol Neural Interface*. 2017;20(3):248-255. doi:10.1111/ner.12527

26. Khadka N, Zannou AL, Zunara F, Truong DQ, Dmochowski J, Bikson M. Minimal Heating at the Skin Surface During Transcranial Direct Current Stimulation. *Neuromodulation Technol Neural Interface*. 2018;21(4):334-339. doi:10.1111/ner.12554

27. Khadka N, Bikson M. Role of skin tissue layers and ultra-structure in transcutaneous electrical stimulation including tDCS. *Phys Med Biol*. Published online September 11, 2020. doi:10.1088/1361-6560/abb7c1

28. Dundas JE, Thickbroom GW, Mastaglia FL. Perception of comfort during transcranial DC stimulation: Effect of NaCl solution concentration applied to sponge electrodes. *Clin Neurophysiol*. 2007;118(5):1166-1170. doi:10.1016/j.clinph.2007.01.010

29. Kuo H-I, Bikson M, Datta A, et al. Comparing cortical plasticity induced by conventional and high-definition 4 × 1 ring tDCS: a neurophysiological study. *Brain Stimulat*. 2013;6(4):644-648. doi:10.1016/j.brs.2012.09.010

30. Bikson M, Datta A, Rahman A, Scaturro J. Electrode montages for tDCS and weak transcranial electrical stimulation: role of "return" electrode's position and size. *Clin Neurophysiol Off J Int Fed Clin Neurophysiol*. 2010;121(12):1976-1978. doi:10.1016/j.clinph.2010.05.020

31. Knotkova H, Riggs A, Berisha D, et al. Automatic M1-SO Montage Headgear for Transcranial Direct Current Stimulation (TDCS) Suitable for Home and High-Throughput In-Clinic Applications. *Neuromodulation J Int Neuromodulation Soc*. 2019;22(8):904-910. doi:10.1111/ner.12786

32. DaSilva AF, Volz MS, Bikson M, Fregni F. Electrode Positioning and Montage in Transcranial Direct Current Stimulation. *J Vis Exp JoVE*. 2011;(51). doi:10.3791/2744

33. De Witte S, Klooster D, Dedoncker J, Duprat R, Remue J, Baeken C. Left prefrontal neuronavigated electrode localization in tDCS: 10-20 EEG system versus MRI-guided neuronavigation. *Psychiatry Res Neuroimaging*. 2018;274:1-6. doi:10.1016/j.pscychresns.2018.02.001

34. Rich TL, Menk JS, Rudser KD, et al. Determining Electrode Placement for Transcranial Direct Current Stimulation: A Comparison of EEG- Versus TMS-Guided Methods. *Clin EEG Neurosci*. 2017;48(6):367-375. doi:10.1177/1550059417709177

35. Seibt O, Brunoni AR, Huang Y, Bikson M. The Pursuit of DLPFC: Non-neuronavigated Methods to Target the Left Dorsolateral Pre-frontal Cortex With Symmetric Bicephalic Transcranial Direct Current Stimulation (tDCS). *Brain Stimulat*. 2015;8(3):590-602. doi:10.1016/j.brs.2015.01.401

36. Dmochowski JP, Koessler L, Norcia AM, Bikson M, Parra LC. Optimal use of EEG recordings to target active brain areas with transcranial electrical stimulation. *NeuroImage*. 2017;157:69-80. doi:10.1016/j.neuroimage.2017.05.059

37. Minhas P, Datta A, Bikson M. Cutaneous perception during tDCS: Role of electrode shape and sponge salinity. *Clin Neurophysiol Off J Int Fed Clin Neurophysiol*. 2011;122(4):637-638. doi:10.1016/j.clinph.2010.09.023

38. Kronberg G, Bikson M. Electrode assembly design for transcranial Direct Current Stimulation: a FEM modeling study. *Conf Proc Annu Int Conf IEEE Eng Med Biol Soc IEEE Eng Med Biol Soc Annu Conf*. 2012;2012:891-895. doi:10.1109/EMBC.2012.6346075

39. Khadka N, Woods AJ, Bikson M. Transcranial Direct Current Stimulation Electrodes. In: Knotkova H, Nitsche MA, Bikson M, Woods AJ, eds. *Practical Guide to Transcranial Direct Current Stimulation: Principles, Procedures and Applications*. Springer International Publishing; 2019:263-291. doi:10.1007/978-3-319-95948-1_10

40. Weber MJ, Messing SB, Rao H, Detre JA, Thompson‐Schill SL. Prefrontal transcranial direct current stimulation alters activation and connectivity in cortical and subcortical reward systems: A tDCS-fMRI study. *Hum Brain Mapp*. 2014;35(8):3673-3686. doi:10.1002/hbm.22429

41. Opitz A, Paulus W, Will S, Antunes A, Thielscher A. Determinants of the electric field during transcranial direct current stimulation. *NeuroImage*. 2015;109:140-150. doi:10.1016/j.neuroimage.2015.01.033

42. Khadka N, Truong DQ, Bikson M. Principles of Within Electrode Current Steering. *J Med Devices*. 2015;9(2):020947-020947-2. doi:10.1115/1.4030126

43. Khadka N, Bikson M. Neurocapillary-Modulation. *Neuromodulation J Int Neuromodulation Soc*. Published online December 19, 2020. doi:10.1111/ner.13338

44. Huang Y, Liu AA, Lafon B, et al. Measurements and models of electric fields in the in vivo human brain during transcranial electric stimulation. Ivry R, ed. *eLife*. 2017;6:e18834. doi:10.7554/eLife.18834

45. Datta A, Bansal V, Diaz J, Patel J, Reato D, Bikson M. Gyri-precise head model of transcranial direct current stimulation: improved spatial focality using a ring electrode versus conventional rectangular pad. *Brain Stimulat*. 2009;2(4):201-207, 207.e1. doi:10.1016/j.brs.2009.03.005

46. Halko MA, Datta A, Plow EB, Scaturro J, Bikson M, Merabet LB. Neuroplastic changes following rehabilitative training correlate with regional electrical field induced with tDCS. *NeuroImage*. 2011;57(3):885-891. doi:10.1016/j.neuroimage.2011.05.026

47. Tyler WJ, Boasso AM, Mortimore HM, et al. Transdermal neuromodulation of noradrenergic activity suppresses psychophysiological and biochemical stress responses in humans. *Sci Rep*. 2015;5:13865. doi:10.1038/srep13865

48. Minhas P, Bansal V, Patel J, et al. Electrodes for high-definition transcutaneous DC stimulation for applications in drug delivery and electrotherapy, including tDCS. *J Neurosci Methods*. 2010;190(2):188-197. doi:10.1016/j.jneumeth.2010.05.007

49. Charvet LE, Shaw MT, Bikson M, Woods AJ, Knotkova H. Supervised transcranial direct current stimulation (tDCS) at home: A guide for clinical research and practice. *Brain Stimulat*. 2020;13(3):686-693. doi:10.1016/j.brs.2020.02.011

50. Charvet LE, Kasschau M, Datta A, et al. Remotely-supervised transcranial direct current stimulation (tDCS) for clinical trials: guidelines for technology and protocols. *Front Syst Neurosci*. 2015;9:26. doi:10.3389/fnsys.2015.00026

# 9
# Transcranial Magnetic Stimulation (TMS)

**Shreyas Harita**
Shreyas is a Ph.D. student at the University of Toronto. His research interests lie in the use of connectome based neural mass modeling to study neural population activity, and how it changes in response to brain stimulation and in neuropathological conditions. The primary aims of his research project are to investigate the stimulation-induced network propagation and connectivity patterns in the human brain. He hopes to achieve a better understanding of this using brain stimulation techniques like TMS and multimodal brain imaging techniques such as structural MRI, fMRI, DTI, and EEG. He also wishes to study how individual variability in brain geometry affects responses to brain stimulation, and how this information can inform neuronavigation techniques to improve the identification of potential TMS targets.

**Frank Mazza**
Frank is a M.Sc. student at the University of Toronto. Frank is interested in identifying electrophysiological signals for diagnosis of depression and transcranial magnetic stimulation (TMS) protocols for treatment of depression, using computer simulations of detailed brain circuits and whole-brain networks. With previous work in identifying EEG correlates of response in a novel rTMS stimulation paradigm (OFC-rTMS), he now focuses on identifying biomarkers in brain signals for diagnosis of depression by linking cellular, circuit, and connectivity changes to signals relevant for clinical diagnosis. In addition, he is working to optimize TMS protocols using computer simulations at the local and global brain scales by simulating protocol effects on local circuits, such as circuit inhibition, and the propagation of activity to other regions in the brain.

**John D. Griffiths**
Dr. Griffiths has a strong technical expertise in multimodal neuroimaging data analysis, scientific computing, and numerical simulations of large-scale brain dynamics. Through his work with Dr. Mcintosh and colleagues in Europe and the US, he is an active contributor to the scientific, software development, and educational missions of the Virtual Brain Project.

## 9.1 Introduction

The ability to accurately and effectively stimulate the brain noninvasively (i.e., without surgically opening the skull) is one of the holy grails of modern clinical and experimental neuroscience. Noninvasive brain stimulation techniques in use today may be grouped broadly into three types: electrical (e.g., transcranial electric stimulation; TES), magnetic (e.g., transcranial magnetic stimulation; TMS), and acoustic (e.g., transcranial ultrasound stimulation; TUS). Of these, TMS is, by far, the most successful and widely used stimulation technique in research and clinical practice. Its success is owed in substantial part to the vision and brilliance of a few key individuals over the past half-century, as well as to the wonderful physical fact that extremely strong magnetic fields can be passed through the skull with relative ease, safety, and focality. This chapter will examine the history, physiology, clinical applications, and practicalities of TMS technology and its many fascinating applications.

## 9.2 How It Works

In 1831, Michael Faraday discovered the principles of electromagnetic induction, whereby an electric current flowing through a wire coil produces a magnetic field. The rate of change of this magnetic field causes the induction of a secondary current in a nearby conductor. With TMS, a current flows through the stimulating coil, which induces an electric current in the subject's brain (the secondary current in a nearby conductor).[1]

The design of a typical TMS stimulator is rather simple. It consists of a stimulating coil held against the subject's head and the main unit that powers the coil. The main unit houses a charging system, multiple energy storage capacitors, a switch to control the shape and flow of current, and other flexible functionalities customized as required (Figure 9.1). Critical factors that determine the effectiveness of the coil stimulator are the maximization of peak coil energy while minimizing power consumption and device heating and the speed of magnetic field rise time. As a result, high-energy storage capacitors and dynamic energy transfer between the capacitor to the coil are essential.

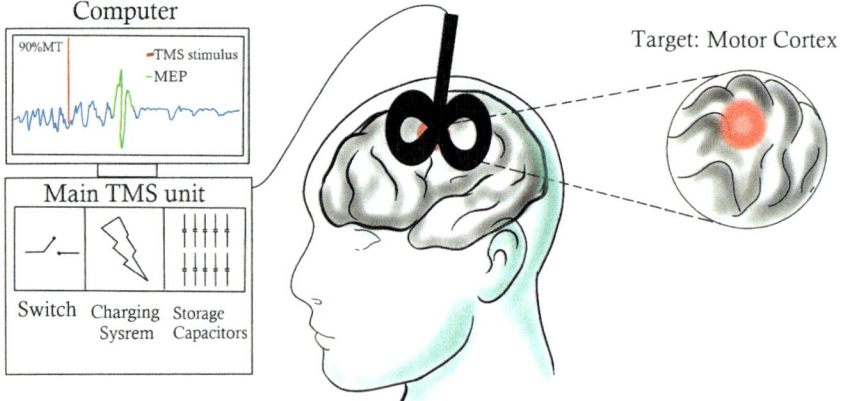

Figure 9.1 Schematic of a standard TMS device and experimental setup for eliciting MEPs through primary motor cortex stimulation.

Advantages of TMS over other noninvasive stimulation technologies include that it can induce the depolarization (i.e., firing) of neurons at sufficiently high stimulation amplitudes. This is possible because magnetic fields can easily pass through the human skull with little to no resistance and produce relatively large secondary currents in the underlying cortical tissue. The peak discharge current needs to be about 10mA/cm2 to elicit neuronal depolarization and firing.[1] Neuronal depolarization caused by the induced current leads to unique physiological and behavioral outcomes depending on the brain area targeted. The TMS-induced electrical currents flow in parallel to the stimulation coil plane; therefore, TMS mainly stimulates neurons that are horizontally aligned relative to the brain surface. However, the extent of activation and the activated neurons' specificity remain unclear and could vary across subjects and the areas stimulated.[2,3]

## 9.3 Typical Usage

### 9.3.1 TMS Stimulation Paradigms

Over the last twenty-five years, TMS has evolved into a powerful clinical and research tool due to its concentrated and noninvasive stimulation of cortical brain regions. Over this time, two principal modes of TMS stimulation delivery have become established: *single-pulse* and *repetitive*.

Single-pulse TMS paradigms apply an individual (typically relatively high-amplitude) stimulation pulse, immediately preceding some behavioral or physiological response such as a reaction time or electroencephalograph (EEG)/electromyograph (EMG) measurement. The most straightforward use of single-pulse TMS is as a method for studying *axonal conduction*. Single-pulse TMS is done at various levels, from individual nerve fibers to small, well-defined chains of neurons, all the way to propagation across large-scale distributed brain networks. Single-neuron conduction can be achieved in some rare cases, such as direct stimulation of the motor nerves in the arm. With single-pulse TMS applied to the brain, however, most described phenomena result from conduction along small polysynaptic pathways. Polysynaptic pathways are characterized as having multiple points (synapses) at which nerve impulses can pass from one neuron to the other.

Studies have used single-pulse TMS in cognitive neuroscience research to *inactivate* regions of the cortex to investigate functional brain organization. The general approach used in these studies is to apply a TMS pulse during a cognitive task or sensory stimulus at a specific location and with very specific timing.

The second principal mode of TMS delivery is not as a single pulse but a consistent stream of pulses, for sustained periods of minutes to tens of minutes. This is known as *repetitive* TMS (rTMS). With single-pulse TMS, the physiological and neurocognitive effects of interest are generally fast and transient activity patterns in brain circuits. With rTMS, the focus is, typically, on *neural plasticity* (i.e., brain changes that outlast — by minutes, hours, days, weeks, or months — the stimulation session itself). One of the most striking (and consistent) observations in all of human neurophysiology is that rTMS can induce neural plasticity that is either excitatory (i.e., long-term potentiation [LTP]) or inhibitory (i.e., long-term depression [LTD]), depending on the frequency and other temporal characteristics of the stimulation waveform. Investigations have determined that low-frequency (<1Hz) rTMS is inhibitory, whereas high-frequency (>5Hz) rTMS is excitatory.[4]

An important variant of rTMS is theta-burst stimulation (TBS). Generally, this protocol includes a series of short high-frequency (50Hz) pulses, with an inter-burst interval of 200 ms (or 5 Hz), which lies within the conventional "theta" frequency range of 4-8Hz.[5] In general, TBS has proved much more potent than standard rTMS at inducing neural plasticity and has garnered major interest from clinicians. The two principal subtypes of TBS are continuous theta-burst (cTBS) and intermittent theta-burst (iTBS), which (for conventional parameters) have also been found to have nominally inhibitory and excitatory effects, respectively.[6]

In addition to single-pulse TMS and rTMS, two other important and related TMS paradigms should be highlighted: *paired-pulse stimulation* and *paired associative stimulation* - both of which can be thought of as variants or extensions of single-pulse TMS. Paired-pulse stimulation involves using not one but two TMS pulses — a test pulse followed by a conditioning pulse, separated by an inter-stimulus interval (ISI). This pairing of the test and conditioning pulses is used to study cortical excitation and inhibition, which could reflect the activity of glutamatergic and GABAergic neurons, respectively.[7]

There are three commonly used paired-pulse approaches, which vary according to the timing and amplitude of the two pulses, and the distinct physiological effects recruited: 1) short-interval intracortical inhibition (SICI), 2) long-interval intracortical inhibition (LICI), and 3) intracortical facilitation (ICF). Reduced cortical inhibition has been seen in psychiatric disorders using paired-pulse stimulation techniques. For example, patients were found to have reduced SICI associated with positive symptoms of schizophrenia.[8] Paired-associate stimulation has a similar approach and rationale to paired-pulse stimulation.

Like paired-pulse stimulation, paired-associative designs are often used to study sensorimotor plasticity.[9] Although technically difficult, twin- and multi-coil TMS experiments, in general, have proved to be an excellent tool for directly studying brain connectivity,[10] and long-studied phenomena like interhemispheric inhibition, where one half of the brain hinders or constrains the other half.[11] Multi-focal rTMS has also received considerable interest in recent years because it can design therapeutic strategies that target distributed networks rather than individual brain regions.[12] Moving forward, improvements in stimulator technology and, in particular, roboticized coil targeting[13] will be key for rapid progress in these areas.

## 9.3.2 Clinical Applications

In addition to being a powerful research tool for studying various aspects of human neurophysiology, TMS (specifically, rTMS) has proven to be a highly effective therapeutic technique across a wide range of neurological and neuropsychiatric conditions. TMS has demonstrated this in large scale, placebo-controlled randomized trials for major depressive disorder (MDD), Parkinson's Disease (PD), obsessive-compulsive disorder, pain, epilepsy, tremors, dystonia, and tinnitus.[14] RTMS has also shown positive behavioral outcomes in post-traumatic stress disorder, addiction, and schizophrenia. It has also demonstrated its utility as a neuro-rehabilitation tool for patients with various central nervous system disorders such as stroke and trauma.14 In its application to neuro-rehabilitation, rTMS therapy has been shown to have a positive outcome for up to 6 months following treatment discontinuation.[15] However, despite the breadth and depth of the research conducted, it is important to note that the exact mechanisms that offer therapeutic benefits from rTMS therapies are still largely unknown and may differ by disorder and individual patients.

RTMS therapy has approval from the US food and drug administration (FDA) for MDD cases where the patients are resistant to traditional treatment (drugs and psychotherapy). One of the brain circuits that may be responsible for the positive outcomes in MDD with rTMS is the meso-cortico-limbic dopamine pathway (Figure 9.2). This pathway is essential for reward processing, learning, and incentive-based actions.[16] Typically, rTMS therapy involves stimulation at the left dorso-lateral prefrontal cortex (dlPFC). The left dlPFC is known to be involved in multiple executive functions, including organization, planning, attention,[17] and response inhibition.[18]

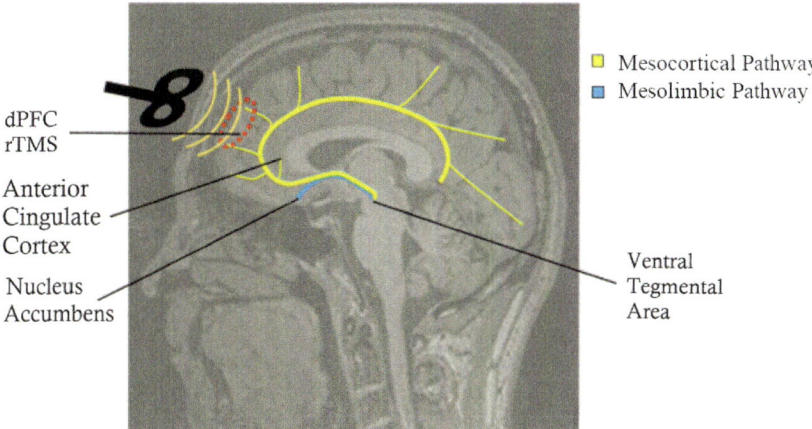

Figure 9.2 A potential driver of the therapeutic effects of rTMS at the dlPFC is its impact on the meso-cortico-limbic dopaminergic pathway.

Research to date suggests that rTMS therapy can be effectively used to improve the slowed movements and tremors seen in PD patients. Results are achieved with the use of high frequencies in the motor cortex (>5 Hz) or low frequencies in the prefrontal motor areas (<1 Hz).[19] Two ways in which cortical rTMS stimulation therapy may obtain its desired effects include modulating functional connectivity between the subcortical structures and the cortex and improving the abnormal cortical changes associated with PD (such as the dysfunction of the cortico-thalamo-cortical motor circuits).[20] However, a systematic review and meta-analysis by Fregni et al. (2005) showed that not every study reports having a positive effect.[21] Some studies even report negative results. Fregni et al. proposed that these negative results may be due to the interaction of rTMS effects with antiparkinsonian drugs and argued that medication could reduce the effects of rTMS, as they act via different mechanisms.21 While the mechanisms above are based on several studies, it is important to note that work remains to establish these mechanisms' roles and how they interact to elicit a therapeutic effect.[22]

### 9.3.3 Neuroprotective effects of rTMS

A key outcome of rTMS therapy is its neuroprotective effects, such as general and disease-specific cell production. One study showed an increase in grey matter volume, with no changes seen in patients receiving sham rTMS.[23] In studies using rodent models, very high frequency (25Hz) rTMS was seen to improve neurogenesis, the process of forming new neurons, in part of the temporal lobe of the brain (the dentate gyrus, specifically) over two weeks.[24]

The neuroprotective effects of rTMS have also been studied in stroke, specifically its anti-apoptotic (i.e., cell death-resistant) properties. Many studies looking at transient ischemic attack models in rodents have shown that rTMS prevents neuron death and alters metabolism and blood flow in the brain around the affected region.[25] RTMS therapy also improves glucose metabolism and reduces the number of caspase-3 positive neurons (caspase-3 is a protein that regulates apoptosis [cell death, destruction of neurons]), compared to the control group - implying that rTMS inhibits neuronal cell death in the affected area.[26] This anti-apoptotic effect of rTMS has helped design clinical therapies for stroke patients. It has also led to clinical studies investigating its efficacy in treating other neurological conditions like epilepsy.

## 9.4 History

The earliest reliable TMS device was developed between 1984-1985 by Anthony Barker and colleagues.[27] Before this, in the late 1970s, a few clinicians started using TES in patients with multiple sclerosis to record motor conduction times.[1]

While useful, this technique was highly uncomfortable for healthy subjects and patients alike and also far riskier due to the possibility of brain damage, epileptic episodes, adverse cognitive effects, electric burn injuries, scalp burns, pain, and headaches. A few years later, Barker and his colleagues would help solve this issue through the invention of TMS. Similar motor conduction tests with single-pulse TMS could now be performed in a much safer and less painful environment. While some risks of pain and headaches remained, for the large part, TMS was considered safer than tES. TMS was mainly used as a diagnostic tool in the following years, and little was done to evaluate its short-term versus Long-term effects. The primary focus was directed towards patient safety, and patient-reported side effects were thoroughly recorded, especially patients with epilepsy or epilepsy-like symptoms (i.e., seizures).

Following these initial developments in the early 1990s, rTMS paradigms started gaining traction, as opposed to single-pulse TMS therapies. The new rTMS paradigm allowed for a longer, more sustained brain stimulation. The fact that the neurological and physiological effects of rTMS lasted well after cessation made it more useful in therapeutic medicine, whereas single-pulse TMS had only been usefully applied in diagnostic medicine. As rTMS grew in popularity, so did the ethical issues surrounding it. In addition to patient safety, with rTMS, additional issues included "how patients would respond to rTMS vs. TMS" and "which disorders might respond to rTMS."

Furthermore, the potential interaction between rTMS and medication and whether it would be harmful to the patient had to be considered. Kolbinger et al. (1995) conducted one of the first studies to focus on clinical applications of rTMS on MDD patients who did not respond to drug-based interventions. In this study, the authors noted that all ten patients receiving non-sham stimulation showed improved outcomes. While the results of this proof-of-principle study were certainly promising, the long-term cortical effects of rTMS protocols on patients were and are yet to be fully understood.[28]

As a result, in 1996, the world's leading TMS authorities published safety and ethical guidelines for TMS usage in both the clinic and the research laboratory. With these guidelines in place, several studies began looking at and confirming the benefits of TMS therapy, and TMS as a clinical tool became increasingly established. Initially, rTMS patient groups were restricted to those who required it as a "last resort" (i.e., patients who did not respond to any other previously established forms of treatment). This last resort connotation again raised the ethical problem: how to efficiently study the effects of TMS therapy if it is only used on patients desperate for some relief? Patients' tendency to self-research, often finding misleading information from non-peer-reviewed sources, exacerbated this problem and continues to do so. Thus, additional safeguards to protect vulnerable populations were put in place.[1]

New rTMS stimulation paradigms were developed along with clinical expansion, which positively impacted the risk-to-benefit ratio for rTMS. An example of this is theta-burst rTMS, which led to longer-lasting and more significant modulation (i.e., more powerful effects) of cortical circuitry and excitability, with a shorter treatment length. These effects, coupled with the pulse characteristics, coil shapes, and stimulation target sites, led to the need for a well-trained technician and a medical expert with procedural training and certification. With a significant increase in those seeking rTMS therapy, it is of the utmost importance that we ensure that patients receive efficient and safe treatment. To this end, guidelines were established in 1998 that require doctors and technicians to be well-versed in the appropriate rTMS methodology and relevant safety features.

In 2008, these guidelines were reviewed and updated to minimize the risk of seizure by limiting potentially dangerous combinations of rTMS frequencies, intensities, and durations. Since then, TMS and rTMS research has grown exponentially, extending into new clinical domains and exploring new and advanced hardware and software. One example of such advancement is the plethora of studies in recent years that combine rTMS with functional MRI.[29],[30] It is important to continually review and update guidelines for the safe and effective use of rTMS in clinical and research labs. These guidelines also ensure that steps are taken to avoid potential problems and that any issues that may arise would be addressed appropriately.

## 9.5   Risks and adverse effects

Following the guidelines established in 1998, a review of the literature conducted by Machii et al. (2006) revealed that rTMS applied to non-motor cortical areas has relatively minor adverse effects, seemingly dependent on individual patient characteristics.[31] A common method of tailoring TMS treatment is to set the stimulation intensity based on the patient's motor threshold (MT). As noted earlier, MT refers to the minimum stimulation intensity required to produce a motor output from a resting muscle (for example, a finger twitch).

Some other studies also use the phosphene threshold (PT). A phosphene occurs when an individual 'sees' light without light actually entering the eye, typically seen when stimulating the visual cortex with TMS. Both MT and PT are useful values to consider. However, these values may vary between regions for other non-motor or non-visual areas of the cortex. Some studies use a stimulus intensity value of less than MT and a frequency of less than 1 Hz to avoid possible seizure risks. Therefore, it would be prudent to take caution in using measures like MT and PT as proxies for the regional threshold.[31]

There are few adverse effects when using rTMS therapy; this is either because potentially adverse effects have not been considered serious or because they have not been reported. Minor side-effects, such as acute headache and neck pain, are the most common medical complaints connected to rTMS therapy. However, these reactions may not necessarily be reported in studies carrying out rTMS therapy or dismissed as trivial due to their common occurrence. Depending on the stimulation site and type, roughly 40% of patients experience side-effects at some point.[31] It has been found that low-frequency rTMS generally causes these side effects more often than high-frequency rTMS. A potential explanation lies in the long treatment length of low-frequency rTMS, with headaches and neck pain resulting from holding one's head and neck in a relatively restrained position for an extended period.

In some cases, a mouth guard is used since rTMS causes the jaw muscles to flex. Sustained flexion of the jaw muscles can lead to a headache in some cases. In addition, some report a strong tingling sensation on the scalp, which may be due to the coil's recurring contact to the same region on the scalp throughout the rTMS session. As a side effect, nausea is rare, with only two known incidents at the time of this writing. Both cases were rTMS stimulation therapies centered on the cerebellum.

Serious negative side effects include seizures and symptoms of bipolar psychosis. In one study, extremely short inter-train intervals (250 ms) were suspected of causing seizures in the patient undergoing rTMS therapy. At the time, there was a lack of safety guidelines about how long inter-train intervals should have been.[32] Following this study, research into inter-train intervals has determined that shorter intervals (<1s) using repeated trains of rTMS stimulation could be problematic.[33] In a separate study, the patient had a history of a maprotiline-induced seizure.

Furthermore, this patient was taking multiple medications for MDD. The authors suggest that a combination of her previous seizure and any potential drug interactions could have led to a seizure following rTMS.[34] It is to be noted that the epileptic episode subsided with the cessation of rTMS treatment in both these cases. Therefore, it is important to note each medical history and tailor the rTMS stimulation paradigm to suit patients' needs accordingly. Concerning psychosis as a side effect: three patients with bipolar depression reported manic symptoms following rTMS to the dlPFC.[35,36] In another case, a patient suffered from delusions following rTMS application.[37] It is important to note that the patients mentioned above were all on medication. However, it should be noted that the patients' specific medications, as reported, could have had interactions with the effects of rTMS therapy and led to such side effects. Nevertheless, the data from these studies are still insufficient and cannot tell us with certainty that the patients' medications led to or increased the risk of an adverse effect. In general, these kinds of events are extremely rare, and if they do occur, warrant an investigation on a case-by-case basis.[31]

## 9.6 Costs & Setup

Today, the main clinical uses of rTMS are to treat patients with treatment-resistant MDD, PD and assist with recovery following stroke. As mentioned previously, rTMS is a form of brain stimulation with no surgery required for its use. An average rTMS device costs around US $50,000.[38] It is used in a clinic to treat patients and research labs to study the effects of rTMS therapy and further improve outcomes by updating the guidelines for rTMS use.

The typical TMS device can be broken down into a current generator, a control board used to modify the electromagnetic field intensity and duration, and a figure-eight coil used to direct the electromagnetic field. While this is the basic set of parts needed, a rTMS device can be customized by altering the coil shape (e.g., H-coil instead of a figure-of-eight coil). Any other adjustments can be made as needed depending on use (i.e., clinical or research). A single session of rTMS in the US typically costs between $200$300 USD, with full course treatments costing between $6,000-$12,000 USD,38 depending on the treatment plan. One study looked at the effects of rTMS therapy and antidepressant medication on the patient's quality of life (QOL) following treatment in terms of cost-effectiveness.[39] According to the study, lifetime costs and QOL analysis revealed that rTMS was far superior to antidepressant medication, which means that rTMS treatment costs less and has better outcomes. This result was found to be consistent across all age ranges. Further studies are required to evaluate rTMS therapy's cost-effectiveness in patients with other conditions (PD, stroke, etc.).

## 9.7 Conclusion

In conclusion, TMS is a fascinating and powerful technology for researchers, clinicians, and patients alike. As one of the three types of noninvasive brain stimulation, TMS has the ability to activate areas of the brain through magnetic stimulation. Widely used and one of the most successful means of brain stimulation, TMS works safely and effectively in clinical and research settings with multiple application modes. As our understanding of and ability to measure and monitor the neurobiological mechanisms engaged by TMS progresses, and this understanding becomes increasingly integrated with the engineering and design of TMS devices, patients can look forward to increasingly precise, effective, and personalized TMS-based therapeutic options.

## Endnotes

1. Horvath, Jared C., Jennifer M. Perez, Lachlan Forrow, Felipe Fregni, and Alvaro Pascual-Leone. "Transcranial magnetic stimulation: a historical evaluation and future prognosis of therapeutically relevant ethical concerns." *Journal of medical ethics* 37, no. 3 (2011): 137-143.

2. Allen, Elena A., Brian N. Pasley, Thang Duong, and Ralph D. Freeman. "Transcranial magnetic stimulation elicits coupled neural and hemodynamic consequences." *Science* 317, no. 5846 (2007): 1918-1921.

3. Wagner, Timothy, Antoni Valero-Cabre, and Alvaro Pascual-Leone. "Noninvasive human brain stimulation." *Annual Review of Biomedical Engineering*. 9 (2007): 527-565.

4. Klomjai, Wanalee, Rose Katz, and Alexandra Lackmy-Vallée. "Basic principles of transcranial magnetic stimulation (TMS) and repetitive TMS (rTMS)." *Annals of physical and rehabilitation medicine* 58, no. 4 (2015): 208-213.

5. Oberman, Lindsay, Dylan Edwards, Mark Eldaief, and Alvaro Pascual-Leone. "Safety of theta burst transcranial magnetic stimulation: a systematic review of the literature." *Journal of Clinical Neurophysiology* 28, no. 1 (2011): 67.

6. Huang, Ying-Zu, Mark J. Edwards, Elisabeth Rounis, Kailash P. Bhatia, and John C. Rothwell. "Theta burst stimulation of the human motor cortex." *Neuron* 45, no. 2 (2005): 201-206.

7. McClintock, Shawn M., Catarina Freitas, Lindsay Oberman, Sarah H. Lisanby, and Alvaro Pascual-Leone. "Transcranial magnetic stimulation: a neuroscientific probe of cortical function in schizophrenia." *Biological psychiatry* 70, no. 1 (2011): 19-27.

8. Daskalakis, Zafiris J., Bruce K. Christensen, Robert Chen, Paul B. Fitzgerald, Robert B. Zipursky, and Shitij Kapur. "Evidence for impaired cortical inhibition in schizophrenia using transcranial magnetic stimulation." *Archives of General Psychiatry* 59, no. 4 (2002): 347-354.

9. Stefan, Katja, Erwin Kunesch, Leonardo G. Cohen, Reiner Benecke, and Joseph Classen. "Induction of plasticity in the human motor cortex by paired associative stimulation." *Brain* 123, no. 3 (2000): 572-584.

10. Shields, Jessica, Jung E. Park, Prachaya Srivanitchapoom, Rainer Paine, Nivethida Thirugnanasambandam, Sahana N. Kukke, and Mark Hallett. "Probing the interaction of the ipsilateral posterior parietal cortex with the premotor cortex using a novel transcranial magnetic stimulation technique." *Clinical Neurophysiology* 127, no. 2 (2016): 1475-1480.

11. Rogasch, Nigel C., Zafiris J. Daskalakis, and Paul B. Fitzgerald. "Cortical inhibition, excitation, and connectivity in schizophrenia: a review of insights from transcranial magnetic stimulation." *Schizophrenia bulletin* 40, no. 3 (2014): 685-696.

12. Chiu, David, C. David McCane, Jason Lee, Blessy John, Lisa Nguyen, Kayla Butler, Rajan Gadhia et al. "Multifocal transcranial stimulation in chronic ischemic stroke: A phase 1/2a randomized trial." *Journal of Stroke and Cerebrovascular Diseases* (2020): 104816.

13. Kantelhardt, Sven Rainer, Tommaso Fadini, Markus Finke, Kai Kallenberg, Jakob Siemerkus, Volker Bockermann, Lars Matthaeus et al. "Robot-assisted image-guided transcranial magnetic stimulation for somatotopic mapping of the motor cortex: a clinical pilot study." *Acta neurochirurgica* 152, no. 2 (2010): 333-343.

14. Lefaucheur, Jean-Pascal, Nathalie André-Obadia, Andrea Antal, Samar S. Ayache, Chris Baeken, David H. Benninger, Roberto M. Cantello et al. "Evidence-based guidelines on the therapeutic use of repetitive transcranial magnetic stimulation (rTMS)." *Clinical Neurophysiology* 125, no. 11 (2014): 2150-2206.

15. Chervyakov, Alexander V., Andrey Yu Chernyavsky, Dmitry O. Sinitsyn, and Michael A. Piradov. "Possible mechanisms underlying the therapeutic effects of transcranial magnetic stimulation." *Frontiers in human neuroscience* 9 (2015): 303.

16. Feil, Jodie, and Abraham Zangen. "Brain stimulation in the study and treatment of addiction." *Neuroscience & Biobehavioral Reviews* 34, no. 4 (2010): 559-574.

17. Tekin, Sibel, and Jeffrey L. Cummings. "Frontal–subcortical neuronal circuits and clinical neuropsychiatry: an update." *Journal of psychosomatic research* 53, no. 2 (2002): 647-654.

18. Blasi, Giuseppe, Terry E. Goldberg, Thomas Weickert, Saumitra Das, Philip Kohn, Brad Zoltick, Alessandro Bertolino, Joseph H. Callicott, Daniel R. Weinberger, and Venkata S. Mattay. "Brain regions underlying response inhibition and interference monitoring and suppression." European Journal of Neuroscience 23, no. 6 (2006): 1658-1664.

19. Chou, Ying-hui, Patrick T. Hickey, Mark Sundman, Allen W. Song, and Nan-kuei Chen. "Effects of repetitive transcranial magnetic stimulation on motor symptoms in Parkinson disease: a systematic review and meta-analysis." *JAMA neurology* 72, no. 4 (2015): 432-440.

20. Pan, PingLei, Yang Zhang, Yi Liu, He Zhang, DeNing Guan, and Yun Xu. "Abnormalities of regional brain function in Parkinson's disease: a meta-analysis of resting state functional magnetic resonance imaging studies." *Scientific reports* 7, no. 1 (2017): 1-10.

21. Fregni, F., D. K. Simon, A. Wu, and A. Pascual-Leone. "Non-invasive brain stimulation for Parkinson's disease: a systematic review and meta-analysis of the literature." Journal of Neurology, *Neurosurgery & Psychiatry* 76, no. 12 (2005): 1614-1623.

22. Fricke, Christopher, Charlotte Duesmann, Timo B. Woost, Judith von Hofen-Hohloch, Jost-Julian Rumpf, David Weise, and Joseph Classen. "Dual-site transcranial magnetic stimulation for the treatment of Parkinson's disease." *Frontiers in neurology* 10 (2019): 174.

23. May, Arne, Gören Hajak, S. Gänssbauer, Thomas Steffens, Berthold Langguth, Tobias Kleinjung, and Peter Eichhammer. "Structural brain alterations following 5 days of intervention: dynamic aspects of neuroplasticity." *Cerebral cortex* 17, no. 1 (2007): 205-210.

24. Ueyama, Eiko, Satoshi Ukai, Asao Ogawa, Masakiyo Yamamoto, Shunsuke Kawaguchi, Ryouhei Ishii, and Kazuhiro Shinosaki. "Chronic repetitive transcranial magnetic stimulation increases hippocampal neurogenesis in rats." *Psychiatry and clinical neurosciences* 65, no. 1 (2011): 77-81.

25. Fujiki, Minoru, Hidenori Kobayashi, Tatsuya Abe, and Tohru Kamida. "Repetitive transcranial magnetic stimulation for protection against delayed neuronal death induced by transient ischemia." *Journal of neurosurgery* 99, no. 6 (2003): 1063-1069.

26. Gao, Feng, Shuang Wang, Yi Guo, Jing Wang, Min Lou, Jimin Wu, Meiping Ding, Mei Tian, and Hong Zhang. "Protective effects of repetitive transcranial magnetic stimulation in a rat model of transient cerebral ischaemia: a microPET study." *European Journal of Nuclear Medicine and Molecular Imaging* 37, no. 5 (2010): 954-961.

27. Barker, Anthony T., Reza Jalinous, and Ian L. Freeston. "Non-invasive magnetic stimulation of human motor cortex." *The Lancet* 325, no. 8437 (1985): 1106-1107.

28. Kolbinger, Hans Martin, Gereon Höflich, Andreas Hufnagel, Hans-Jürgen Müller, and Siegfried Kasper. «Transcranial magnetic stimulation (TMS) in the treatment of major depression—a pilot study.» *Human Psychopharmacology: Clinical and Experimental* 10, no. 4 (1995): 305-310.

29. Fox, Michael D., Randy L. Buckner, Matthew P. White, Michael D. Greicius, and Alvaro Pascual-Leone. "Efficacy of transcranial magnetic stimulation targets for depression is related to intrinsic functional connectivity with the subgenual cingulate." *Biological psychiatry* 72, no. 7 (2012): 595-603.

30. Opitz, Alexander, Michael D. Fox, R. Cameron Craddock, Stan Colcombe, and Michael P. Milham. "An integrated framework for targeting functional networks via transcranial magnetic stimulation." *Neuroimage* 127 (2016): 86-96.

31. Machii, Katsuyuki, Daniel Cohen, Ciro Ramos-Estebanez, and Alvaro Pascual-Leone. "Safety of rTMS to non-motor cortical areas in healthy participants and patients." *Clinical Neurophysiology* 117, no. 2 (2006): 455-471.

32. Wassermann, EricM, LeonardoG Cohen, StephenS Flitman, Robert Chen, and Mark Hallett. "Seizures in healthy people with repeated" safe" trains of transcranial magnetic stimuli." *The Lancet* 347, no. 9004 (1996): 825-826.

33. Chen, Robert, Christian Gerloff, Joseph Classen, Eric M. Wassermann, Mark Hallett, and Leonardo G. Cohen. "Safety of different inter-train intervals for repetitive transcranial magnetic stimulation and recommendations for safe ranges of stimulation parameters." *Electroencephalography and Clinical Neurophysiology/Electromyography and Motor Control* 105, no. 6 (1997): 415-421.

34. Conca, A., P. König, and A. Hausmann. "Transcranial magnetic stimulation induces 'pseudoabsence seizure'." *Acta Psychiatrica Scandinavica* 101, no. 3 (2000): 246-249.

35. Dolberg, Ornah T., Shaul Schreiber, and Leon Grunhaus. "Transcranial magnetic stimulation-induced switch into mania: a report of two cases." *Biological Psychiatry* 49, no. 5 (2001): 468-470.

36. Garcia-Toro, M. "Acute manic symptomatology during repetitive transcranial magnetic stimulation in a patient with bipolar depression." *The British Journal of Psychiatry* 175, no. 5 (1999): 491-491.

37. Zwanzger, Peter, Robin Ella, Martin E. Keck, Rainer Rupprecht, and Frank Padberg. "Occurrence of delusions during repetitive transcranial magnetic stimulation (rTMS) in major depression." *Biological Psychiatry* 51, no. 7 (2002): 602-603.

38. Raeburn, Paul. "Wise Buy? Repetitive Transcranial Magnetic Stimulation." *MedPage Today*. February 12, 2016. https://www.medpagetoday.com/psychiatry/depression/56168

39. Voigt, Jeffrey, Linda Carpenter, and Andrew Leuchter. "Cost effectiveness analysis comparing repetitive transcranial magnetic stimulation to antidepressant medications after a first treatment failure for major depressive disorder in newly diagnosed patients–A lifetime analysis." *PloS one* 12, no. 10 (2017): e0186950.

# 10 Deep Brain Stimulation

**Irene E. Harmsen**
*Irene Harmsen is an MD/PhD student at the University of Toronto. Her research is in neurosurgery and focuses on deep brain stimulation to treat patients with movement disorders. She aspires to become a neurosurgeon-scientist to advance therapies for patients with neurodegenerative disorders. Outside of her professional life, she enjoys travelling and staying active as a triathlete!*

## 10.1 Introduction

Deep brain stimulation (DBS) is a neurosurgical procedure that involves the insertion of a "brain pacemaker" through the skull (see figure 10.1). This pacemaker-like neurostimulation device is programmed to send electrical signals to certain areas of the brain to relieve symptoms associated with motor, mood, or cognitive circuit disorders. Given its relative safety and therapeutic effects, DBS has become a mainstream surgical procedure. To date, approximately 150,000 patients have been implanted at over 700 centers worldwide. While DBS is most commonly indicated for the treatment of movement disorders, particularly Parkinson's disease, DBS is now being applied to different brain circuits to investigate its potential in treating other neurological and psychiatric disorders.[1]

## 10.2 How It Works

### 10.2.1 Possible Mechanisms of DBS

Despite its use for almost 60 years, the relationship between DBS and its effect on brain networks remains unclear. As the use of DBS continues to expand beyond movement disorders, determining the precise mechanisms by which DBS works is becoming increasingly important. Historically, the stimulated deep target was thought to undergo net inhibition or net excitation.[2] However, recent studies focus attention on the modulatory effects of DBS on cortical networks.[3]

An overview of the mechanism(s) of DBS includes hypotheses such as depolarization blockade, synaptic modulation, and desynchronization of pathological

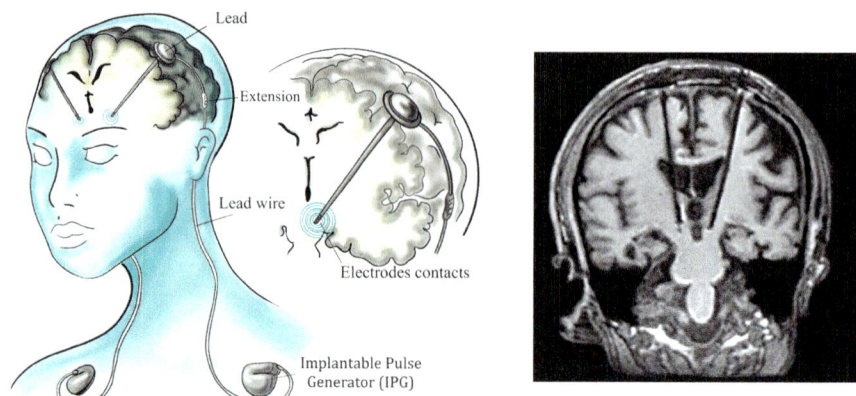

Figure 10.1 Illustration (left) and magnetic resonance image (MRI) (right) of a deep brain stimulation device implanted in a patient. A deep brain stimulation implant consists of four main components: (1) electrode contacts, (2) lead, (3) extension and lead wire, and (4) neurostimulator or implantable pulse generator (IPG), (diagram by D. Ashouri Vajari) Ashouri Vajari, Danesh, Maria Vomero, Johannes B. Erhardt, Ali Sadr, Juan S. Ordonez, Volker A. Coenen, and Thomas Stieglitz. "Integrity assessment of a hybrid DBS probe that enables neurotransmitter detection simultaneously to electrical stimulation and recording." Micromachines 9, no. 10 (2018): 510.

oscillatory activity. While most of these hypotheses are framed in the context of Parkinson's disease — for which DBS is most commonly indicated — they also apply to other disorders treated with DBS. Firstly, depolarization blockade refers to the direct blocking of neuronal output at or near the site of the DBS electrode by electrical currents generated from the implanted system. Since the clinical effects of DBS are similar to those of a surgical lesion, the basis of this hypothesis centers on silencing neurons of the stimulated brain structure. Similarly, the synaptic modulation hypothesis is based on the indirect regulation of neuronal output by activating axon terminals near the stimulating electrode. This action can result in local synaptic inhibition or excitation, depending on the specific pathway being stimulated. If DBS-activated axon terminals release GABA neurotransmitters, the downstream effect is inhibitory, whereas the release of glutamate would be excitatory.

Beyond the level of single neurons and synapses, there exists a macroscale organization of the brain that defines brain regions and large-scale communication pathways. The proposed mechanisms of DBS have more recently focused on this larger, overall system level to explore the regulating effects of DBS on abnormal neuronal oscillatory activity. Neuronal oscillations, or brainwaves, are rhythmic or repetitive patterns of neural activity in the central nervous system. Brainwaves are generated by interactions between neurons that produce visible oscillations that can be observed by functional neuroimaging techniques such as electroencephalography (EEG) and magnetoencephalography (MEG). The synchronization of neural firing patterns give rise to brainwaves at different frequencies (e.g., delta wave, 1-3 Hz; theta wave, 4-8 Hz; alpha wave, 8-12 Hz; beta wave, 13-30 Hz; gamma wave, 30-50 Hz). Brainwaves are thought to play an important role in processing neural information and may be involved in feature binding, information transfer mechanisms, and the generation of movement. As such, abnormal brainwaves are implicated in human diseases such as Parkinson's disease (beta wave disruption) and Alzheimer's (alpha and beta wave disruption).[4,5] In the context of Parkinson's disease, DBS is thought to desynchronize or reduce abnormally high levels of beta activity in the basal ganglia-thalamocortical motor circuit. Clinically, there exists a relationship between the amount of beta reduction and improvement in motor symptoms.

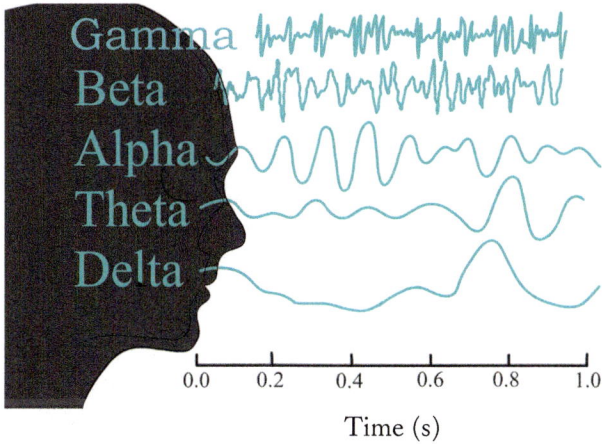

**Figure 10.2** Brainwaves (neuronal oscillations) are repetitive patterns of neural activity in the brain. They are dependent on the frequency of oscillation and can be classified into different bands (from lowest to highest frequency: delta, theta, alpha, beta, and gamma).

## 10.2.2 Mechanistic Insights from Human & Animal Studies

Many human and animal studies are being conducted worldwide to gain a better understanding of how DBS works. Human DBS studies are clinically focused and assess the feasibility and efficacy of DBS for new indications and brain targets through clinical trials.[6] Various neuroimaging and neurophysiological techniques are also being used to examine how the brain responds to DBS. These techniques include imaging modalities such as computerized tomography (CT), structural or functional magnetic resonance imaging (MRI), diffusion tensor imaging (DTI), and positron emission tomography (PET). Physiological modalities focus more on recording the electrical (or associated magnetic) activity of the brain using local field potentials (LFP), electroencephalography (EEG), and magnetoencephalography (MEG). For a review of DBS-MEG studies, see Harmsen et al. (2018).[6]

Research is becoming increasingly multimodal, whereby many of these techniques are used simultaneously to provide both spatial and temporal insights into the brain's response to DBS.

Clinical research is complemented by animal studies that examine the underlying mechanisms of DBS and evaluate new indications and technology. Electrodes have been developed using translational methods for use in animal models ranging from rats to non-human primates. DBS is possible under anesthesia and in freely moving conditions in these animals, for which stimulation parameters have been adjusted according to brain size and structural differences. Some interesting areas of active research determine the possible effects of DBS on neural growth (neurogenesis) and the formation of neural connections (synaptogenesis).

## 10.3 Typical Usage

DBS was approved for use in movement disorders since the early 2000s because of its safety and therapeutic benefit. Patients with Parkinson's disease (PD) who have received DBS report overall improvements in quality of life due to improved mobility and increased independence. Good clinical outcomes and high levels of patient satisfaction are attributed to the proper selection of the brain target and DBS settings. In comparison, DBS for non-movement disorders is still very much experimental and, as such, has mixed patient outcomes.

Table 10.1 Brain targets for DBS by disorder.

| Neural circuit | Disorder | DBS target |
| --- | --- | --- |
| Motor | Parkinson's disease | STN, GPi |
|  | Essential tremor | VIM |
|  | Dystonia | GPi, VIM |
| Motor/limbic | Obsessive-compulsive disorder | ITP |
|  | Tourette syndrome | CM-Pf |
| Limbic | Treatment-resistant depression | SCC |
| Reward/limbic | Anorexia, morbid obesity | SCC, hypothalamus |
| Memory | Alzheimer's disease | Fornix |
| Sensory/interoceptive awareness | Chronic pain | Vc, PVG |
| Various | Epilepsy | ATN |

Legend: ATN, anterior thalamic nucleus; CM-Pf, centromedian-parafascicular; DBS, deep brain stimulation; GPi, globus pallidus internus; ITP, inferior thalamic peduncle; PVG, periventricular gray matter; SCC, subcallosal cingulate; STN, subthalamic nucleus; Vc, ventrocaudalis thalamic nucleus; VIM, ventromedial nucleus of the thalamus.

In 1997, thalamic DBS for essential tremor and PD-related tremor was approved by the Food and Drug Administration (FDA), followed by the approval for subthalamic nucleus (STN) and globus pallidus internus (GPi) DBS for PD in 2003. A humanitarian device exemption for STN DBS and GPi DBS for dystonia was granted in 2003 and for the anterior limb of the internal capsule (ALIC) for obsessive-compulsive disorder in 2009.

Other disorders treated with DBS include major depression, Alzheimer's disease, epilepsy, anorexia, obesity, chronic pain, and addiction.[7] Case reports and small clinical trials suggest that DBS is successful for most of these indications; however, larger randomized controlled trials must completed before FDA approval can be granted. Since DBS effects are reversible (i.e., the procedure does not cause lesioning of the brain tissue), the exploration of new targets and applications is endless.

## 10.4 History

### 10.4.1 Early Technologies - Paving the Way

Since ancient times, electrical stimulation has been used to modulate the nervous system and treat neurological disorders.[8] In the year 46 AD Scribonius Largo, physician to the Roman emperor Claudius, suggested putting an electric ray on the brain's surface as a remedy for headaches. These fish were known to produce an electric discharge that numbs those who handle them. Up until the 18th-century, electric fish were used to treat pain, seizures, and depression.

In the 19th-century, Giovanni Aldini conducted experiments that suggested the cortical surface could be electrically stimulated, supporting the idea that electricity could have therapeutic effects in treating many neuropsychiatric disorders. This idea eventually led to therapeutic brain stimulation in the form of electroshock or electroconvulsive therapy (ECT) for the treatment of severe psychosis, introduced by Ugo Cerletti in 1938.

### 10.4.2 Early Years

Early work on electrical stimulation and studies that utilized selective lesions of specific deep brain structures (thalamic and cerebellar nuclei) for the treatment of movement disorders led to the development of DBS.

In the mid-1980s, a French team led by Alim-Louis Benabid realized that the motor benefits achieved by permanently lesioning a brain region with radio frequencies could also be achieved by electrically stimulating the region. Benabid and colleagues carried out clinical trials of chronic neurostimulation to develop it as a therapy in its own right. The success of treating Parkinson's patients with DBS led the field to adopt stimulating techniques over ablative surgeries.

### 10.4.3 Improvements and Advances

The advancement of technology has also led to new DBS devices and novel stimulating techniques to optimize therapeutic outcomes for patients. As with many therapies, whether pharmacologic or non-pharmacologic, DBS relies on the optimal dosing of electrical current delivery to the brain. Each individual has a unique therapeutic window for stimulation that varies based on symptom presentation, disease severity, and progression. In a heterogeneous clinical syndrome such as Parkinson's disease, patients can present with several clinical phenotypes including tremor-dominant, akinetic-rigid, or mixed subtypes. As such, DBS programming is individualized to maximize therapeutic benefit and reduce stimulation-induced adverse effects. This individualized programming has been made possible with the combined efforts of academic and industry-led innovation.

One such example is the development of directional electrodes, which offers more programming possibilities to optimize patient settings. Directional electrodes allow stimulation to be steered in a particular direction, closer or farther from the DBS target, based on the individual patient's needs. This steering is particularly useful if electrode placement is not optimal or to avoid stimulating a nearby structure that produces adverse effects. Advances in DBS electrode technology are also promising for treating patients with complex disorders that involve symptoms from different neural circuits. In disorders such as Parkinson's disease dementia (PDD) or dementia with Lewy bodies (DLB), patients have a combination of motor and cognitive symptoms. With the advent of longer, dual-frequency electrodes, brain structure can be stimulated simultaneously from both the motor and cognitive circuits using a single electrode (e.g., GPi-NBM multi-targeting).

Advances in technology also lead to new stimulation paradigms that could further optimize patient settings. A recent study explored the effect of stimulating patients at kilohertz frequencies using a novel ultra-high-frequency neurostimulator (Nevro Inc., CA, USA).[9] In patients with Parkinson's disease or essential tremor, a stimulation frequency of 10 kHz was applied to deep brain targets. Motor outcome improvement was similar to that of conventional 130 Hz stimulation; however, kilohertz-frequency stimulation suggested a reduction in the occurrence of stimulation-induced adverse effects such as paresthesia (i.e., numbness, tingling) and speech impairment. Another novel stimulation protocol is interleaving stimulation, whereby two or more groups of settings (and electrodes) are activated in rapid alternation to provide the patient with a more customized volume of tissue activation. Similarly, research groups are exploring patterned stimulation that can alter the regularity and duration of the stimulation to optimize DBS's efficacy and preserve the neurostimulator's battery life.[11]

Typically, DBS systems rely on a fixed-life (non-rechargeable) neurostimulator or implantable pulse generator (IPG) that needs to be replaced every 3-5 years. This battery life estimate is based on regular stimulator use in Parkinson's disease. However, in patients with more severe symptoms or indications requiring higher amplitudes of stimulation (e.g., treatment-resistant depression), battery replacement surgeries are required more frequently. With each IPG replacement, there is a risk of infection of the DBS hardware; explantation may be necessary if the system becomes infected and initial disease symptoms recur. As a solution, rechargeable batteries have been developed that last up to 15 years.

## 10.5 Properties

### 10.5.1 Precision and Accuracy

Good clinical outcomes are a function of the accurate positioning of the DBS electrode in the deep brain target. Functional neurosurgeons use a three-dimensional coordinate system to locate small targets in the patient's brain. This form of surgery, known as stereotaxy, relies on computed tomography (CT) or magnetic resonance imaging (MRI) to guide the procedure. Micro-electrode recordings (MER) are also used in DBS procedures to ensure that the electrode is correctly placed within the target structure. MER is a neurophysiological technique that records the activity of a single neuron. Since neurons in different brain structures have unique and identifiable firing patterns, the location within the brain can be determined by recording neuronal activity.

After electrode placement, its position is usually confirmed in the operating room using fluoroscopy. Fluoroscopy is an imaging technique that uses X-rays to obtain real-time images of the interior of an object. Patients undergo final MRI or CT imaging the morning after DBS insertion to confirm electrode location and ensure no bleeding has occurred. At some DBS centers, operating rooms have built-in MRI machines that enable surgeons to image the patient while performing surgery.

DBS settings are individually programmed to account for differences in electrode location, symptoms, disease severity, and individual thresholds for stimulation-induced adverse reactions to optimize symptom improvement and reduce adverse effects. DBS programming starts six weeks after surgery, once swelling from the surgery has subsided, and usually requires 4-8 clinical visits over 3-6 months.

### 10.5.2 Invasiveness

While deep brain stimulation is an open-skull procedure, it is considered minimally invasive compared to many other neurosurgical procedures and is performed while the patient is awake. Patients are awake during DBS as brain mapping is much more difficult if the patient is under a general anesthetic or strong sedative. In addition, the procedure is safer if the patient's neurological function (speech and voluntary movement) can be checked periodically during the procedure.

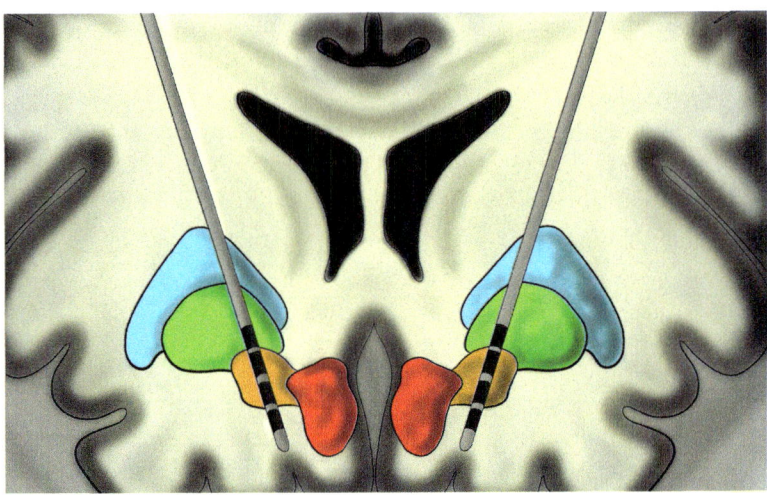

Figure 11.3 Reconstruction and localization of DBS electrodes for research purposes using Lead-DBS software. Electrodes have been implanted in the subthalamic nucleus (STN) in each hemisphere of a patient with Parkinson's disease. The patient's T1-weighted MRI image is superimposed on a neuroimaging atlas to show important motor circuit brain regions such as the globus pallidus externus (blue) and internus (green), STN (orange), and red nucleus (red).

### 10.5.3 Setup Requirements

DBS is primarily conducted in larger hospitals with well-trained interdisciplinary teams due to the nature of the procedure, its invasiveness, the neuroimaging requirements, and the neurophysiological equipment needed to perform these procedures. Teams typically include a neurologist, a psychiatrist, and a neurosurgeon to perform neurological and psychiatric screenings to assess patients prior to surgery. Once the DBS electrodes are in place, a team consisting of an experienced neurologist, neurosurgeon, and a dedicated programming nurse should be available for continued care. This team adjusts DBS settings and changes medications, as well as deals with potential device failures.

## 10.6 Logistics

### 10.6.1 Risks

Risks and complications are inherent with any surgical procedure; however, DBS is safe, and the overall risk of the procedure — and adverse hardware-related events, is acceptably low. A study on 728 patients who received DBS found that the risks of severe adverse events that could occur during the operation include bleeding in the brain (1.6%), stroke (0.4%), and seizures (0.3%).[12] Possible side effects after surgery include infection, headache, confusion, hardware complications, temporary pain, and swelling at the implantation site. Once the DBS device is turned on, some settings may cause adverse effects, but these often improve with further adjustment of the device. Possible stimulation-induced adverse effects include numbness or tingling sensations (paresthesia), muscle tightness of the face or arm, speech problems, balance problems, light-headedness, and unwanted mood changes (e.g., mania, depression). Many of these associated risks are mitigated by inclusion and exclusion criteria and the interdisciplinary healthcare team that screens patients based on neurological, neurosurgical, and psychiatric eligibility.

### 10.6.2 Costs

DBS for movement disorders has been used for over a decade and is typically offered to patients when medications no longer help. Despite the benefits of DBS, surgery and post-operative care are expensive. The surgery costs $30,000-50,000, and each battery replacement, required every three years on average, for the neurostimulator costs $10,000-20,000. DBS is usually covered by insurance. Research grants cover the costs of DBS procedures used as treatments on patients for non-approved diseases, such as Alzheimer's disease and treatment-resistant depression.

### 10.6.3 Limitations

Although DBS reduces symptoms significantly and improves the patient's quality of life, DBS is not a cure or a means to change disease progression. DBS settings require adjustment as symptoms worsen due to disease progression in neurodegenerative disorders such as Parkinson's disease and Alzheimer's disease. Similarly, not all symptoms may be resolved by DBS. When treating Parkinson's disease, symptoms typically alleviated by the gold-standard Parkinson's medication levodopa will respond best to DBS. In contrast, other symptoms not managed by levodopa, such as speech, will not improve (and may worsen) with DBS. Symptom reduction is also not immediate, and programming DBS settings can take months, requiring numerous patient visits. Other limitations include the invasive and awake procedure, which could be unpleasant and scary for some, and risks associated with the surgery. It is also possible for the hardware to malfunction, wires to disconnect, and electrodes to shift. The neurostimulator battery also requires monitoring and surgical replacement before its full depletion to avoid the return of symptoms. Some DBS devices are also currently incompatible with MRI, which limits post-operative imaging.

### 10.6.4 Notable Use Cases

While DBS is effective for movement disorders, DBS's therapeutic benefit for other indications is still being determined. Early clinical trials of fornix stimulation in patients with Alzheimer's disease suggested that patients with mild Alzheimer's disease had better outcomes than those with a more severe form.[13] These findings shaped the inclusion and exclusion criteria for performing DBS in Alzheimer's disease. Interestingly, DBS for Alzheimer's disease was born out of a serendipitous finding when a team of Canadian doctors attempted to treat a morbidly obese patient with DBS.[14] Instead of causing weight loss, the electrical stimulation caused the patient to experience vivid memories from childhood. Even after a year, the patient performed better on memory tests when the electrodes were stimulated.

Unique indications for which DBS is currently being explored include decreased level of consciousness, schizophrenia, and drug and alcohol addictions. To date, phase 1 clinical trials with few subjects have been conducted to assess the feasibility of DBS in these disorders. Recruitment for these trials is often more difficult than in DBS trials for movement disorders. Often, patients cannot provide fully informed consent and must rely on a substitute decision-maker. Patient non-adherence to study protocols and loss to follow-up are also common in some of these patient populations. Nevertheless, DBS has been applied to patients in a persistent vegetative state and has shown some promise in helping patients emerge from a coma.[15] In a clinical trial for treatment-resistant schizophrenia, four out of seven patients showed symptom improvements (reduced occurrences of delusions and hallucinations) with stimulation of the nucleus accumbens or subgenual anterior cingulate cortex.[16] Moreover, in the crossover phase of the study, these patients all showed worsening when stimulation was discontinued.

Given the increases in opioid-related deaths over the last two decades (from 2000-2020), DBS for drug addictions is an area of great interest. Beyond opioid addiction, DBS has been applied to treat alcohol, nicotine, and cocaine addiction. Although studies showed promise, results are limited to case series or case reports that are not controlled. Stimulation is also often used during active drug use, so information on the effect of DBS during withdrawal in preventing relapse is limited. Interestingly, the use of DBS for the treatment of addiction happened by chance rather than design. In the mid-late 2000s, observations of patients with Parkinson's disease treated with subthalamic DBS suggested that stimulation could reduce symptoms of dopamine dysregulation syndrome (DDS). DDS refers to compulsive patterns of behavior such as pathological gambling, hypersexuality, and the overuse of dopamine-replacement therapy. It is a dysfunction of the reward system seen in individuals with prolonged use of dopaminergic medications.

## 10.7 The Future of DBS

As the population increases in age, we can expect the need for DBS to increase, especially to treat neurodegenerative disorders such as Parkinson's disease and Alzheimer's disease. Continued research on the safety and efficacy of current and novel indications will also increase demand for this therapy. In 2015, the global market value of DBS devices was estimated at USD 664.4 million and was projected to increase by 8.2% during the forecast period of 2016 to 2024.[17]

Use and satisfaction with DBS therapy can also be improved by further optimizing settings to increase therapeutic benefit, reduce stimulation-induced adverse effects, and prolong battery life. In its current form, conventional DBS settings employ constant stimulation independent of functional status and need. This constant stimulation can be detrimental and has been associated with speech impairments and an increased risk of falling in patients with Parkinson's disease treated with subthalamic DBS. Ideally, stimulation should only be delivered when needed. This concept forms the basis of next-generation closed-loop DBS systems. Also known as adaptive DBS, stimulation delivery is dosed based on the patient's clinical state at a certain point in time. It relies on biofeedback signals that are recorded in real-time. The focus of ongoing research in this field is finding a reliable signal that can be used to control stimulation. In the context of Parkinson's disease, examples of possible feedback variables include neurochemical signals such as dopamine fluctuations, external movement-related signals such as tremors (detected by wearable accelerometers), and neurosignals such as oscillatory beta activity (detected by implanted electrodes).

Adaptive DBS is highly applicable for conditions of an episodic nature in which symptoms occur as discrete episodes. In Parkinson's disease, this could manifest as the freezing of gait when starting to move, and in essential tremor, as an action tremor when reaching for a cup. In neuropsychiatric diseases, tics occur in Tourette syndrome, compulsions in obsessive-compulsive disorder, and flashbacks in post-traumatic stress disorder. Through the simultaneous recording of brain activity and stimulation delivery, adaptive DBS could provide improved symptom control. Epilepsy researchers have already tested closed-loop systems that detect and terminate focal epileptiform discharges before the onset of a global seizure.[18]

Adaptive DBS technology has the potential to improve clinical practice and therapeutic outcomes for patients. Importantly, it can be developed in parallel to other advancements in the field of DBS, such as the discovery of novel brain targets for new and existing indications, refining targeting and post-operative programming techniques, and developing a better understanding of the mechanisms of DBS.

# Endnotes

1. Lozano, Andres M., and Nir Lipsman. "Probing and regulating dysfunctional circuits using deep brain stimulation." Neuron 77, no. 3 (2013): 406-424.

2. Welter, Marie-Laure, Jean-Luc Houeto, Anne-Marie Bonnet, Paul-Boulos Bejjani, Valérie Mesnage, Didier Dormont, Soledad Navarro, Philippe Cornu, Yves Agid, and Bernard Pidoux. "Effects of high-frequency stimulation on subthalamic neuronal activity in parkinsonian patients." Archives of neurology 61, no. 1 (2004): 89-96.

3. De Hemptinne, Coralie, Nicole C. Swann, Jill L. Ostrem, Elena S. Ryapolova-Webb, Marta San Luciano, Nicholas B. Galifianakis, and Philip A. Starr. "Therapeutic deep brain stimulation reduces cortical phase-amplitude coupling in Parkinson's disease." Nature neuroscience 18, no. 5 (2015): 779-786.

4. Little, Simon, and Peter Brown. "The functional role of beta oscillations in Parkinson's disease." Parkinsonism & related disorders 20 (2014): S44-S48.

5. Koelewijn, Loes, Aline Bompas, Andrea Tales, Matthew J. Brookes, Suresh D. Muthukumaraswamy, Antony Bayer, and Krish D. Singh. "Alzheimer's disease disrupts alpha and beta-band resting-state oscillatory network connectivity." Clinical Neurophysiology 128, no. 11 (2017): 2347-2357.

6. Harmsen, Irene E., Nathan C. Rowland, Richard A. Wennberg, and Andres M. Lozano. "Characterizing the effects of deep brain stimulation with magnetoencephalography: a review." Brain stimulation 11, no. 3 (2018): 481-491.

7. Lozano, Andres M., and Nir Lipsman. "Probing and regulating dysfunctional circuits using deep brain stimulation." Neuron 77, no. 3 (2013): 406-424.

8. Holtzheimer, Paul E., and Helen S. Mayberg. "Deep brain stimulation for psychiatric disorders." Annual review of neuroscience 34 (2011): 289-307.

9. Rossi, Umberto. "The history of electrical stimulation of the nervous system for the control of pain." Pain research and clinical management 15 (2003): 5-16.

10. Harmsen, Irene E., Darrin J. Lee, Robert F. Dallapiazza, Philippe De Vloo, Robert Chen, Alfonso Fasano, Suneil K. Kalia, Mojgan Hodaie, and Andres M. Lozano. "Ultrahigh Frequency Deep Brain Stimulation at 10 000 Hz Improves Motor Function." Neurosurgery 66, no. Supplement_1 (2019): nyz310_367.

11. Horn, Martin A., Alessandro Gulberti, Eileen Gülke, Carsten Buhmann, Christian Gerloff, Christian KE Moll, Wolfgang Hamel, Jens Volkmann, and Monika Pötter-Nerger. "A New Stimulation Mode for Deep Brain Stimulation in Parkinson's Disease: Theta Burst Stimulation." Movement Disorders (2020).

12. Fenoy, Albert J., and Richard K. Simpson. "Risks of common complications in deep brain stimulation surgery: management and avoidance." Journal of neurosurgery 120, no. 1 (2014): 132-139.

13. Laxton, Adrian W., David F. Tang-Wai, Mary Pat McAndrews, Dominik Zumsteg, Richard Wennberg, Ron Keren, John Wherrett et al. "A phase I trial of deep brain stimulation of memory circuits in Alzheimer's disease." Annals of neurology 68, no. 4 (2010): 521-534.

14. Hamani, Clement, Mary Pat McAndrews, Melanie Cohn, Michael Oh, Dominik Zumsteg, Colin M. Shapiro, Richard A. Wennberg, and Andres M. Lozano. "Memory enhancement induced by hypothalamic/fornix deep brain stimulation." Annals of Neurology: Official Journal of the American Neurological Association and the Child Neurology Society 63, no. 1 (2008): 119-123.

15. Tsubokawa, Takashi, Takamitsu Yamamoto, Yoichi Katayama, Teruyasu Hirayama, Sadahio Maejima, and Takashi Moriya. "Deep-brain stimulation in a persistent vegetative state: follow-up results and criteria for selection of candidates." Brain Injury 4, no. 4 (1990): 315-327.

16. Corripio, Iluminada, Alexandra Roldán, Salvador Sarró, Peter J. McKenna, Anna Alonso-Solís, Mireia Rabella, Anna Díaz et al. "Deep brain stimulation in treatment resistant schizophrenia: A pilot randomized cross-over clinical trial." EBioMedicine 51 (2020): 102568.

17. Shah, S. "Global deep brain stimulation devices market, by application (Parkinson's disease, essential tremor, dystonia, others), and by geography-trends, outlook, and forecast from 2016-2024 2017: 1–69."

18. Ma, Brandy B., Madeline C. Fields, Robert C. Knowlton, Edward F. Chang, Jerzy P. Szaflarski, Lara V. Marcuse, and Vikram R. Rao. "Responsive neurostimulation for regional neocortical epilepsy." Epilepsia 61, no. 1 (2020): 9

# 11
# Focused Ultrasound

**Irene E. Harmsen**
*Irene Harmsen is an MD/PhD student at the University of Toronto. Her research is in neurosurgery and focuses on deep brain stimulation to treat patients with movement disorders. She aspires to become a neurosurgeon-scientist to advance therapies for patients with neurodegenerative disorders. Outside of her professional life, she enjoys travelling and staying active as a triathlete!*

## 11.1  Introduction/The Basics

Focused ultrasound (FUS) is a noninvasive, image-guided surgical technology that uses ultrasound energy to target specific areas of the brain. FUS is an emerging technology that has ablative and non-ablative applications for neurological and psychiatric diseases.[1] FUS is primarily used to create brain lesions to treat essential tremors and Parkinson's disease.[1,2] FUS is also used to open the blood-brain barrier to improve the delivery of chemotherapy to brain tumors and promote the clearance of beta-amyloid plaques in Alzheimer's disease.[3]

## 11.2  How it Works

FUS achieves lesioning via thermal ablation. An ultrasound transducer is used to convert electrical energy into mechanical (sound) energy and back again. The mechanical waves transmit energy through molecular movements. Focusing this energy on a single target can result in heating and subsequent lesioning of the brain tissue. Where the beams converge, the ultrasound produces a variety of therapeutic effects enabling treatment without incisions or radiation. The biological consequences of FUS are dependent on intensity, frequency, and duration of exposure. Low-intensity ultrasound can produce reversible transient clinical results that may last for a few minutes and are useful for target localization. Sub-threshold intensities are also used for the reversible opening of the blood-brain barrier with the use of microbubbles. Microbubbles are injected into the bloodstream, and when the brain is sonicated, these bubbles oscillate and temporarily disrupt the blood-brain barrier. At high intensity, sonication becomes therapeutic as the brain tissue reaches temperatures greater than 55°C, which denatures cellular protein and produces permanent lesions.

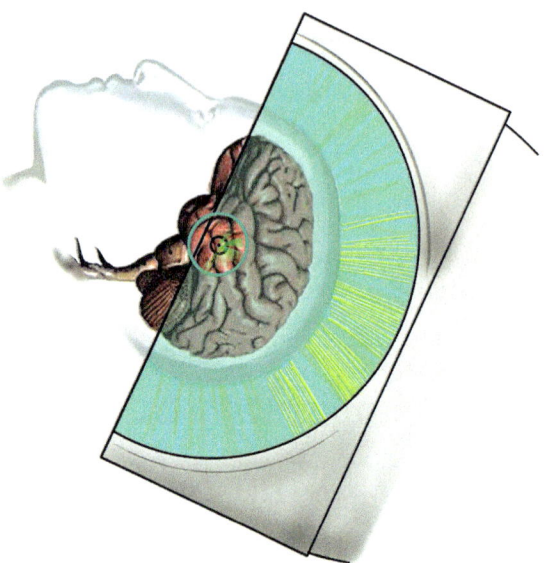

Figure 11.1 High-intensity ultrasound waves are targeted at a precise area of the brain under MRI guidance. More than 1,000 ultrasound beams converge to generate heat that destroys the unwanted tissue without an incision. Krishna V, Sammartino F, Rezai A. A Review of the Current Therapies, Challenges, and Future Directions of Transcranial Focused Ultrasound Technology: Advances in Diagnosis and Treatment. JAMA Neurol. 2018;75(2):246-54.

## 11.3 Typical Usage

High-intensity focused ultrasound is typically used to treat neurological disorders such as essential tremor, neuropathic pain, and Parkinsonian tremor.[1,2,4] It became an approved therapy for essential tremor in 2016 according to American FDA regulations. The safety and efficacy of FUS for other movement disorders and psychiatric conditions are being studied, and FUS is also an effective therapy in the field of oncology for tumor ablation. Since it does not involve ionizing radiation, FUS is considered low risk, and repeat treatments are possible. Furthermore, its noninvasiveness reduces toxicity compared to other ablation techniques, and surgical risks, including blood vessel damage, are mitigated.

In contrast, low-intensity FUS uses acoustic energy to oscillate gas-filled microbubbles that are administered simultaneously. This FUS-mediated technique temporarily disrupts the blood-brain barrier (BBB), allowing previously impenetrable agents to enter or exit the central nervous system (CNS). More commonly,

FUS is used in the delivery of drug or gene therapeutics across the BBB. These therapeutics are usually contained within encapsulated nanoparticles to enhance targeted cellular uptake and control rates of drug release, distribution, and removal. Surface modifications of nanoparticles are engineered to determine these pharmacokinetic properties.

## 11.4 History

### 11.4.1 Early Technologies - Paving the Way

Ablative brain surgery was first introduced in the early 1800s by a physiologist named Pierre Flourens. Through the surgical destruction of parts of animal brains, he observed that physical and behavioral effects implied the loss of function from the ablated brain tissue.[5] The lesioning of brain tissue to treat neurological disorders, such as Parkinson's disease, took place from 1939 to the late-1950s before the development of levodopa medications and again from the mid-1980s to the late-1990s before the advent of deep brain stimulation (DBS).[6] Ablative surgeries were performed to destroy the motor thalamus (thalamotomy) and globus pallidus (pallidotomy), both of which are structures forming the motor circuit and implicated in movement disorders.

The use of focused ultrasound as an ablative mechanism arose from observations during World War II when high-intensity ultrasound waves used to navigate submarines were found to kill marine life. Ever since the early 1940s, ultrasound waves have been focused on body tissues for ablative purposes.

### 11.4.2 First Release and Inventor(s)

The first historical application of FUS was in 1947 and attributed to brothers William and Francis Fry. Their extensive work throughout the 1950s and 1960s culminated in the clinical treatment of neurological disorders. In 1992, the use of magnetic resonance-guided FUS was first cited and patented. In 1998, this technology was transferred to INSIGHTEC (Haifa, Israel), which developed the first FUS system. FUS ablation was FDA-approved for essential tremor in 2016 and is currently being investigated for other indications, including Parkinson's disease, dystonia, neuropathic pain, obsessive-compulsive disorder, epilepsy, treatment-resistant depression, Alzheimer's disease, and brain tumors.

### 11.4.3 Improvements Since Release

As a relatively new technology, the field of FUS is rapidly undergoing new advancements to improve its efficacy and applicability to a multitude of conditions. Technical developments in high-intensity FUS for ablation therapy focus on equipment design to improve electronic control, ablation focusing, and target imaging. For example, researchers are developing a new method of guiding and controlling focused ultrasound exposure to increase the delivery speed of therapy. This method involves the replacement of mechanically steered FUS transducers with those that are electronically steered.[7] Various beam designs have also been explored to overcome limitations such as beam scattering and diffraction and the unwanted high-energy deposition to tissues in the ultrasound pathway, which causes burns. Ablative tissue performance has been enhanced with the use of piezo-active materials with specific acoustic properties and transducer arrays that favor many elements. FUS systems are also being designed to provide flexible and controllable multi-focus patterns, leading to improved targeting and helping users avoid obstacles or regions that should not be sonicated.[8]

Advancements in nanoparticle design have also greatly improved the use of FUS and nanoparticles for the optimal delivery of therapeutics to the brain. For example, the use of polymers (e.g., polyethylene glycol, PEG) in nanoparticles has increased its ability to escape detection by immune cells, increase its biocompatibility and half-life, and increase its distribution within the target tissue.[9] Lipid-based nanoparticles (e.g., nanoemulsions) have also been used for brain-targeted drug delivery using FUS. Nanoemulsions have the unique ability to change phases from a liquid to a gas upon exposure to the FUS pressure waves. This expansion causes the drug to be released at the focal site while producing on-demand microbubbles for improved spatial and temporal delivery of therapeutics.[10]

Ongoing animal research is also exploring the use of FUS and nanoparticles to administer gene therapy to treat neurological disorders such as Parkinson's disease. Nanoparticles are also being designed to carry genes, which requires striking a balance between decreasing cytotoxicity and increasing transfection rates.[11]

Beyond the therapeutic applications of FUS with nanoparticles, techniques using this pair are also being assessed for a possible role in disease screening and functional studies of the brain. For example, the detection and diagnosis of CNS disorders is limited and relies mainly on the onset of symptoms for diagnoses, indicative of disease processes that have already been long underway. Screening processes could include FUS using antibody-conjugated nanoparticles to detect or enhance imaging of disease markers.[12] In neurodegenerative disorders, this could consist of detecting protein aggregates such as alpha-synuclein in Parkinson's disease, tau protein and amyloid-beta plaques in Alzheimer's disease, and huntingtin protein in Huntington's disease.

## 11.5 Properties

### 11.5.1 Precision and Accuracy

Studies suggest that the accuracy of FUS is less than 2 mm.[2] FUS achieves precise lesioning with the use of advanced technologies and intraoperative imaging. The ultrasound transducers that are used circulate degassed water for coupling and tissue cooling. Algorithms also ensure an in-phase ultrasound convergence for precise lesioning. Furthermore, intraoperative MRI guidance is important for monitoring brain anatomy and real-time temperature. The transducer focal point is centered on the intended sonication target to maximize accuracy. If slight adjustments need to be made, electronic steering for up to 2 mm can be accurately performed. Other factors that affect the precision and accuracy of FUS include the transducer shape and number of elements. The heterogeneity and thickness of the patient's skull must also be taken into consideration; bone tends to absorb and reflect the ultrasound waves, which alters its velocity and phase.

### 11.5.2 Invasiveness

FUS enables the treatment of the brain without incisions or radiation. In both ablative and non-ablative applications, FUS is noninvasive, making it suitable for select patients who are not candidates for conventional surgical options. Ablative FUS and deep brain stimulation (DBS) share the same patient population. Despite its excellent efficacy, DBS has lower patient acceptability due to its invasive approach, the need for implanted hardware, and the required long-term programming and battery replacement. FUS ablation is a treatment option for patients who either have contraindications for DBS surgery or prefer not to have a DBS implant.

### 11.5.3 Setup Requirements

FUS is usually performed in academic teaching hospitals that include interdisciplinary teams of clinical and research experts in medical biophysics, biology, and the clinical sciences. The procedure is led by a functional neurosurgeon and conducted in an MRI-suite. MRI is used to guide ultrasound delivery using real-time imaging and is necessary to ensure the treatment's safety and efficiency. Sonography, or ultrasound imaging, can also be used for image guidance, but only for the pre-procedural positioning of the target tumor or brain region. Before the procedure, patients are screened and assessed for eligibility by a neurologist, neuropsychologist, neurosurgeon, and psychiatrist. Medical oncology teams are also involved in tumor ablation and the delivery of chemotherapeutics using low-intensity FUS and nanoparticles.

## 11.6 Logistics

### 11.6.1 Risks

Although FUS is noninvasive, the procedure does have associated risks. High sonication pressure delivered for long durations may result in cavitation (the rapid compression and expansion of entrapped gas in the tissue), which may lead to hemorrhage if it occurs near blood vessels. Since bone absorbs ultrasound energy, the skull is susceptible to heating. Patients have experienced transient headaches and scalp burns; additionally, asymptomatic necrosis of the skull may occur. Sonication can also induce dizziness and nausea. Neurological adverse effects associated with FUS ablation include gait disturbances (9%) and sensory deficits (14%) that can be permanent, unlike DBS.[4,13]

For non-ablative FUS in which nanoparticles are used to deliver chemotherapeutics to brain tumors, symptoms associated with chemotoxicity can still occur (although much less due to the targeted therapy). However, other treatments for brain tumors such as surgery, radiation therapy, and chemotherapy all have many more limitations and side effects than FUS. Surgery is associated with risk for infection, blood clots, and mechanical tissue damage; radiation therapy relies on ionizing radiation; and chemotherapy has systemic side effects including fatigue, nausea and vomiting, and hair loss, to name a few.

### 11.6.2 Costs

FUS procedures cost approximately $40,000. Since FUS was approved by the FDA for essential tremor in 2016, public and private health insurance plans now cover the procedure in the USA. Europe, Korea, Canada, Japan, Russia, Taiwan, and the Middle East have also approved FUS for essential tremor, and most procedures are covered. Patients that receive FUS for other disorders are usually enrolled in clinical trials through which research grants cover the procedure.

### 11.6.3 Limitations

Ablative FUS is an effective and permanent treatment option for patients with neurological and psychiatric disorders. While there is a benefit to having a permanent lesion and not having to deal with DBS-related hardware, the procedure cannot be undone, and any adverse effects will also be permanent. Other limitations of the technique include skull heterogeneity and thickness, whereby some patients may not be good candidates for FUS if they have a low skull density ratio.[14] Currently, FUS for essential tremor is only approved for patients with a skull density ratio of >0.4. The FUS system also has a limited treatment envelope, which refers to the location of the brain target that can be sonicated. Targets that are more than

3 cm from the mid-commissural point may not be treatable. Thus, the efficiency of sonication substantially decreases for brain regions close to the skull, such as cortical or surface targets. Fortunately, this limitation makes FUS ideal for lesioning deep thalamic and basal ganglia targets, areas of a common surgical focus for movement disorders, chronic pain, epilepsy, and psychiatric disorders.

## 11.6.4 Notable Use Cases

Since FUS is an emerging technology with the potential to treat many neurological and psychiatric disorders, pilot trials that demonstrate the feasibility and safety of FUS are important. An ablative FUS study conducted in 2014 on four patients with obsessive-compulsive disorder (OCD) reported improvements in symptoms and no adverse neurological events.[15] Similarly, 2015 saw the first patients treated with high-intensity FUS for treatment-resistant depression.[16] Both these procedures were bilateral thermal anterior capsulotomies where magnetic resonance (MR)-guided FUS was used to lesion the anterior limb of the internal capsule (thalamo-frontal white-matter tracts implicated in psychiatric disorders). In another phase 1 clinical trial, 12 patients with chronic neuropathic pain underwent central lateral thalamotomies (ablation of the thalamic nucleus). Patients benefitted from an average pain reduction of about 40%, sustained after one year of follow-up.[17] The next step will be for larger numbers of patients to receive FUS in randomized controlled trials to determine the long-term safety and efficacy of FUS for these new indications.

The application of high-intensity FUS is also being investigated for treating ischemic and hemorrhagic stroke. For ischemic (embolic) stroke, the goal is for ultrasound waves to dissolve blood clots that block arteries and reduce blood flow and oxygen delivery to brain tissues, leading to damage or the death of neurons. Research has been conducted in rabbit models of embolic stroke and shows promising results for causing effective thrombolysis (clot dissolution) without immediate damage to the targeted blood vessels.[18] For intracerebral hemorrhage, MR-guided FUS has been shown to liquify large-volume blood clots to improve blood drainage.[19] Interest also exists in the clearance of protein aggregations that are characteristic of many neurodegenerative disorders. In mouse models of Alzheimer's disease, FUS has been used to reduce amyloid-beta plaques via the delivery of endogenous antibodies and subsequent glia activation.[20] Research is ongoing to translate the positive findings from animal studies to humans.

## 11.7 Future of FUS

Ablative high-intensity FUS is expected to take off as a noninvasive therapy. Larger clinical trials will be needed to determine its safety and efficacy in various neurological and psychiatric disorders so that FUS can be approved and publicly funded. As for the use of FUS with nanoparticles to deliver therapeutics to the brain, beyond more effective drug delivery, there is interest in immunotherapy, gene therapy, and sono-optogenetics. Immunotherapy is a type of cancer treatment that helps the immune system fight cancer. It works to heighten the immune system's response and better recognize and target cancer cells. MR-guided FUS immunotherapy uses nanoparticles to deliver tumor-targeting antibodies directly to the tumor site. FUS can also be used to deliver DNA-loaded microbubbles or nanoparticles to a target site for gene therapy. The use of this technique has been proposed for Parkinson's disease to restore dopaminergic function. Finally, sono-optogenetics represents a new field that provides optogenetic neuromodulation in the brain. Optogenetics is the use of light to control the activity of individual neurons; however, the delivery of light sources within the brain is limited because photons do not travel well through tissue. The use of FUS and nanoparticles that deliver nanoscopic light sources to tissue could be used to overcome this challenge and allow for optogenetic neuromodulation.

## Endnotes

1. Elias, W. Jeffrey, Diane Huss, Tiffini Voss, Johanna Loomba, Mohamad Khaled, Eyal Zadicario, Robert C. Frysinger et al. "A pilot study of focused ultrasound thalamotomy for essential tremor." *New England Journal of Medicine* 369, no. 7 (2013): 640-648.

2. Magara, Anouk, Robert Bühler, David Moser, Milek Kowalski, Payam Pourtehrani, and Daniel Jeanmonod. "First experience with MR-guided focused ultrasound in the treatment of Parkinson's disease." *Journal of therapeutic ultrasound* 2, no. 1 (2014): 11.

3. Silva, Inaê Carolline Silveira da, Anna Beatriz Temoteo Delgado, Pedro Hugo Vieira da Silva, and Victor Ribeiro Xavier Costa. "Focused ultrasound and Alzheimer's disease A systematic review." *Dementia & neuropsychologia* 12, no. 4 (2018): 353-359.

4. Jeanmonod, Daniel, Beat Werner, Anne Morel, Lars Michels, Eyal Zadicario, Gilat Schiff, and Ernst Martin. "Transcranial magnetic resonance imaging–guided focused ultrasound: noninvasive central lateral thalamotomy for chronic neuropathic pain." *Neurosurgical focus* 32, no. 1 (2012): E1.

5. Carlson, Neil R., William Buskist, and G. Neil Martin. "Psychology: The science of behavior." (1997).

6. Cif, Laura, and Marwan Hariz. "Seventy years of pallidotomy for movement disorders." *Movement Disorders* 32, no. 7 (2017): 972-982.

7. Krishna V, Sammartino F, Rezai A. A Review of the Current Therapies, Challenges, and Future Directions of Transcranial Focused Ultrasound Technology: Advances in Diagnosis and Treatment. *JAMA Neurol.* 2018;75(2):246-54.

8. Lu, Mingzhu, Xiaodong Wang, Mingxi Wan, Yi Feng, Feng Xu, Hui Zhong, and Jinwen Tan. "Image-guided 256-element phased-array focused ultrasound surgery." *IEEE Engineering in Medicine and Biology Magazine* 27, no. 5 (2008): 84-90.

9. Aggarwal, Parag, Jennifer B. Hall, Christopher B. McLeland, Marina A. Dobrovolskaia, and Scott E. McNeil. "Nanoparticle interaction with plasma proteins as it relates to particle biodistribution, biocompatibility and therapeutic efficacy." *Advanced drug delivery reviews* 61, no. 6 (2009): 428-437.

10. Yildirim, Adem, Nicholas T. Blum, and Andrew P. Goodwin. "Colloids, nanoparticles, and materials for imaging, delivery, ablation, and theranostics by focused ultrasound (FUS)." *Theranostics* 9, no. 9 (2019): 2572.

11. Price, R. J., Fisher, D. G., Suk, J. S., Hanes, J., Ko, H. S., Kordower, J. H. (2019). Parkinson's disease gene therapy: will focused ultrasound and nanovectors be the next frontier? *Mov. Disord.* 34, 1279–1282. doi: 10.1002/mds.27675

12. Manoutcharian, Karen, Roxanna Perez-Garmendia, and Goar Gevorkian. "Recombinant antibody fragments for neurodegenerative diseases." *Current neuropharmacology* 15, no. 5 (2017): 779-788.

13. Elias, W. Jeffrey, Nir Lipsman, William G. Ondo, Pejman Ghanouni, Young G. Kim, Wonhee Lee, Michael Schwartz et al. "A randomized trial of focused ultrasound thalamotomy for essential tremor." *New England Journal of Medicine* 375, no. 8 (2016): 730-739.

14. Kyung Won Chang, Yong-Sook Park, Jin Woo Chang. Skull Factors Affecting Outcomes of Magnetic Resonance-Guided Focused Ultrasound for Patients with Essential Tremor. *Yonsei Med J.* 2019 Aug 1; 60(8): 768–773. doi: 10.3349/ymj.2019.60.8.768

15. Jung HH, Kim SJ, Roh D, et al. Bilateral thermal capsulotomy with MR-guided focused ultrasound for patients with treatment-refractory obsessive-compulsive disorder: a proof-of-concept study. *Mol Psychiatry.* 2015;20(10):1205-11.

16. Kim M, Kim CH, Jung HH, et al. Treatment of Major Depressive Disorder via Magnetic Resonance-Guided Focused Ultrasound Surgery. *Biol Psychiatry.* 2018;83(1):e17-e18.

17. Jeanmonod, Daniel, Beat Werner, Anne Morel, Lars Michels, Eyal Zadicario, Gilat Schiff, and Ernst Martin. "Transcranial magnetic resonance imaging–guided focused ultrasound: noninvasive central lateral thalamotomy for chronic neuropathic pain." *Neurosurgical focus* 32, no. 1 (2012): E1.

18. Burgess, Alison, Yuexi Huang, Adam C. Waspe, Milan Ganguly, David E. Goertz, and Kullervo Hynynen. "High-intensity focused ultrasound (HIFU) for dissolution of clots in a rabbit model of embolic stroke." *PloS one* 7, no. 8 (2012): e42311.

19. Monteith, Stephen J., Neal F. Kassell, Oded Goren, and Sagi Harnof. "Transcranial MR-guided focused ultrasound sonothrombolysis in the treatment of intracerebral hemorrhage." *Neurosurgical focus* 34, no. 5 (2013): E14.

20. Jordão, Jessica F., Emmanuel Thévenot, Kelly Markham-Coultes, Tiffany Scarcelli, Ying-Qi Weng, Kristiana Xhima, Meaghan O'Reilly et al. "Amyloid-β plaque reduction, endogenous antibody delivery and glial activation by brain-targeted, transcranial focused ultrasound." *Experimental neurology* 248 (2013): 16-29.

# 12 Hybrid Neurotechnology Systems

## Hubert Banville

Hubert Banville is a PhD student in Computer Science at Inria, Université Paris-Saclay, and a researcher at InteraXon Inc. With a background in Biomedical Engineering (Polytechnique Montréal), he previously conducted research on functional neuroimaging and hybrid brain-computer interfaces at the MuSAE Lab (INRS, Université du Québec). His current research focuses on learning representations from EEG and other biosignals using self-supervised learning, with a focus on consumer neurotechnology applications.

## Lucas Trambaiolli

Lucas Trambaiolli is a Research Fellow at McLean Hospital - Harvard Medical School, U.S.A. He received the B.Sc. degree in Biomedical Engineering in 2011 and the M.Sc. and Ph.D. degrees in Neuroscience and Cognition in 2014 and 2018, respectively, from the Federal University of ABC, Brazil. In 2017, he was a visiting researcher at the Institut National de la Recherche Scientifique (INRS) - University of Quebec, Canada. His research interests include brain connectivity analysis and machine learning to identify neuroimaging-based biomarkers and develop new brain-computer interfaces and neurofeedback protocols for clinical applications.

## Tiago H. Falk

Prof. Tiago H. Falk is an Associate Professor at the Institut national de la recherche scientifique (INRS-EMT), University of Quebec, in Montreal, Quebec, Canada. His research interests are on the use of signal processing to provide context-awareness to machine learning algorithms, with particular focus on real-world applications involving noisy data. He is a Senior Member of the IEEE, alumni of the Global Young Academy, member of the Sigma Xi Research Society, Academic Chair of the Canadian Medical and Biomedical Engineering Society, Co-Chair of the IEEE SMC Brain-Machine Interface TC, and a member of the IEEE SMC Society Board-of-Governors. He is (co-) editor of the book "Signal Processing and Machine Learning for Biomedical Big Data," published in 2018 by CRC Press. Together with his research team, he has published over 300 papers in top-tiered journals, conference proceedings and book chapters. He has 5 patents involving noisy sensor data analysis and enhancement.

## 12.1 Introduction

As described in the previous chapters of this book, two main groups of noninvasive brain imaging technologies are commonly used to compose a BCI system. The first and most popular is based on measurements of electrical or magnetic resultants from neural and synaptic activity, and includes methods such as electroencephalography (EEG) and magnetoencephalography (MEG). The high temporal resolution of these methods is fundamental to measure fast neural activities including event-related potentials (ERP), steady-state evoked potentials (SSEP), event-related desynchronization (ERD) or synchronization (ERS), as well as slow cortical potentials (SCP). For a complete overview related to these responses, please refer to chapter 2.

The second group includes functional magnetic resonance imaging (fMRI), functional near-infrared spectroscopy (fNIRS), and functional transcranial Doppler (fTCD). These methods measure relative changes in local blood oxygenation due to the metabolic activity of brain cells. This local blood oxygenation level-dependent (BOLD) change is commonly explored in experiments using fMRI, while fNIRS measures relative concentrations of oxyhemoglobin and deoxyhemoglobin (for a deeper discussion, please refer to chapters 4 and 5). Although hemodynamic-based methods usually present lower temporal resolution, they have higher spatial information that allows the selection of specific brain targets.

Hybrid BCI (hBCI) systems merge two or more monitoring methods (with at least one type of neural signal) to achieve an optimal BCI design.[1] More recently, hybrid systems have also included the combination of neuroimaging with neuromodulation, such as transcranial magnetic stimulation (TMS) and transcranial direct current stimulation (tDCS),[2] with emerging applications in sleep enhancement and brain-to-brain interfacing.[3,4]

In this chapter, we discuss the rationale for using hybrid neurotechnology systems, introduce basic hybridization concepts, and conclude with a brief overview of current hybrid BCI applications.

## 12.2 The Rationale for Hybrid Systems

As detailed by Nijholt et al. (2011), seven critical points should be addressed in future setups to achieve an optimal BCI system.[5] Hybrid BCIs are useful across all points, as detailed below:

- **Reliability:** It is known that BCI accuracy varies with factors such as mental and physical fatigue. In this context, an hBCI can be used to monitor the user's cognitive states and adjust internal parameters accordingly. For example, monitoring peripheral information in parallel to the main BCI system would provide instant information about stress and fatigue.

- **Proficiency:** There is no BCI system based on a single modality that works properly for all users. An hBCI can help with this limitation, and thus if one modality does not recognize the desired command, the second modality could allow the volitional control of the BCI setup. Moreover, with an hBCI, one modality could be used to remove artifacts from the other and improve accuracy.
- **Bandwidth:** Conventional BCIs present information transfer rates (ITR) around 100 bits per second. An hBCI can be used to accelerate the ITR by selecting the first occurrence of two redundant neural responses or by correcting unwanted selections and constantly measuring error potentials.
- **Utility:** Many single-modality BCI applications target only one task (for example, wheelchair control). Using a sequential hBCI, the user could select between different imaging modalities and increase the number of tasks, consequently improving the final accuracy and utility. As an example, wheelchairs could also include a robotic arm or communication device controlled by the hBCI.
- **Convenience:** Traditionally, BCI systems rely on lengthy preparation times and laboratory setups. Despite requiring multiple modalities, hBCIs can be more convenient. For example, given the complementarity of measures, a few pairs of electrodes from different modalities may provide the same information as multiple electrodes from a single method. In fact, recent technological advances have allowed for the development of miniaturized hybrid EEG-fNIRS sensors.
- **Support:** Real-world BCIs should require low to no configuration, preparation, or maintenance. With an hBCI approach, different portable and plug-and-play devices working in parallel can be used as a backup system to reduce the maintenance frequency.
- **Training:** Training conventional BCIs can be tedious, repetitive, and without progress during the training sessions. Recent advances in subject-independent protocols or artificially generated training sets have shown to be valuable options to reduce the training duration of hBCIs. Also, studies applying hybrid approaches showed reduced training time compared to a single modality BCI.

## 12.3 Concepts of hybrid BCIs

An hBCI setup is characterized by the combination of different imaging modalities of brain tasks, the type of synchronization between modalities or tasks, and the level of fusion between the modalities or tasks. Given this number of options, the multimodal system should be carefully designed,[6] or the hBCI may underperform when compared to a single modality setup.[1]

### 12.3.1 Hybridization approaches

The most intuitive hBCI setup is to combine two or more streams of data-carrying neural activity. This approach is termed pure hBCI (Figure 12.1). It can be achieved by integrating multiple neuroimaging modalities[7] or merging multiple cognitive tasks from the same imaging method, for example, two different patterns from EEG.

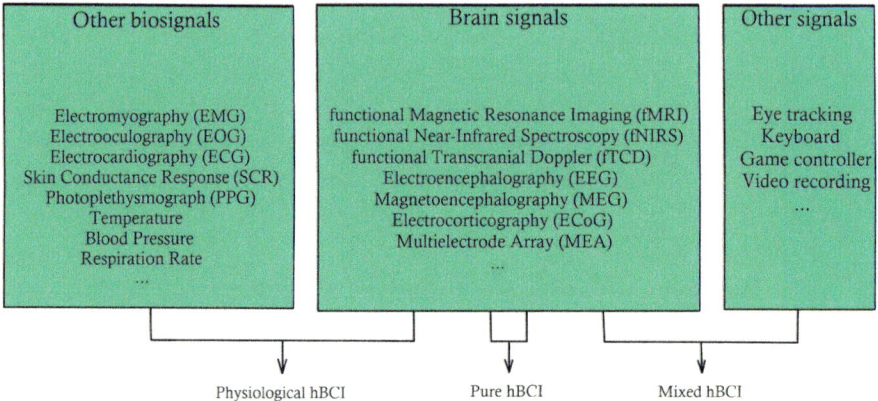

Figure 12.1 Different types of hybrid BCI, according to the combination of data modalities.

The use of other physiological signals in addition to neural data was proven a valuable addition to hBCI protocols.[8] Signals such as electromyography (EMG), electrooculography (EOG), electrocardiography (ECG), galvanic skin response (GSR), and blood pressure, among others, can provide valuable information about the participant's level of stress, attention, or affective responses.[9] The combination of neural data with other biosignals is termed physiological hBCI.[10] Lastly, non-physiological data can also be used to create an hBCI in a category named mixed hBCI.[20] This approach can include data from different equipment, such as a keyboard or an eye tracker to provide extra information to the hBCI setup.[11]

### 12.3.2 Synchronization

Given the possible combinations previously listed, an hBCI can also be categorized according to the synchronization between the chosen components. The first group includes approaches based on a sequential organization, in which two or more components work in series. As illustrated in figure 12.2, a possible implementation of this approach uses an initial element as a switch to activate or deactivate a second component.[12] Another implementation would use the first component as a selector to choose between two or more possible options, such as selecting different sets of movements in wheelchairs (e.g., moving straight or taking turns). The second group is composed of protocols in which its components work in parallel, adding complementary information about the desired effect. One example is the parallel combination of EEG and EMG techniques that can be alternated to reduce the influence of fatigue on control performance of either component.[13]

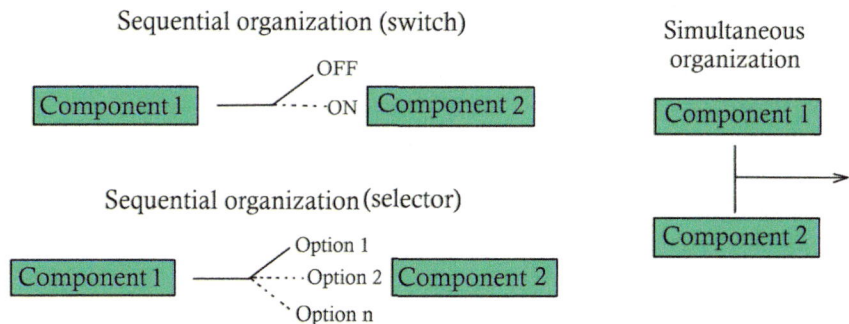

Figure 12.2 Examples of different synchronization between components.

## 12.3.3 Fusion levels

Every BCI system follows four main steps: data acquisition, preprocessing of the acquired information, decision making, and output presentation.[14] In an hBCI protocol, information fusion can occur at any one of these steps (Figure 12.3.), according to the components of the system.[15]

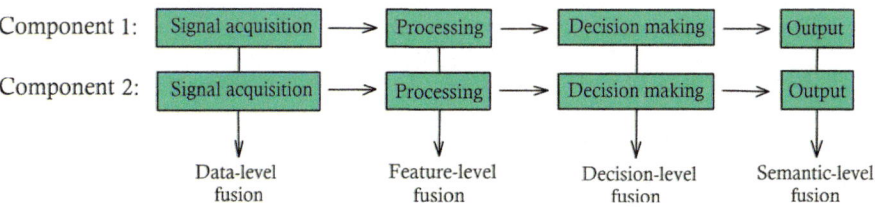

Figure 12.3 Example of fusion strategies in a sequential hBCI. Horizontal arrows represent the common BCI steps, while vertical arrows show the steps in which the different types of fusion occur.

Protocols merging unprocessed data are said to rely on data-level fusion. This approach is commonly employed by systems with components providing similar information or systems using one modality to improve the quality of a second one. For example, a common data fusion approach uses EMG or EOG signals to reduce noise in EEG data before feature extraction.[25]

Systems merging features from different components are said to perform feature-fusion level. This approach is popular for protocols combining data that requires separate processing pathways. One example is the extraction of features from EEG and fNIRS data separately, followed by combining these features as inputs for a classifier. Although higher robustness can be achieved, this fusion level usually presents higher dimensionality, which can harm performance when only a few data points are available.

Designs with decision-level fusion apply independent data processing methods and decision-making algorithms for each component before combining these labels. This structure is particularly useful for setups based on "voting algorithms," which combine the outputs from multiple classifiers as votes to reach a final decision. In a particular case of decision-level fusion, protocols combining modalities that control different outputs, but work together toward the same high-level task, are also said to use semantic-level fusion. This structure is typically used when combining neural data with non-physiological inputs.

## 12.4 Applications

This section briefly presents three promising application areas of hBCI systems: wheelchair control, speller and GUI control, and passive and affective BCIs. Additionally, we discuss the up-and-coming area of research on hybrid neurostimulation-neuroimaging systems.

### 12.4.1 Wheelchair control

A popular application of BCIs is the control of wheelchairs.[16] The first hBCI used for wheelchair control relied on detecting a P300 wave to select a destination in a predefined list and EEG-based changes in brain power for fast-stop movements.[17] Since EEGs can be portable and have high temporal resolution, they have been the most popular modality for wheelchair control,[18] with many applications relying on pure hBCI implementations, including the combination of visual P300 or motor imagery to control movement direction and steady-state-visually evoked potentials (SSVEPs) to control acceleration.[19,20,21]

Several studies have aimed at improving robustness by designing mixed hBCI systems based on the wheelchair's positioning and navigation sensors. The sensors' inputs can be used to correct the trajectory while the subject controls the chair (for example, using motor imagery to move left or right) or stop an ongoing movement if the subject fails to do so.[22,23,24,25,26,27] Physiological signals have also been used to improve wheelchair control with, for example, using EMG-measured teeth-gritting for forward or backward movement control[28] and eye blinks to stop the wheelchair.

## 12.4.2 Hybrid BCI Spellers and GUI control

BCI spellers allow spelling words and sentences based on brain activity and have the potential to give locked-in patients a way to communicate again. Studies focusing on spelling devices usually present a significant number of inputs (at least 36 commands, corresponding to different available characters). The high number of inputs thus requires modalities that can allow the precise selection of a target character out of many. One of the most common approaches to this challenge is the combination of SSVEP and P300 stimuli. Studies use this combination to split sets of stimuli (e.g., identifying on which part of the screen the user is focusing) or preselecting and expanding subgroups of characters, or even using both stimuli redundantly (waiting for both neural responses to identify a selection).[29,30,31,32] Other strategies include comparing the selected character with tracked eye movements;[33,34] or adapting the classifier decision based on the detection of an error-related potential (ErrP).[35,36]

More generally speaking, the problem of controlling a computer interface (e.g., cursor, buttons, lists, etc.) is also an active area of BCI research. For instance, hBCIs merging P300 and motor imagery tasks were applied to control a cursor,[37,38] a web browser,[39] and an email client system.[40] Other solutions use a larger number of modalities, with SSVEP and ERD/ERS neural responses combined with eye-tracking and environmental camera monitoring to control a graphical user interface (GUI).[41]

## 12.4.3 Hybrid passive and affective BCIs

As opposed to using neural signatures to control a device (known as active BCI), passive BCIs can be used to monitor implicit mental states of the user, such as their affective state, so that their environment can be adapted accordingly. Many affective states take their roots in deeper brain regions, making it challenging to measure neurophysiological correlates of emotions with techniques such as EEG and fNIRS.[42] Emotions, however, are known to modulate other physiological signals, such as heart rate or breathing patterns.[43] This realization has opened doors for new passive hBCI applications.

Seminal work showed the usefulness of combining peripheral physiological signals to classify emotions in a single user.[44] More recently, a series of work on multimodal affective monitoring was sparked by the release of open-source datasets such as the DEAP dataset.[45] For instance, in Clerico et al., (2018),[46] new EEG and GSR amplitude modulation features and phase-amplitude coupling features were introduced. In Gupta et al., (2016),[47] the authors fused several features extracted from EEG, fNIRS, physiological signals (themselves derived from fNIRS) to predict the reported quality of experience of 21 subjects listening to synthetic speech. Emotions are often confounded by other factors, such as fatigue or physical activity. Parent et al., (2019)[48] addressed this by combining EEG and physiological signals to monitor stress under physical activity.

## 12.4.4 Combining neuroimaging and neurostimulation

In a recording and stimulation hybrid system, also known as brain state-dependent brain stimulation (BSDBS),[49] various roles can be played by both halves of the system. The imaging part (e.g., EEG or fNIRS) helps reduce the inter- and intra-subject variability inherent to applying neurostimulation: finding the right location, timing, and stimulation parameters are simplified by monitoring brain states in real-time. In turn, neurostimulation (e.g., TMS, tDCS) can evoke, interfere with, or modulate neuronal activity, allowing manipulations to shed light on brain function.[50] In some applications, it can also be a way to transmit information directly to one's brain.

A recent application that combines brain stimulation and neuroimaging is called Brain-to-Brain Interfacing (BTBI) where direct communication from an individual to another is made possible; to do so, a recording modality needs to detect the brain activity of a "sender" (using a BCI), while a stimulation modality is necessary for delivering the information to the brain of a "receiver."

One of the first implementations of a BTBI was demonstrated in rats using intracortical microelectrode arrays.[51] A system was presented that linked two rats kept separate in two different locations — an "encoder" rat and a "decoder" rat — tasked with pressing a lever as indicated by an LED. Using the encoder rat's somatosensory activity, information was sent to the decoder rat via electrical brain stimulation to motivate it to press the lever at the same time as the encoder rat; only then would both get rewards.

The first published account of BTBI involving humans was of an interface between a human and a rat.[13] In Yoo et al., (2013), a human used an SSVEP BCI to control the tail of an anesthetized rat through transcranial focused ultrasound (FUS), a non-invasive stimulation technique that induces brain activation electro-mechanically (see di Biase et al., [2019][52] for an introduction).

Human-to-human BTBI was only reported in 2014 independently by two groups. In Grau et al., (2014),[54] a system combining a motor imagery BCI on a first individual and robotized TMS stimulation of the visual cortex of a second individual was presented. The "emitter" was then able to send bits (0 or 1) by performing motor imagery, which was relayed by email and used to control a TMS machine to induce phosphenes (a sensation of light in the visual field) in the "receiver." The BTBI was used to transmit the words "Hola" and "Ciao" from India-based emitters to France-based receivers.

In Rao et al., (2014),[53] motor imagery BCI and TMS stimulation were combined. This time, instead of using visual stimulation, the system directly induced a motor reaction in the receiver.[54] This communication channel was used in the context of a video game, where a first individual (the emitter) could see the current state of the game but not control it, whereas a second individual (the receiver) could not see the game but could actually control it.

More recently, Jiang et al., (2019) reported the use of both stimulation and recording modalities on a single individual in the context of a multi-person BTBI.[55] Their approach combined two senders with SSVEP BCIs and one receiver with TMS and an SSVEP BCI in a Tetris-like game scenario. The two senders, who could see the game state, had to pick a move through their SSVEP BCI. Their suggestions were then sent to the receiver through occipital TMS, who had to decide, without seeing the game screen, how to rotate a game piece (done with an SSVEP BCI) based on the sender's suggestions.

## 12.5 Final considerations

In this chapter, we introduced the concepts of BCI hybridization and the rationale for using hybrid systems. We then briefly reviewed multiple applications based on hybrid systems in various areas, such as mobility, communication, and imaging-stimulation integration. Although hybridization opens the door to improved performance and new applications, the novelty of this field implies that research is still needed before hybrid systems are fully translatable to real-world contexts.

## Endnotes

1. Allison, Brendan Z., Clemens Brunner, Vera Kaiser, Gernot R. Müller-Putz, Christa Neuper, and Gert Pfurtschler. "Toward a hybrid brain–computer interface based on imagined movement and visual attention." *Journal of neural engineering* 7, no. 2 (2010): 026007.

2. Siebner, Hartwig R., Til O. Bergmann, Sven Bestmann, Marcello Massimini, Heidi Johansen-Berg, Hitoshi Mochizuki, Daryl E. Bohning et al. "Consensus paper: combining transcranial stimulation with neuroimaging." *Brain stimulation* 2, no. 2 (2009): 58-80.

3. Marshall, Lisa, Halla Helgadóttir, Matthias Mölle, and Jan Born. "Boosting slow oscillations during sleep potentiates memory." *Nature* 444, no. 7119 (2006): 610-613.

4. Yoo, Seung-Schik, Hyungmin Kim, Emmanuel Filandrianos, Seyed Javid Taghados, and Shinsuk Park. "Non-invasive brain-to-brain interface (BBI): establishing functional links between two brains." *PloS one* 8, no. 4 (2013): e60410.

5. Nijholt, Anton, Brendan Z. Allison, and Rob JK Jacob. "Brain-computer interaction: can multimodality help?." In *Proceedings of the 13th international conference on multimodal interfaces*, pp. 35-40. 2011.

6. Lorenz, Romy, Javier Pascual, Benjamin Blankertz, and Carmen Vidaurre. "Towards a holistic assessment of the user experience with hybrid BCIs." *Journal of neural engineering* 11, no. 3 (2014): 035007.

7. Allison, Brendan Zachary, Robert Leeb, Clemens Brunner, G. R. Müller-Putz, Günther Bauernfeind, John W. Kelly, and Christa Neuper. "Toward smarter BCIs: extending BCIs through hybridization and intelligent control." *Journal of neural engineering* 9, no. 1 (2011): 013001.

8. Banville, H., and T. H. Falk. "Recent advances and open challenges in hybrid brain-computer interfacing: a technological review of non-invasive human research." *Brain-Computer Interfaces* 3, no. 1 (2016): 9-46.

9. Liberati, Giulia, Stefano Federici, and Emanuele Pasqualotto. "Extracting neurophysiological signals reflecting users' emotional and affective responses to BCI use: a systematic literature review." *NeuroRehabilitation* 37, no. 3 (2015): 341-358

10. Allison, Brendan Zachary, Robert Leeb, Clemens Brunner, G. R. Müller-Putz, Günther Bauernfeind, John W. Kelly, and Christa Neuper. "Toward smarter BCIs: extending BCIs through hybridization and intelligent control." *Journal of neural engineering* 9, no. 1 (2011): 013001.

11. Choi, Inchul, Ilsun Rhiu, Yushin Lee, Myung Hwan Yun, and Chang S. Nam. "A systematic review of hybrid brain-computer interfaces: Taxonomy and usability perspectives." *PloS one* 12, no. 4 (2017): e0176674.

12. Pfurtscheller, Gert, Teodoro Solis-Escalante, Rupert Ortner, Patricia Linortner, and Gernot R. Muller-Putz. "Self-paced operation of an SSVEP-Based orthosis with and without an imagery-based "brain switch:" a feasibility study towards a hybrid BCI." *IEEE transactions on neural systems and rehabilitation engineering* 18, no. 4 (2010): 409-414.

13. Leeb, Robert, Hesam Sagha, Ricardo Chavarriaga, and José del R Millán. "A hybrid brain–computer interface based on the fusion of electroencephalographic and electromyographic activities." *Journal of neural engineering* 8, no. 2 (2011): 025011.

14. Chaudhary, Ujwal, Niels Birbaumer, and Ander Ramos-Murguialday. "Erratum: Corrigendum: Brain–computer interfaces for communication and rehabilitation." *Nature Reviews Neurology* 13, no. 3 (2017): 191-191.

15. Gürkök, Hayrettin, and Anton Nijholt. "Brain–computer interfaces for multimodal interaction: A survey and principles." *International Journal of Human-Computer Interaction* 28, no. 5 (2012): 292-307.

16. Fernández-Rodríguez, Álvaro, Francisco Velasco-Álvarez, and Ricardo Ron-Angevin. "Review of real brain-controlled wheelchairs." *Journal of neural engineering* 13, no. 6 (2016): 061001.

17. Rebsamen, Brice, Etienne Burdet, Q. Zeng, Haihong Zhang, M. Ang, C. L. Teo, C. Guan, and C. Laugier. "Hybrid P300 and Mu-Beta brain computer interface to operatea brain controlled wheelchair." In *Proceedings of the 2nd International Convention on Rehabilitation Engineering & Assistive Technology*, pp. 51-55. 2008.

18. Min, Byoung-Kyong, Matthew J. Marzelli, and Seung-Schik Yoo. "Neuroimaging-based approaches in the brain–computer interface." *Trends in biotechnology* 28, no. 11 (2010): 552-560.

19. Li, Yuanqing, Jiahui Pan, Fei Wang, and Zhuliang Yu. "A hybrid BCI system combining P300 and SSVEP and its application to wheelchair control." *IEEE Transactions on Biomedical Engineering* 60, no. 11 (2013): 3156-3166.

20. Long, Jinyi, Yuanqing Li, Hongtao Wang, Tianyou Yu, and Jiahui Pan. "Control of a simulated wheelchair based on a hybrid brain computer interface." In *2012 Annual International Conference of the IEEE Engineering in Medicine and Biology Society*, pp. 6727-6730. IEEE, 2012.

21. Li, Jie, Hongfei Ji, Lei Cao, Di Zang, Rong Gu, Bin Xia, and Qiang Wu. "Evaluation and application of a hybrid brain computer interface for real wheelchair parallel control with multi-degree of freedom." *International journal of neural systems* 24, no. 04 (2014): 1450014.

22. Lin, C. T., Craig Euler, Po-Jen Wang, and Ara Mekhtarian. "Indoor and outdoor mobility for an intelligent autonomous wheelchair." In *International Conference on Computers for Handicapped Persons*, pp. 172-179. Springer, Berlin, Heidelberg, 2012.

23. Lopes, Ana, Joao Rodrigues, Jorge Perdigao, Gabriel Pires, and Urbano Nunes. "A new hybrid motion planner: Applied in a brain-actuated robotic wheelchair." *IEEE Robotics & Automation Magazine* 23, no. 4 (2016): 82-93.

24. Punsawad, Yunyong, and Yodchanan Wongsawat. "Hybrid SSVEP-motion visual stimulus based BCI system for intelligent wheelchair." In *2013 35th Annual International Conference of the IEEE Engineering in Medicine and Biology Society (EMBC)*, pp. 7416-7419. IEEE, 2013.

25. Iturrate, Iñaki, Javier M. Antelis, Andrea Kubler, and Javier Minguez. "A noninvasive brain-actuated wheelchair based on a P300 neurophysiological protocol and automated navigation." *IEEE transactions on robotics* 25, no. 3 (2009): 614-627.

26. Puanhvuan, Dilok, and Yodchanan Wongsawat. "Semi-automatic P300-based brain-controlled wheelchair." In *2012 ICME International Conference on Complex Medical Engineering (CME)*, pp. 455-460. IEEE, 2012.

27. Carlson, Tom, and Jose del R. Millan. "Brain-controlled wheelchairs: a robotic architecture." *IEEE Robotics & Automation Magazine* 20, no. 1 (2013): 65-73.

28. Li, Zhijun, Shuangshuang Lei, Chun-Yi Su, and Guanglin Li. "Hybrid brain/muscle-actuated control of an intelligent wheelchair." In *2013 IEEE International Conference on Robotics and Biomimetics (ROBIO)*, pp. 19-25. IEEE, 2013.

29. Chang, Min Hye, Jeong Su Lee, Jeong Heo, and Kwang Suk Park. "Eliciting dual-frequency SSVEP using a hybrid SSVEP-P300 BCI." *Journal of neuroscience methods* 258 (2016): 104-113.

30. Panicker, Rajesh C., Sadasivan Puthusserypady, and Ying Sun. "An asynchronous P300 BCI with SSVEP-based control state detection." *IEEE Transactions on Biomedical Engineering* 58, no. 6 (2011): 1781-1788.

31. Xu, Minpeng, Hongzhi Qi, Baikun Wan, Tao Yin, Zhipeng Liu, and Dong Ming. "A hybrid BCI speller paradigm combining P300 potential and the SSVEP blocking feature." *Journal of neural engineering* 10, no. 2 (2013): 026001.

32. Yin, Erwei, Zongtan Zhou, Jun Jiang, Fanglin Chen, Yadong Liu, and Dewen Hu. "A speedy hybrid BCI spelling approach combining P300 and SSVEP." *IEEE Transactions on Biomedical Engineering* 61, no. 2 (2013): 473-483.

33. Yong, Xinyi, Mehrdad Fatourechi, Rabab K. Ward, and Gary E. Birch. "The design of a point-and-click system by integrating a self-paced brain–computer interface with an Eye-tracker." *IEEE Journal on Emerging and Selected Topics in Circuits and Systems 1*, no. 4 (2011): 590-602.

34. Zander, Thorsten O., Matti Gaertner, Christian Kothe, and Roman Vilimek. "Combining eye gaze input with a brain–computer interface for touchless human–computer interaction." *Intl. Journal of Human–Computer Interaction* 27, no. 1 (2010): 38-51.

35. Combaz, Adrien, Nikolay Chumerin, Nikolay V. Manyakov, Arne Robben, Johan AK Suykens, and Marc M. Van Hulle. "Towards the detection of error-related potentials and its integration in the context of a P300 speller brain–computer interface." *Neurocomputing* 80 (2012): 73-82.

36. Zeyl, Timothy, Erwei Yin, Michelle Keightley, and Tom Chau. "Adding real-time Bayesian ranks to error-related potential scores improves error detection and auto-correction in a P300 speller." *IEEE transactions on neural systems and rehabilitation engineering* 24, no. 1 (2015): 46-56.

37. Yu, Tianyou, Yuanqing Li, Jinyi Long, and Zhenghui Gu. "Surfing the internet with a BCI mouse." *Journal of neural engineering* 9, no. 3 (2012): 036012.

38. Bai, Lijuan, Tianyou Yu, and Yuanqing Li. "A brain computer interface-based explorer." *Journal of neuroscience methods* 244 (2015): 2-7.

39. Long, Jinyi, Yuanqing Li, Tianyou Yu, and Zhenghui Gu. "Target selection with hybrid feature for BCI-based 2-D cursor control." *IEEE Transactions on biomedical engineering* 59, no. 1 (2011): 132-140.

40. Yu, Tianyou, Yuanqing Li, Jinyi Long, and Feng Li. "A hybrid brain-computer interface-based mail client." *Computational and mathematical methods in medicine* 2013 (2013).

41. Malechka, Tatsiana, Tobias Tetzel, Ulrich Krebs, Diana Feuser, and Axel Graeser. "Sbci-headset—Wearable and modular device for hybrid brain-computer interface." *Micromachines* 6, no. 3 (2015): 291-311.

42. Lindquist, Kristen A., Tor D. Wager, Hedy Kober, Eliza Bliss-Moreau, and Lisa Feldman Barrett. "The brain basis of emotion: a meta-analytic review." *The Behavioral and brain sciences* 35, no. 3 (2012): 121.

43. Shu, Lin, Jinyan Xie, Mingyue Yang, Ziyi Li, Zhenqi Li, Dan Liao, Xiangmin Xu, and Xinyi Yang. "A review of emotion recognition using physiological signals." *Sensors* 18, no. 7 (2018): 2074.

44. Picard, Rosalind W., Elias Vyzas, and Jennifer Healey. "Toward machine emotional intelligence: Analysis of affective physiological state." *IEEE transactions on pattern analysis and machine intelligence* 23, no. 10 (2001): 1175-1191.

45. Koelstra, Reinder Alexander Lambertus. "Affective and Implicit Tagging using Facial Expressions and Electroencephalography." PhD diss., Queen Mary University of London, 2012.

46. Clerico, Andrea, Abhishek Tiwari, Rishabh Gupta, Srinivasan Jayaraman, and Tiago H. Falk. "Electroencephalography amplitude modulation analysis for automated affective tagging of music video clips." *Frontiers in Computational Neuroscience* 11 (2018): 115.

47. Gupta, Rishabh, Hubert J. Banville, and Tiago H. Falk. "Multimodal physiological quality-of-experience assessment of text-to-speech systems." *IEEE Journal of Selected Topics in Signal Processing* 11, no. 1 (2016): 22-36.

48. Parent, Mark, Abhishek Tiwari, Isabela Albuquerque, Jean-François Gagnon, Daniel Lafond, Sébastien Tremblay, and Tiago H. Falk. "A Multimodal Approach to Improve the Robustness of Physiological Stress Prediction During Physical Activity." In *2019 IEEE International Conference on Systems, Man and Cybernetics (SMC)*, pp. 4131-4136. IEEE, 2019.

49. Bergmann, Til O. "Brain state-dependent brain stimulation." *Frontiers in psychology* 9 (2018): 2108.

50. Bergmann, Til Ole, Anke Karabanov, Gesa Hartwigsen, Axel Thielscher, and Hartwig Roman Siebner. "Combining non-invasive transcranial brain stimulation with neuroimaging and electrophysiology: current approaches and future perspectives." *Neuroimage* 140 (2016): 4-19.

51. Pais-Vieira, Miguel, Mikhail Lebedev, Carolina Kunicki, Jing Wang, and Miguel AL Nicolelis. "A brain-to-brain interface for real-time sharing of sensorimotor information." *Scientific reports* 3 (2013): 1319.

52. di Biase, Lazzaro, Emma Falato, and Vincenzo Di Lazzaro. "Transcranial focused ultrasound (tFUS) and transcranial unfocused ultrasound (tUS) neuromodulation: from theoretical principles to stimulation practices." *Frontiers in neurology* 10 (2019): 549.

53. Rao, Rajesh PN, Andrea Stocco, Matthew Bryan, Devapratim Sarma, Tiffany M. Youngquist, Joseph Wu, and Chantel S. Prat. "A direct brain-to-brain interface in humans." *PloS one* 9, no. 11 (2014): e111332.

54. Grau, Carles, Romuald Ginhoux, Alejandro Riera, Thanh Lam Nguyen, Hubert Chauvat, Michel Berg, Julià L. Amengual, Alvaro Pascual-Leone, and Giulio Ruffini. "Conscious brain-to-brain communication in humans using non-invasive technologies." *PloS one* 9, no. 8 (2014): e105225.

55. Jiang, Linxing, Andrea Stocco, Darby M. Losey, Justin A. Abernethy, Chantel S. Prat, and Rajesh PN Rao. "BrainNet: a multi-person brain-to-brain interface for direct collaboration between brains." *Scientific reports* 9, no. 1 (2019): 1-11.

# Brain Stimulation Methods Comparison Chart

| Stimulation Method | Transcranial Electrical Stimulation | Transcranial Magnetic Stimulation | Deep Brain Stimulation | Focused Ultrasound |
|---|---|---|---|---|
| Modality | Electric Current | Magnetic Fields | Electrical Impulses | Concentrated Sound Waves |
| Generally Treats... | Depression[1] | Mood Disorders[2] | Movement Disorders, Epilepsy[3] | Alzheimer's disease, Essential Tremors[4] |
| Primary Target Sites | Cerebral Cortex[5] | Pre-Frontal Cortex, Motor Cortex[6] | Thalamus, Subthalamic Nucleus, Globus Pallidus Interna[7] | Blood-Brain Barrier, Thalamus[4] |
| Treatment Duration | ~30 min[8] | ~40 minutes[9] | 3-6 hrs surgery, then indefinitely[10] | ~3 hrs.[11] |
| Average Total Cost in U.S.[1] | ~$12,000[12] | ~$15,000[13] | ~$40,000[3] | ~$40,000[14] |
| Invasiveness | Noninvasive | Noninvasive | Invasive | Noninvasive |
| Risks | Itching, tingling, headache, burning[15] | Scalp irritation, headaches[13] | May worsen cognitive symptoms[10] | Temporary nausea, headache, numbing[16] |

[1]Individual treatment costs greatly contrast across the U.S. and across the world.

## Endnotes

1. Pérez, Carolina, Jorge Leite, Sandra Carvalho, and Felipe Fregni. "Transcranial electrical stimulation (tES) for the treatment of neuropsychiatric disorders across lifespan." *European Psychologist* (2016): 21 (1): 78–95.

2. Kim, Yong-ku, and So-young Oh. "Transcranial Magnetic Stimulation: A Brief Conspectus and Area of Therapeutic Application." *TRANSCRANIAL MAGNETIC STIMULATION* (2013): 3.

3. Goodman, Brenda. "Deep Brain Stimulation May Offer Lasting Benefits for Parkinson's Disease." WebMD. August 8, 2011. https://www.webmd.com/parkinsons-disease/news/20110808/deep-brain-stimulation-may-offer-lasting-benefits-parkinsons-disease#1.

4. Sunnybrook Hospital. "What Is Focused Ultrasound?" Accessed July 4, 2019. https://sunnybrook.ca/content/?page=focused-ultrasound-treatment-research.

5. Reed, Thomas, and Roi Cohen Kadosh. "Transcranial electrical stimulation (tES) and its effects on cortical excitability and connectivity." *Journal of inherited metabolic disease* 41, no. 6 (2018): 1123-1130.

6. Chou, Ying-hui, Patrick T. Hickey, Mark Sundman, Allen W. Song, and Nan-kuei Chen. "Effects of repetitive transcranial magnetic stimulation on motor symptoms in Parkinson disease: a systematic review and meta-analysis." *JAMA neurology* 72, no. 4 (2015): 432-440.

7. National Institute of Neurological Disorders and Stroke. "Deep Brain Stimulation for Movement Disorders Fact Sheet." 2019. https://www.ninds.nih.gov/Disorders/PatientCaregiver-Education/Fact-Sheets/Deep-Brain-Stimulation-Movement-Disorders-Fact.

8. Pavlova, Elena L., Alexandra A. Menshikova, Roman V. Semenov, Ekaterina N. Bocharnikova, Galina N. Gotovtseva, Tatiana A. Druzhkova, Anna G. Gersamia, Anna A. Gudkova, and Alla B. Guekht. "Transcranial direct current stimulation of 20-and 30-minutes combined with sertraline for the treatment of depression." *Progress in Neuro-Psychopharmacology and Biological Psychiatry* 82 (2018): 31-38.

9. National Alliance on Mental Illness. "ECT, TMS, and Other Brain Stimulation Therapies." Accessed July 4, 2019. https://www.nami.org/Learn-More/Treatment/ECT,-TMS-and-Other-Brain-Stimulation-Therapies.

10. National Tremor Association. "Deep Brain Stimulation Frequently Asked Q & A's." Accessed July 4, 2019. https://tremor.org.uk/deep-brain-stimulation-faq.html.

11. Ghanouni, Pejman, Kim Butts Pauly, W. Jeff Elias, Jaimie Henderson, Jason Sheehan, Stephen Monteith, and Max Wintermark. "Transcranial MRI-guided focused ultrasound: a review of the technologic and neurologic applications." *American Journal of Roentgenology* 205, no. 1 (2015): 150-159.

12. Zaghi, Soroush, Nikolas Heine, and Felipe Fregni. "Brain stimulation for the treatment of pain: a review of costs, clinical effects, and mechanisms of treatment for three different central neuromodulatory approaches." *Journal of pain management* 2, no. 3 (2009):39.

13. Hersh, Julie K. "TMS or ECT? A Mental Health Consumer Weighs the Options." Psychology Today. 2013. https://www.psychologytoday.com/ca/blog/struck-living/201306/tms-or-ect-mental-health-consumer-weighs-the-options.

14. Focused Ultrasound Foundation. "Essential Tremor." Accessed July 4, 2019. https://www.fusfoundation.org/diseases-and-conditions/neurological/essential-tremor.

15. Thomas, Liji. "Transcranial Direct Current Stimulation Risks." News Medical. August 23, 2018. https://www.news-medical.net/health/Transcranial-Direct-Current-Stimulation-Risks.aspx.

16. Cleveland Clinic. "MR-Guided Focused Ultrasound for Treatment of Tremor Risks /Benefits." 2019. https://my.clevelandclinic.org/health/treatments/21087-mr-guided-focused-ultrasound-for-treatment-of-tremor/risks--benefits.

# 13 Market Drivers

## Alvaro Fernandez

*Alvaro Fernandez, named a Young Global Leader, runs SharpBrains, an independent market research firm tracking applied neuroscience. A recognized public speaker, he has been quoted by The New York Times, The Wall Street Journal, CNN, Reuters, and Associated Press, among others. Alvaro is the Editor-in-chief of seminal market reports on Pervasive Neurotechnology and Digital Brain Health, and co-author of the books The SharpBrains Guide to Brain Fitness and El Cerebro Que Cura. He enjoys serving in the World Economic Forum's Council on the Future of Neurotechnology, and in the Global Teacher Prize Academy run by the Varkey Foundation. Alvaro holds an MBA and MA in Education from Stanford University and a BA in Economics from Universidad de Deusto, in his native Spain.*

## 13.1 Neurotechnology is Going Noninvasive and Pervasive

Everyone has heard that Elon Musk has ambitious plans for a new brain-computer interface platform, which will require implanting a chip in one's brain.

What not everyone has heard is that most of the action these days is happening in noninvasive neurotechnologies.

For example, in May 2019, DARPA awarded significant funding to six research teams to support the Next-Generation Nonsurgical Neurotechnology (N3) program, first announced in March 2018.[1] The Battelle Memorial Institute, Carnegie Mellon University, Johns Hopkins University Applied Physics Laboratory, Palo Alto Research Center (PARC), Rice University, and Teledyne Scientific are all developing practical yet high-resolution brain-machine interfaces for use by the military using optics, acoustics, and electromagnetics to record neural activity and send signals back to the brain at high speed and at high-resolution.

All this with no surgery or implantable chips whatsoever.

In just a few years, soldiers, sailors, and airmen could command their respective vehicles and weapons without touching a button — intuitively via their thoughts and mental commands. They could even feel incoming threats and preempt them, via their thoughts, before occurring.

The good news is, the military is not the only group innovating at the frontier of neurotechnology and human performance.

Superathlete Tom Brady has revealed his "brain resiliency program" to increase his athletic edge,[2] as have multiple elite sports teams in the US and Europe. Hundreds of research labs and firms are working on ways to "harness neuroplasticity for good" via neurocognitive assessments and therapies (Akili, BrainHQ, CogniFit, Pear Therapeutics, MyndYou, Click Therapeutics, Cogniciti), mindfulness apps (Headspace, Calm, Claritas Mindsciences), EEG (Emotiv, InteraXon, NeuroSky) virtual reality (MindMaze), and more.

Assuming we harness the opportunity well, I believe the future of neurotechnology is noninvasive, pervasive, and deeply beneficial.

Everyone needs (and deserves) wise access to neurotechnology. Technology surrounds us. But it is "dumb" technology — even talking about "smartphones" is quite a stretch. What if, thanks to advances like the ones above, systems around us could read our thoughts and emotions; and respond to them in real-time? And what if, even better, they could help us enhance ourselves as human beings, harnessing the natural properties of the brain?

Globally, over 264 million people suffer from depression, as reported by the World Health Organization in 2020.[3] Add to that substance abuse and other mental health conditions, learning and cognitive disabilities, concussions, dementia...

Dr. Tom Insel, a well-known scientist, turned policy-maker, turned entrepreneur, often talks about how over $15 billion has been invested in health technology since 2012 and more in over a thousand new companies.[4] Yet, brain and mental healthcare has not truly improved, even though brain and mental disorders remain among the costliest conditions in the US, with an annual burden estimated at more than $200 billion.[5] The same is true regarding population aging and brain health: the need is very real and substantial, both in developed and emerging countries.

While we have historically failed to bend the curve in other areas of health — often because, as Peter Drucker stated, "you can't manage what you can't measure." Emerging digital and neurological monitoring technologies finally allow us to remedy that fundamental issue so that we can identify problems early and intervene early.

Lifelong neurogenesis and neuroplasticity offer much promise at the individual and population levels.

The potential to improve our brains and minds is enabled by recent findings around lifelong neurogenesis — the creation of new neurons — and neuroplasticity: the human brain continually changes itself through experience.[6]

Neuroplasticity, also known as brain plasticity, refers to the brain's ability to rewire itself based on experience by forming new and stronger connections between neurons, among other factors.[6] It was believed for a long time that, after a certain

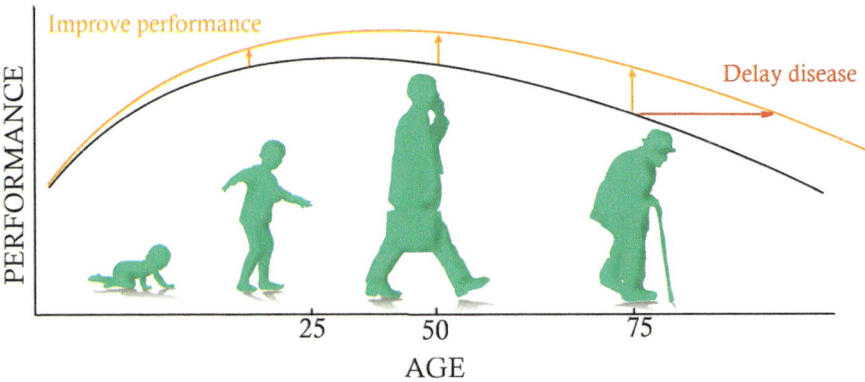

Figure 13.1 The opportunity to increase cognitive performance across the lifespan. Source: research analysis performed for The SharpBrains Guide to Brain Fitness, second edition (2013).

age, the brain became "fixed." However, now we know that the brain never stops changing and generating new neurons (albeit at a lower rate). As a result, there is now great interest and hope surrounding ways to harness neuroplasticity to better lives, improve brain performance throughout the lifespan, and delay disease and the decline of brain health.

We can strengthen specific circuits of the brain (through education, our jobs and lifestyles, and targeted interventions from meditation to noninvasive neurotechnologies) to learn faster, better, and become more resilient.[7]

However, there is a growing perceptive divide between those with access to the latest knowledge and tools and those without that same connection.

Proper access to neurotechnologies should not be a luxury for the few; it is a must for the many facing increasing demands on our brains and minds given longer and more complex lives.

## 13.2 Noninvasive neurotechnologies provide a new and scalable avenue to monitor and harness that promise.

While we are in the early days, we are already witnessing the coming of age of a very promising neurotech toolkit. NeuraMetrix, one of the winners of the 2017 Brainnovations Pitch Contest put together by SharpBrains, is developing an AI-based method of monitoring typing cadence to enable early detection of neurodegenerative diseases, from Alzheimer's Disease to Parkinson's.[8] The system can run silently (yes, permission and privacy will be critical issues to address) in the background of a personal computer or smartphone, integrating hundreds of variables in a persons' keyboard cadence and flagging unusual intraindividual patterns.

Digital Cognition Technologies has adapted a traditional neuropsychological test (the 'Clock Drawing Task') and combined it with machine learning to provide fast, affordable, and scalable detection of cognitive changes.

At the forefront of digital phenotyping, Mindstrong Health is finding ways to analyze 'digital exhaust' - data taken from smartphones - to provide objective, continuous, and proactive markers of mood, cognition, and behavior.[9] Variables extracted through machine learning can be as good at predicting cognitive function as the test-retest reliability of numerous cognitive tests, presenting an opportunity for scalable and noninvasive solutions to detect brain and mental health challenges early. Further, the information gained from these methods could be used by clinicians and patients to enable early intervention and monitor progress over time, something which is rarely done today.

On the intervention side, Akili Interactive Labs has completed impressive research supporting the use of "prescription" video games to target symptoms of attention deficit hyperactivity disorder (ADHD).[10] The FDA approved the prescription video game, EndeavorRX, created by Akili in 2020, the first of its kind. Akili CEO Eddie Martucci said in a statement. "We're using technology to help treat a condition in an entirely new way as we directly target neurological function through medicine that feels like entertainment."[10]

Other firms like Click Therapeutics, Sincrolab, and MyndYou are commercializing a new wave of personalized cognitive training therapy programs. And researchers at Neuroscape, AUGMENTx, and UCSF are working on virtual and augmented reality platforms for multimodal bio-sensing, adaptive evaluation, and brain-body training, which could help upgrade brain healthcare and cognitive rehab in the near term.

With private and public investments backing innovation in the space and an explosion in pervasive neurotechnology IP filings since 2010, it is not hard to see that this neurotech toolkit will grow broader and deeper.

M Ventures — an evergreen $300 million (Euro) digital health fund backed by Merck — has five investments in brain-related companies,[11] including a sizeable one in Akili Interactive Labs. Akili's vision is to have additional FDA-approved monitoring and treatment environments (in essence, "videogames") that certify the validity of efficacy against mental health issues such as autism spectrum disorders, sensory processing, depression, Alzheimer's, dementia, and Parkinson's disease.

Sana Health won the 2019 Brainnovations Pitch Contest by presenting a novel combination of audio-visual stimulation and neurofeedback training to alleviate chronic pain.[12]

Pear Therapeutics is on-track to commercialize FDA-cleared app-based monitoring and gamification to tackle challenges such as substance abuse disorder, PTSD, anxiety, insomnia, traumatic injury, and ADHD.[11]

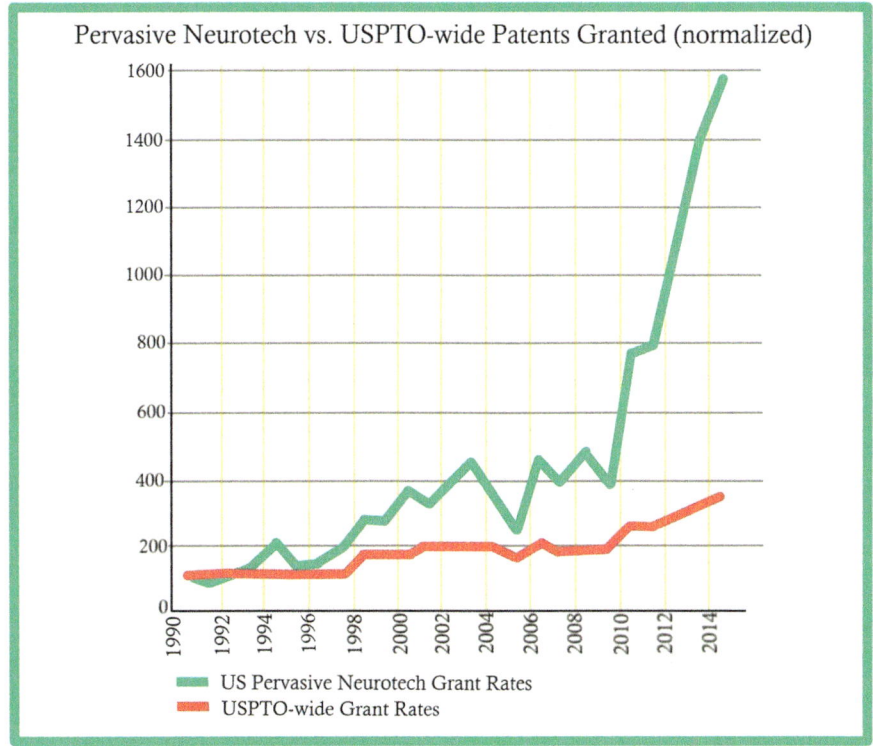

Figure 13.2 Pervasive Neurotech vs. USPTO-wide Patents Granted. Source: SharpBrains Analysis, USPTO Web Patent Databases, AcclaimIP Database Queries, and USPTO Patent Technology and Monitoring Team Reports (2015) (SharpBrains).

MindMaze has raised over $100 million to develop platforms based on virtual reality, augmented reality, computer graphics, brain imaging, and neuroscience.[11]

And investments are growing from public sources.

In the US, the National Institute of Mental Health runs the Small Business Innovation Research Program and the Small Business Technology Transfer Research Program, which help start-ups commercialize research. The majority of funding since 2005 has been aimed at supporting IT-based (as opposed to drug-based) initiatives.[13]

Up north, Baycrest recently secured over $120 million from the governments of Canada and Ontario, industry, and various donors to build the new Canadian Centre for Aging & Brain Health Innovation,[14] with a mission to accelerate, innovate, and drive adoption of validated brain health products.

## 13.3 Pay attention to these ten areas of expected rapid growth

How can we connect all these dots and predict, as much as humanly possible, which specific noninvasive neurotechnologies and applications are likely to grow faster in the short and medium-term?

To answer that question, we examined the global landscape of Pervasive Neurotechnology patents, given that investment in intellectual property is a crucial signal in the life-cycle of technology commercialization. We paid extra attention to neurotechnologies, which, being digital, scalable, relatively inexpensive, and noninvasive, pose few if any negative side effects — at least much lower than traditional pharmacological interventions. Within those four major neurotechnology classes, these are ten areas where we expect rapid growth (see Figure 13.3).

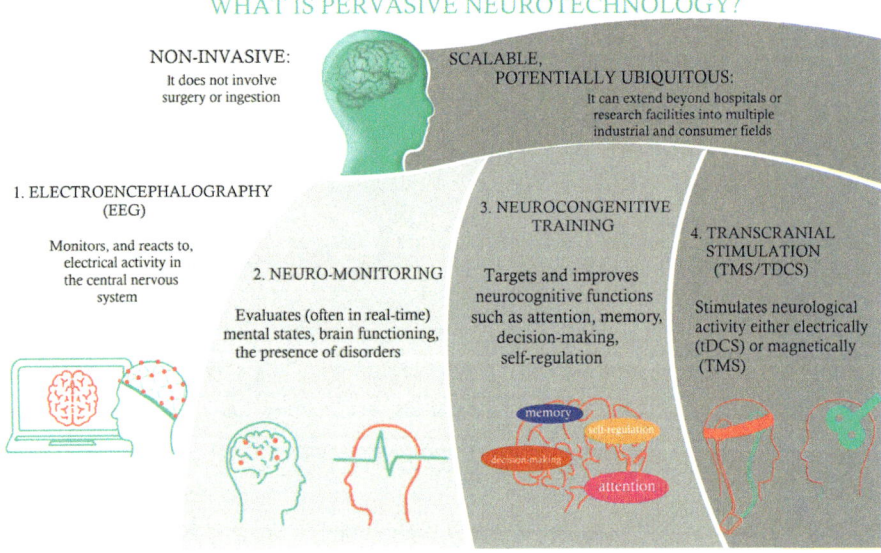

Figure 13.3 The four major neurotechnology classes (SharpBrains).

## 13.4 Big Data-enhanced diagnostics and treatments

As the costs of computing power, cloud accessibility, and hardware sensors dwindle, neurotech-based systems can leverage measurements taken from a far broader swath of the population than ever before possible. Which can help understand precisely where an individual's readings lie on the distribution curve of health to disease, understand with nuance how one's readings change over time, and better discern proper diagnoses and treatments based on the efficacy of treatments with others having similar brain signatures.

"Companies like CNS Response and Advanced Brain Monitoring are already deploying systems that harness the power of big data. (Fernandez, 2015)"[15]

### 13.4.1 Brain-Computer Interfaces for device control

As illustrated with the DARPA funding mentioned earlier, Brain-Computer Interfaces (BCIs) link the commands of our thoughts to the devices of the world. The global BCI market is expected to reach close to $1.5 billion by 2020 (of which 85% is estimated to be noninvasive) and may reach $3.85 Billion by 2027.[16]

"Companies like Emotiv and NeuroSky are advancing the state of BCI technology, while other organizations are developing the external systems and ecosystems to interact with BCIs."[15] "Phillips is developing home medical systems that remotely monitor health via EEG, helping patients suffering from ALS (commonly known as Lou Gehrig's disease), for example, to control home appliances via BCIs.[15]"

### 13.4.2 Real-time neuromonitoring (plus robotic aids)

"A good number of companies, including Medtronic, Neuropace, and St. Jude Medical, are developing systems to actively monitor brain activity and respond in real-time" with appropriate treatments.[15]

"These systems can discern symptoms leading up to an undesirable brain event (such as a seizure) and provide pre-emptive treatments to mitigate or altogether thwart epileptic activity. Some monitoring systems are coupled with other assistive devices, such as robotic aids to enable patients suffering from neurological disorders (such as ALS) to regain lost motor control.[15]"

### 13.4.3 Neurosensor-based vehicle operator systems

Multiple patients have described neurosensory-based vehicle operator systems that employ neural detection devices to monitor vehicle operator alertness (or a lack thereof) and take preventative measures with driver stimulation and vehicle autopilot/shutdown.

Whether due to inattentiveness (for example, texting while driving) or drowsiness, new vehicle-integrated systems can assess real-time operator fitness. The US Army, automotive companies like Toyota, start-ups like Freer Logic, medical device makers, and insurers are all patenting inventions addressing this concern.

### 13.4.4 Brain-responsive computing systems

As Microsoft CEO Sataya Nadella says:

"We are moving from a world where computing power was scarce to a place where it now is almost limitless and where the true scarce commodity is increasingly human attention."

A recent study by Microsoft finds that 68% of early tech adopters and 67% of heavy social media users must concentrate hard to stay focused on tasks.[15] So large tech companies are patenting systems to improve productivity and worker output, for example, by using EEG signals or eye-tracking to recognize the user's mental state and tailor the computing experience.

### 13.4.5 Virtual Reality treatments, especially in conjunction with EEG and tDCS

Whether for treating PTSD and phobias through exposure therapy or assisting surgeons in the operating room, virtual reality is quickly gaining momentum.

Medical tech companies, such as Medtronic and Brainlab, and consumer research firms such as Nielsen, are building significant IP portfolios within the industry. Evoke Neuroscience has several patents showing the interplay between virtual reality, EEG, and transcranial direct current stimulation (tDCS).[17]

### 13.4.6 "Mindful" wearables

Wearables are being designed to improve not just physical health but mental well-being as well. Meditation apps in tandem with consumer EEGs like InteraXon's Muse aim to help users build concentration and self-regulation skills.[18]

Even general-purpose fitness wearables are starting to include mental health and training applications. Multiple firms have secured patents that consider physiological and contextual factors.

### 13.4.7 Cognitive training videogames

Software applications accessible online and via mobile devices include gaming systems that target specific cognitive and emotional systems of the brain.

Companies like Akili, Posit Science, Lumos Labs, and Total Brain have secured patent protection (and significant market traction) on products in this area. A patent recently issued to Lumos Labs for enhancing fluid intelligence and working memory through mental manipulation of memorized objects is illustrative.19

### 13.4.8 Collaborative cognitive simulations

These systems focus on improving learning and skill acquisition across the extended workforce through online interactive platforms and cognitive simulation models. Human capital-intensive organizations such as AT&T and Accenture, and start-ups such as Applied Cognitive Engineering are developing multiple applications and securing relevant intellectual property rights.

### 13.4.9 Personalized brain stimulation

Technologies that influence brain activity via magnetic fields or electrical impulses, or even light, are becoming increasingly common, even with concerns about proper use and potential side-effects. Multiple hospitals and clinics already offer treatments based on brain stimulation. DARPA has awarded contracts to develop systems to augment memory with targeted electrical stimulation techniques.[20] Consumers can buy wearable devices such as Halo Neuroscience and Thync, which claim to induce an array of brain states that range from calming to energizing.

Firms like NeuroSigma, VieLight, and Neuroelectrics are developing adaptive and personalized neuromodulation methods that could mean noninvasive, non-pharmacologic treatments for a variety of conditions. The FDA recently cleared NeuroSigma's eTNS SystemTM (delivering Trigeminal Nerve Stimulation) as the first non-drug treatment for ADHD.[21]

Even professional groups are stepping up to spark much-needed innovation. The American Academy of Clinical Neuropsychology recently announced a new Disruptive Technology Initiative to "break down traditional silos in our education models, so the next generation of neuropsychologists embraces engineering, coding, and biotech."[22]

## 13.5 Help us promote responsible innovation and wise adoption

All this flurry of innovation has, inevitably, also led to much confusion and controversy.

Would you (or should you) consider implanting electrodes in your brain (as proposed by Elon Musk's new venture) when noninvasive methods could deliver many benefits with little to no risk? Even among the noninvasive methods, how will people know what to use and what not to use — and how and when? How can we educate all citizens to prioritize the multiple pieces in the brain health puzzle, using technology to augment (but not replace) our lifestyles?

New platforms and devices can produce great benefits but also have the capacity for misuse and harm.

Here is an example. As described above, the US Army, automotive companies, and medical and insurance companies are developing neurosensor-based systems to improve driving safety and employ car-based neural detection devices to monitor driver alertness and take preventative measures (e.g., with driver stimulation or vehicle autopilot/shutdown systems).

Sounds great, right?

But what if that data is shared with your insurance company? Or, with the police, in real-time? Doing so could certainly help reduce accidents due to sleepiness or drinking but could also create a Big Brother-type society in which most of us would not want to live.

Imagine that, despite all safety precautions, you end up having an accident; A horrible accident that leaves you so traumatized that you never want to drive again.

Would you want to erase that memory?

Maybe.

But first, consider potential side effects. Given how our brains work (cells that fire together, wire together), you might also weaken other associated memories. Perhaps you would forget much about the people you were driving with, even breaking the love you felt for your spouse, who too was in the car. And you would also be less likely to learn from that experience, as bad as it was, and less likely to drive more carefully next time.

Instead of erasing the memory, you might want to consider alternatives. What if going through a few weeks of virtual reality-assisted cognitive training and therapy helps you manage the anxiety and the trauma from the accident, and equips you to become a more alert and safer driver?

We live in exciting, transformational times, but we need to be proactive about anticipating and mitigating potential issues, aligning scientific innovation to the interests of people adopting emerging neurotechnologies. We need to step back for a minute and ask, how do we maximize the benefits and minimize the risks? What kind of ecologically valid research and customer protections, given the surge of 'do-it-yourself' home devices and loosely regulated products, do we need to be in place before mainstream adoption of so much neurotech innovation?

Now is the ideal moment for all stakeholders to engage with the noninvasive neurotech revolution in ways that can benefit all, anticipating and addressing major concerns regarding privacy and personal autonomy raised by big data platforms, and potentials way forward.

The task is not easy.

We need to bridge academia and industry. True, we lack clear standards and taxonomies for neurotechnology, but we need to be aspirational rather than "legalistic" — consider diverse perspectives, strive for the widest benefit with the minimum risks, and educate users, so we can enable beneficial innovation in ways that regulation alone, as important as it is, probably cannot.

## 13.6 Fortunately, multiple stakeholders are already working hard on this.

The Digital Medicine Society (DiMe) just announced an initiative, Ethical Considerations in Digital Medicine, aimed at "developing recommendations for the ethical use of mobile technology in research and clinical settings" and "rais[ing] awareness amongst investigators and regulators regarding potential ethical pitfalls in the field of digital medicine, alongside suggested strategies to address those pitfalls."[23]

The World Economic Forum has convened a Global Council on the Future of Neurotechnology, composed of 20+ research and industry leaders, including myself, with an objective to find ways to "improve the quality of life and function of individuals across the life course, and make communities more inclusive and cohesive through technological advances related to the Fourth Industrial Revolution."

And, of course, NeuroTechX is publishing this primer to inspire and educate both the current and the next generation of neurotech enthusiasts.

## 13.7 Conclusion

In conclusion, I would encourage readers to keep three themes in mind as they contemplate research or career moves in the years ahead:

1. The need being immense, this is no time for small thinking. Think big, think of ways to significantly help improve billions of lives
2. While the media may find invasive neurotechnologies like Elon Musk's more exciting to write about, the real action in the short- and medium-term will focus on noninvasive technologies, given they can help address much of the need with a more favorable benefit, safety, and cost profile.
3. Sustainable innovation will require much collaboration and many "joint ventures" between academia and industry. It is time to solve problems together, sometimes fail together, and always learn and grow together.

## Endnotes

1. Wolf, Erik J., Theresa H. Cruz, Alfred A. Emondi, Nicholas B. Langhals, Stephanie Naufel, Grace CY Peng, Brian W. Schulz, and Michael Wolfson. "Advanced technologies for intuitive control and sensation of prosthetics." *Biomedical engineering letters* 10, no. 1 (2020): 119-128.

2. Bishop, Greg. "Tom Brady wants to play 'forever.' With his new-age prep, he might get close." Sports Illustrated. December 15, 2014. https://www.si.com/nfl/2014/12/10/tom-brady-new-england-patriots-age-fitness.

3. Bhide, Amar, Srikant M. Datar, and Katherine Stebbins. "SSRIs and Non-SSRIs: Case Histories of Significant Medical Advances." (2020).

4. Dayak, Meena, and Young, Courtney. "Interview with Thomas Insel: The brain: the last frontier." National Council Magazine, Issue 1, 2012.

5. brain and mental disorders remain among the costliest conditions in the US, with an annual burden estimated at more than $200 billion.

6. Li, Ping, Jennifer Legault, and Kaitlyn A. Litcofsky. "Neuroplasticity as a function of second language learning: anatomical changes in the human brain." *Cortex* 58 (2014): 301-324.

7. Sahakian, Barbara J., Annette B. Bruhl, Jennifer Cook, Clare Killikelly, George Savulich, Thomas Piercy, Sepehr Hafizi et al. "The impact of neuroscience on society: cognitive enhancement in neuropsychiatric disorders and in healthy people." Philosophical Transactions of the Royal Society B: *Biological Sciences* 370, no. 1677 (2015): 20140214.

8. SharpBrains, "Why monitoring Typing Cadence may help detect early Parkinson's and Alzheimer's Disease." January 25, 2018. https://sharpbrains.com/blog/2018/01/25/update-why-monitoring-typing-cadence-may-help-detect-early-parkinsons-and-alzheimers-disease/

9. Martinez-Martin, Nicole, Thomas R. Insel, Paul Dagum, Henry T. Greely, and Mildred K. Cho. "Data mining for health: staking out the ethical territory of digital phenotyping." *NPJ digital medicine* 1, no. 1 (2018): 1-5.

10. Canady, Valerie A. "FDA approves first video game Rx treatment for children with ADHD." *Mental Health Weekly* 30, no. 26 (2020): 1-7.

11. Fernandez, Alvaro. "Four reasons the future of brain health is digital, pervasive and bright." SharpBrains. February 15, 2017. sharpbrains.com/blog/2017/02/15/four-reasons-the-future-of-brain-health-is-digital-pervasive-and-bright/

12. Fernandez, Alvaro. "To Be Involved in Neuroethics: A Must for Entrepreneurs and for Healthcare as a Whole." *AJOB neuroscience* 10, no. 4 (2019): 208-210.

13. In the US, the National Institute of Mental Health runs the Small Business Innovation Research Program and Small Business Technology Transfer Research Program, helps start-ups commercialize research — the majority of funding since 2005 has been aimed at supporting IT-based (as opposed to drug-based) initiatives.

14. Branch, SPB Strategic Policy. "Evaluation of the Contribution to Brain Canada Foundation's Canada Brain Research Fund 2011-12 to 2015-16." (2017).

15. Fernandez, Alvaro. "10 Non-invasive Neurotechnologies About to Transform Brain Enhancement and Brain Health." SharpBrains. November 10, 2015. https://sharpbrains.com/blog/2015/11/10/10-neurotechnologies-about-to-transform-brain-enhancement-and-brain-health/

16. Allied Market Research. "Brain Computer Interface Market Expected to Reach $3.85 Billion by 2027." ND. https://www.alliedmarketresearch.com/brain-computer-interfaces-market

17. Hagedorn, David W., and James WG Thompson. "Transcranial stimulation device and method based on electrophysiological testing." U.S. Patent 8,838,247, issued September 16, 2014.

18. Hoffmann, Alexandra. "The iterative development and evaluation of the gamified stress management app "Stress-Mentor"." (2020).

19. Hinman, Tyler, Benjamin Lee Ahroni, and Aaron Kaluszka. "Systems and methods for a self-directed working memory task for enhanced cognition." U.S. Patent Application 14/579,431, filed July 2, 2015.,

20. DARPA has awarded contracts to develop systems to augment memory with targeted electrical stimulation techniques.

21. US Food and Drug Administration. "FDA permits marketing of first medical device for treatment of ADHD." *FDA News Release. Silver Spring, MD: FDA* (2019).

22. Postal, Karen. "President's Annual State of the Academy Report." The Clinical Neuropsychologist. 2018. 32. 1-9. 10.1080/13854046.2017.1406993.

23. Wicklund, Eric. "New non-profit aims to develop digital medicine research standards." mHealth Intelligence, May 22, 2019. https://mhealthintelligence.com/news/new-non-profit-aims-to-develop-digital-medicine-research-standards.

# 14
# The Neurotech Ecosystem

**Jen Wang**
Jen Wang is a recent graduate from McGill University where she studied neuroscience and computer science. She has a passion for science communication and strongly believes in making scientific concepts accessible to everyone, whether that be through articles or educational infographics. Having joined the NeuroTechX community in 2018, her interests vary between AI, neurotech, and mental health.

As the field of neurotechnology continues to grow, enthusiasts and experts alike have created an ever-changing landscape of new innovations. From consumer devices and startups to academic labs and government initiatives, the neurotechnology ecosystem continues to thrive amongst a wide range of sectors.

The following collection of companies, individuals, and initiatives are far from exhaustive, but they represent a handful of exciting projects in the field today. A more exhaustive list can be found on the NeuroTechX website at https://neurotechx.com/neurotech-ecosystem.

## 14.1 10 Companies in the Spotlight

### 14.1.1 InteraXon/Muse

**Founder:** Ariel Garten, Chris Aimone, and Trevor Coleman

**Year Founded:** 2007. First Muse headband launched in 2014.

**Product:** EEG headbands

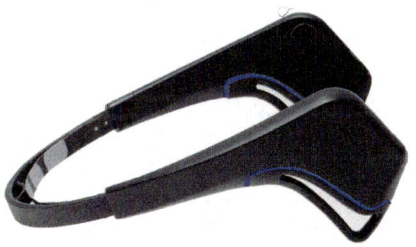

The Muse headband

The *Muse* company creates wearable EEG technology in the form of a headband used in guided meditation. Connecting via Bluetooth to a free phone app, Muse records your brain waves with 7 EEG sensors and uses auditory feedback during a meditation session. The app then allows you to evaluate your sessions with EEG graphs and track your progress over time. Because of its noninvasiveness and lightweight, Muse has also been used heavily in international neuroscience research. These projects include studying the waves of Buddhist monks as they meditate, identifying brain signals involved in pain, integrating the headband into the field of VR, and relating EEG signals to different events such as stress or different emotional states. The entire family of headbands includes variants created for different audiences, ranging from developers and researchers to everyday consumers.

Website: https://choosemuse.com/

## 14.1.2 OpenBCI

Founder: Conor Russomanno, Joel Murphy

Year Founded: 2014

Product: EEG and whole-body BCI hardware

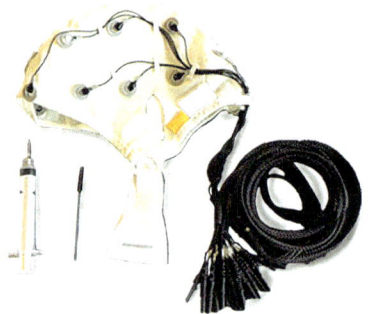

OpenBCI Electrode Cap Kit

*OpenBCI* operates under the belief that "science advancements will only — and should only — be made through an open forum of shared knowledge and concerted effort." Originally funded by a successful Kickstarter campaign, OpenBCI is a community of neurotechnology enthusiasts who participate in making brain-computer interfaces available and accessible to anyone interested. OpenBCI sells various neurotechnology products on its site, such as a variety of starter kits, headwear, accessories, and boards to work with EEG and MEG technologies affordably. They also have an entire educational domain, with tutorials, documentation, articles, code, and forums to get started with neurotechnology.

Website: https://openbci.com/

## 14.1.3 Emotiv

Founder: Tan Le and Dr. Geoff Mackellar

Year Founded: 2011

Location: San Francisco, U.S.A

Product: EEG-based BCI

EMOTIV EPOC X 14 Channel Mobile Brainwear®

Focusing on accessible EEG technologies, *Emotiv* is a company formed in San Francisco with the mission of "[empowering] individuals to understand their own brain and accelerate brain research globally." Through the use of Brain-Computer Interfaces (BCI) Emotiv leads the market in wearable EEG technology, with applications in accessibility design, learning, medicine, robotics, and more.

Website: https://www.emotiv.com/

### 14.1.4 MindMaze

Founder: Tej Tadi

Year Founded: 2012

Location: International, HQ in Switzerland

Product: Gamified rehabilitation system

MindMotion™ GO

*MindMaze* intersects neuroscience, mixed reality, and AI to create a brain-computer interface to accelerate at-home and hospital care. Referred to as a "gamified rehabilitation system," their FDA-approved MindMotion Pro and MindMotion Go tracks patients with motion sensors and provides a virtual environment for hospital or at-home use.

Website: https://www.mindmaze.com/

### 14.1.5 Neuropace

Founder: Frank Fischer

Year Founded: 1997

Location: Silicon Valley

Product: Pacemaker for the brain

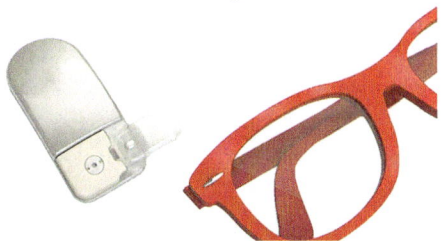

Small device, big innovation

NeuroPace RNS® System

Developers of the RNS® System, *Neuropace*, created a brain-responsive neurostimulation system. Like a "pacemaker for the brain," the RNS System responds to and reads a person's brain waves. As of now, it is mostly used by patients with drug-resistant focal epilepsy, by targeting — in a safe and noninvasive way — the area of the brain where the seizure starts. Neuropace designs, develops, and manufactures this product and hopes to expand to treat other neurological conditions.

Website: https://www.neuropace.com/

## 14.1.6 BrainGate

Year Founded: Clinical trials began in 2009.

Location: Several universities across the US

Products: Mobility aids

BrainGate's wirelessly powered and communicating, integrated neural recording microsystems

*BrainGate* is a research team focused on restoring independence and mobility in those who suffer from neurological diseases, injury, or limb loss using BCI. With a set of micro-electrodes planted in the brain, BrainGate tracks brain signals and runs them through a decoder. As of now, the system is considered "investigative" but has, for example, allowed a person to move a mouse cursor on the screen independently. The company hopes to expand usage to other applications such as prosthetic limbs, neurotherapeutics, and other communication devices.

Website: https://www.braingate.org/

## 14.1.7 eno

Founder: Jacob Flood

Year Founded: 2015

Location: Montreal and Toronto

Product: Headphones

Founded by a McGill alumni, *eno* (previously known as Mindset) makes over-ear headphones that use BCI technology to help you concentrate. By recording EEG signals and responding

enophones

dynamically, eno's current goal is to help users master their concentration by recognizing and tuning-out distractions. Going forward, they plan to augment their offerings to include online education, e-sports and gaming, AR/VR, and mental health instruments.

Website: https://enophone.com/

## 14.1.8 Dreem

Founder: Hugo Mercier and Quentin Soulet de Brugière

Year Founded: 2015

Location: Paris and San Francisco

Product: Sleep headband

The Dreem headband

*Dreem* is a headband that uses EEG to improve a user's sleep by recording brain activity, recognizing sleep patterns and stages, and providing neurofeedback as a relaxation technique. It has also been used extensively in clinical trials and research. In 2016, Dreem had already collected over 7,000 pre-orders of its beta version. After a successful industrialization stage, Dreem announced that it had raised an additional €30 million in 2018. In the future, they hope to improve the headband by making it more lightweight, personalized, and include more features.

Website: https://dreem.com/

## 14.1.9 Brainco

Founder: Bicheng Han

Location: Somerville, MA

Product: EEG headband for learning

BrainCo's neuro headband the FocusCalm

Supported by Harvard Innovation Labs, "*BrainCo* aims [to] [help] people . . . achieve a better life and . . . do better in academics through brain science." Their EEG headband FocusCalm uses BCI to improve concentration and learning skills and has already gone through several promising pilot studies in high schools in China.

Website: https://www.brainco.tech/

### 14.1.10 Neurable

Founder: Ramses Alcaide
Location: Boston, MA
Product: BCI for gaming and other apps

Neurable's DK1

Neurable's main goal is to use BCI to make things like virtual environments controllable by solely recording brain activity. With machine learning, the Neurable platform can process and classify EEG data in real-time. While their focus is currently on mixed-reality experiences, they hope to expand their application to gaming, entertainment, and health.

Website: http://neurable.com/about/science/neurable#

## 14.2 Academia

### 14.2.1 Neuroscape (Adam Gazzaley's Lab) — (University of California San Francisco)

Located at the University of California San Francisco, *Neuroscape* was formed by Adam Gazzaley by merging his three existing entities — *The Gazzaley Lab*, the *Neuroscience Imaging Center,* and the *Neuroscape Lab.* Made up of a core team, along with affiliates, collaborators, and interns, the lab's research and development revolves around using noninvasive neurotechnology, such as video games, virtual reality, and wearable devices, "to help both healthy and impaired populations."

Website: www.neuroscape.ucsf.edu

### 14.2.2 Synthetic Neurobiology Group: Ed Boyden's lab at MIT

Dr. Boyden's Lab at MIT studies and develops neurobiological tools to record the wiring and dynamics of the brain and how it functions when things go wrong. Some of their projects include mapping the molecules of the brain, controlling brain computing via optogenetics, and studying the repair and workings of dysfunctional brains.

Website: https://syntheticneurobiology.org

## 14.2.3 GTNeuro (Georgia Tech)

GTNeuro's lab at the Georgia Institute of technology operates under the belief that scientific research and technology are codependent and must be developed in unison. Focusing on the study and treatment of the nervous system, the GTNeuro community spans multiple schools of Georgia Tech and uses concepts from both the Neuroscience and Neuroengineering fields. They work to understand topics such as "multisensory integration and novel combination repair strategies, unraveling the complex algorithms of the brain from seemingly simple repetitive functions to storing memories, and probing the brain through functional imaging." Partners of the group include Georgia Tech's *Neural Engineering Centre*, the *Center for Advanced Brain Imaging*, and the *Emory Neuromodulation and Innovation Center (ENTICe)*.

Website: https://neuro.gatech.edu/

## 14.2.4 Swartz Center for Computational Neuroscience

According to their website, the goal of the Swartz Center for Computational Neuroscience is to "observe and model how functional activities in multiple brain areas interact dynamically to support human awareness, interaction, and creativity." The Center uses EEG, MEG, and other noninvasive brain imaging technologies to observe the brain — not as a collection of individual neurons but as a single unit that is functionally and dynamically connected. With the advancement of neuroimaging technologies such as fMRI, the Center develops mathematical models, novel signal-processing techniques, and new statistical methods to unravel the complex behaviors of high-level operations like human cognition and awareness.

Website: https://sccn.ucsd.edu/

## 14.2.5 PERFORM Center at Concordia University

PERFORM, which stands for Prevention, Evaluation, Rehabilitation, and Formation, is a community of students, researchers, and educators that have created a clinical research facility at Concordia University focused on promoting healthy living for those with injuries or chronic illnesses to improve quality of life. They look to "leverage the links between exercise, nutrition, physical activity, and lifestyle in an effort to improve health across the population." The Perform Center conducts research projects on a wide range of areas including, how the processes of the brain are impacted by behavior, sleep studies, memory research, energy metabolism of the brain during exercise, the Game Clinic for seniors, and a study on the "Simultaneous high-density EEG/fMRI acquisition during well-controlled tasks and resting states." These brain studies utilize MRI, PET, and EEG, among other neurotechnology means to research ways to improve quality of life.

Website: http://www.concordia.ca/research/perform.html

## 14.3 Notable Individuals

The field of neurotechnology is full of bright minds from several disciplines, both in academia and industry. Though it would be impossible to list them all, here are a handful of the innovators who have shaped the field.

### 14.3.1 Academics

#### 14.3.1.1 Jonathan Wolpaw

Considered the godfather of Brain-Computer Interfaces (BCI), Jonathan Wolpaw is the Director of the National Center for Adaptive Neurotechnologies in New York. His research includes the study of spinal cord learning and conditioning, as well as using BCI to rehabilitate and improve the lives of those with neuromuscular disorders such as Amyotrophic Lateral Sclerosis (ALS).

#### 14.3.1.2 Miguel Ângelo Laporta Nicolelis, M.D., Ph.D.

Miguel Nicolelis is a Brazilian scientist and the Principal Investigator of the Nicolelis Lab at the Duke University Medical Center, and the founder of Duke's Center for Neuroengineering. Dr. Nicolelis is known for his pioneering work in Brain-Machine Interfaces, neuroprosthetics, and measuring neuronal populations. In particular, he established a new multi-site, multi-electrode way to record brain activity in humans and primates. Often thought of as a paradigm in the field, Dr. Nicolelis continues today to use this technique in his research, with the potential to develop new therapies for diseases such as Parkinson's and epilepsy.

#### 14.3.1.3 John Donoghue, PhD

Dr. Donoghue founded the Brown Institute of Brain Sciences at Brown University and has been conducting research in BCI for over 20 years. Having advised for boards such as the National Institute of Health and NASA, and with over 80 published research papers in journals such as Nature and Science, Dr. Donoghue is considered a leader and a founding father of the field of BCI.

#### 14.3.1.4 György Buzsáki

Currently, a professor at the NYU Langone Medical Center, Dr. Buzsáki's main research topics are in "neural syntax" — how numerous brain rhythms and segments organize themselves to produce cognitive functions. He is a pioneer in sleep, memory, and brain oscillations. His recognition of the important brain oscillation frequencies, their hierarchy, and the way they interact with one another have created new implications in the study of brain diseases.

### 14.3.1.5 Alvaro Pascual-Leone, MD, PhD

Dr. Pascual-Leone is a Professor of Neurology and an Associate Dean for Clinical and Translational Research at Harvard Medical School. His research focuses on the mechanisms behind brain plasticity and noninvasive brain stimulation for a variety of applications, such as preventing cognitive decline, reducing dementia risk, and minimizing the impact of neurodevelopmental disorders. Having authored over 600 highly-cited publications, including books, Dr. Pascual-Leone is considered an international leader in his field.

### 14.3.1.6 Marom Bikson, PhD

Dr. Bikson is a research fellow Neurophysiology Unit, University of Birmingham Medical School. His research is based on how electricity affects the human body in pursuit of applying this knowledge to medical technologies and safety procedures. Some of these technologies include biosensors, drug delivery systems, treatments for neurological diseases, electrotherapy devices, and more. He is passionate about education and outreach to underrepresented groups and is a founding member of Neuromodec, which offers free and shared resources to develop an open-source approach to related research.

### 14.3.1.7 Theodore Berger, PhD

Dr. Berger is the David Packard Chair of Engineering & Professor of Biomedical Engineering. A prominent member of neural electronics, Dr. Berger uses theoretical and experimental approaches in his research in mammalian neural systems, especially in the hippocampus. In particular, he pioneered the concept of an electrode-based silicon chip implanted in rat and monkey brains that can process information like actual neurons.

## 14.3.2 Industry

### 14.3.2.1 Adam Gazzaley, MD, PhD

Adam Gazzaley is the Founder and Executive Director of Neuroscape and a Professor of Neurology, Physiology, and Psychiatry. Neuroscape is a "translational neuroscience center at UCSF engaged in both development and research to advance cutting-edge technologies as novel brain assessment and optimization tools." His interests in Neuroscape and his other companies Akili Interactive Labs and JAZZ Venture Partners revolve around BCI, optimization technology for learning and medicine, therapeutic video games, and hardware. He is also a co-author of the book "The Distracted Mind with Dr. Adam Gazzaley."

### 14.3.2.2 Tan Le & Olivier Oullier

Tan Le is the CEO, and Olivier Oullier the President, of the San-Francisco-based company Emotiv, developers of wearable EEG technologies and related software. Le is the recipient of several awards for her innovation, such as the 2018 Innovation Research Interchange (IRI) Achievement Award and being named among the Fast Company's Most Influential Women in Technology for 2010.

Olivier Oullier is a Professor of Behavioral and Brain Sciences at Aix-Marseille University and is a leader in personalized neuroinformatics. After co-authoring more than 200 publications and 20 years of experience in the field, he now leads AI research in cognition and emotion at Emotiv.

### 14.3.2.3 Connor Russomanno

As an original founder and current CEO of the OpenBCI platform, Connor Russomanno has continued to strive for cost-effective BCI technology. Russomanno has a background in engineering and design, studying at Columbia University and Parsons School of Design, respectively. A former student of Joel Murphy, the pair first launched a successful Kickstarter campaign in late 2013 to found OpenBCI, funding more than double their goal. Another equally successful campaign launched in 2015, totaling more than $370,000 across the two projects. Today Russomanno continues to explore his love of teaching through courses at Parsons and with OpenBCI.

### 14.3.2.4 Joel Murphy

Joel Murphy, a co-founder of OpenBCI and former teacher of Russomanno, is an "electro-mechanical designer and fabricator with 15 years of hands-on experience in the design of products and small scale production tooling." As a teacher at Parsons, Murphy has used his experiences with students as inspiration for several startups outside of OpenBCI. His students' interest in biosensing pushed him to create the Pulse Sensor via Kickstarter, a "plug-and-play heart-rate sensor for Arduino." Other startups include Tympan, an open-source hearing aid project, and OpenHak, an open-source fitness tracker.

## 14.4 Government Brain Initiatives

Over the past few decades, governing bodies have begun to recognize the economic and scientific value of neurotechnology. With this, countries have established several new and exciting initiatives that unite scientists, engineers, and communicators in the hope of furthering our understanding of the brain.

### 14.4.1 CONP

In partnership with the Brain Canada and Health Canada, The Canadian Open Neuroscience Platform (CONP) "aims to bring together many of the country's leading scientists in basic and clinical neuroscience to form an interactive network of collaborations in brain research, interdisciplinary student training, international partnerships, clinical translation and open publishing." The platform brings together more than 33 native and international universities, research labs, and corporations; and was first established with a $10M grant in 2018.

The group also offers awards such as the Research Scholar Program and the Student Scholar program with the goal of making neuroscience more open and accessible.

### 14.4.2 Human Brain Project

Started in 2013 and co-funded by the European Union, the Human Brain Project (HBP) gathers several research facilities across Europe in the quest for a greater understanding of the human brain. Their six research areas of focus include neuroinformatics, brain simulation, high-performance analytics & computing, medical informatics, neuromorphic computing (development of brain-inspired computing), and neurorobotics. The group also hosts both online and in-person educational resources through the HBP Education Programme.

### 14.4.3 The National Institutes of Health Blueprint for Neuroscience Research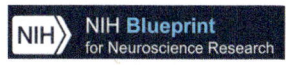

The NIH Blueprint for Neuroscience Research, created in 2004, is an aggregation of several NIH Institutes and Centers with the goal of "[accelerating] transformative discoveries in brain function in health, aging, and disease." The group focuses on three "Grand Challenges." The first Challenge, The Human Connectome Project (HCP), aims to map the entire "structural and functional neural connections of the brain in vivo within and across individuals" (aptly referred to as the connectome) and has led to the publication of over 100 papers. The Grand Challenge on Chronic Neuropathic Pain is a collaboration of several researchers who desire to "understand the changes in the nervous system that cause acute, temporary pain to become chronic."

### 14.4.4 BRAIN Initiative (The Brain Research through Advancing Innovative Neurotechnologies)

Supported by the National Institutes of Health (NIH), the BRAIN Initiative was created by President Barack Obama. According to their 2014 report, BRAIN 2025: A Scientific Vision, the goal of the project is "to map the circuits of the brain, measure the fluctuating patterns of electrical and chemical activity flowing within those circuits, and understand how their interplay creates our unique cognitive and behavioral capabilities."

Research focuses include molecular mappings of the brain, structural mapping, neural dynamics, and various new recording, imaging, and neuroinformatic techniques.

### 14.4.5 Brain Mapping by Innovative Neurotechnologies for Disease Studies Brain/MINDS (Japan)

A newer project started in Japan in 2014, the Brain/MINDS project, aims to "map the structure and function of neuronal circuits to ultimately understand the vast complexity of the human brain." Built largely around the RIKEN Center for Brain Science, the group describes three major research areas:

- The structure and functional mapping of a non-human primate brain.
- The development of innovative neurotechnologies for brain mapping.
- Human brain mapping and clinical research.

### 14.4.6 China Brain Project

The China Brain Project, a 15-year project started in 2016, aims to focus government resources on understanding the neural basis of human cognition to address immediate societal needs. The project aims to enhance and learn from the fields of brain diseases and artificial intelligence. Some of their research focuses include studying the causal mechanisms of the brain, early diagnoses and intervention of brain disorders, non-human primate research, and brain-inspired computing.

### 14.4.7 Israel Brain Technologies

The Israel Brain Technologies (IBT) aims "to position Israel as the global hub for groundbreaking brain research, technology, and significant investment in treating, managing, and curing brain disease." IBT fosters startups through the Brainnovations program. The IBT also works to facilitate collaborations between scientists, physicians, entrepreneurs, and investors for their IBTtech platform. Lastly, the IBT offers prizes to Israeli researchers and holds conferences.

## 14.4.8 Australian Brain Alliance

The Australian Brain Alliance aims to "establish an Australian Brain Initiative that will create advanced industries in neurotechnology, develop treatments for debilitating brain disorders, and produce high-impact transdisciplinary collaborations that will increase our understanding of the brain." With a focus on neurotechnologies, the initiative conducts research in neurostimulation and neuromodulation, neuromorphic (brain-like) computation, and brain-inspired machine learning algorithms. Their site includes a learning section with informational videos and fact sheets (https://www.brainalliance.org.au/).

## 14.4.9 Korean Brain Initiative

Started in 2016, the Korean Brain Initiative (KBI) focuses on the development of neurotechnology and reinforcement of the neuroscience ecosystem with a vision to advance brain science by enhancing the local, national, and global networks. The first half of the project focuses on R&D, with key topics including multi-scale brain mapping, artificial intelligence, personalized medicine for brain disorders, and many multidisciplinary projects. The second half fosters and supports the growth of the neuroscience ecosystem in Korea.

# 15
# Challenges in the Field

**Lohit Velagapudi**

*Lohit Velagapudi is an MD candidate at Sidney Kimmel Medical College at Thomas Jefferson University in Philadelphia. He currently conducts clinical research in machine learning applications to tumor, functional, spine, and vascular neurosurgery and is passionate about developing applicable clinical tools for surgical candidate selection, prognostication, and operative management. He has a degree in neuroscience from Pennsylvania State University and previously worked in computational biology and image analysis research at Cedars-Sinai Hospital and University of California Irvine. He has numerous peer reviewed publications within the fields of neurosurgery, neurology, and interventional neuroradiology and has presented his work at multiple national conferences. He is excited about applying advances in technology and computing to the operating room in order to improve healthcare outcomes.*

## 15.1 Overview

Unfortunately, developing and using neurotechnology is not an easy venture. While developments on the engineering and computational side of neurotech may occur quickly, translating such advances to clinical practice takes time due to the sedentary nature of healthcare advancements as a whole. Handling these challenges sets the pace for innovation in the field, and thus, advancements in ancillary areas that play a part in the development of neurotechnology are key. This section will review some key challenges that developers and healthcare innovators face when creating and working with neurotechnology. An overview of technology regulation and its impact is required to understand some of these challenges.

### 15.1.1 HIPAA

HIPAA (Health Insurance Portability and Accountability Act) is a legislative act that is one of the biggest considerations when creating and sharing data and technology in the healthcare field. HIPAA law covers patients' basic privacy rights and the dissemination of their personal health information (PHI). By regulating who can access and use a patient's data, HIPAA protects and ensures the privacy, confidentiality, motility, and the availability of health information to healthcare users, which is a massive concern considering the rising use of electronic health records (EHRs). In addition, HIPAA compliance must be guaranteed for any new clinical trials, technology, or data-sharing project, and strict measures must be taken if any patient data is used to create or test neurotechnology.

## 15.1.2 IRB

Hand in hand with HIPAA regulation is the concept of the IRB (Institutional Review Board). While more broadly applicable to clinical research, almost every project utilizing patient data from a healthcare center must be approved by an IRB. Created in response to abuses such as the Tuskegee Syphilis Study, IRBs serve as regulatory bodies that approve research and development protocols and conduct risk-benefit analyses when patients may be at risk. Often staffed by senior administrators and research professionals, IRBs protect the rights of patients by advocating for lowest-risk interventions and ensuring that any data that is used is properly stored and shared in accordance with HIPAA guidelines.

## 15.1.3 FDA

The Food and Drug Administration (FDA) also plays a major role in regulating healthcare devices and interventions. Medical devices undergo a stringent quality control evaluation by the FDA, which also mandates clinical trials of various phases to validate a device's efficacy and safety. Also regulated by the FDA, devices may be tested on animal models before being employed in human subjects. By ensuring that healthcare technology maintains high standards of non-malfeasance, the FDA also serves to protect consumers. FDA compliance is a major concern for any neurotechnology developer.

## 15.1.4 Resolution

Resolution refers to the concept that there is an inherent tradeoff between accuracy and precision when creating and testing neurotechnology. Let us consider the example of an EEG (electroencephalography). Accuracy refers to the level at which the EEG can capture the brain's electrical activity and how closely the EEG reading reflects the true pattern of activity. Precision, on the other hand, describes the inter-test reliability of such technology. If an EEG was performed on the same individual, with parameters such as activity and time of day, and controlled, to what degree would the readout be the same. The tradeoff between precision and accuracy is evident when this example is considered: an EEG readout that can track the smallest change in brain activity, demonstrating high accuracy, might vary wildly between measurements due to minute variations in random noise. Likewise, an EEG that can produce the same readout over and over might miss small details in activity necessary for a diagnosis. Toeing the line between a functional level of accuracy and precision is a challenge that many forms of neurotechnology must face.

## 15.1.5 Bias-Variance Tradeoff

The concept of the bias-variance tradeoff is an application of a general resolution problem in data analytics and machine learning. Similar to the problem of resolution, the bias-variance tradeoff describes the inherent difficulty with training machine learning models to an acceptable level of accuracy and precision. In this case, bias refers to the generalization of the model; a machine learning protocol with high bias is very general, with low specificity to the trained dataset. Low specificity has the advantage of being used with other datasets, but in turn, may not accurately predict an outcome and may miss certain features of the dataset. Variance describes the specificity of a model to the training set. A model with high variance can accurately predict an outcome from one dataset but may not be generalizable to other areas. When variance is increased at the expense of bias, a model is described as "overfitted" to a dataset and may yield unacceptable results when applied to new data. Likewise, a model with high bias at the expense of variance is "underfitted," and the model may not provide specific results and may miss crucial patterns.

The bias-variance problem applies to many machine learning protocols used in healthcare and neuroscience. Given the small, heterogeneous nature of the datasets used, overfitting is the most common problem encountered. Scientists and developers may seek the ideal of high AUC (area under the curve), a performance measure for the classification of tasks, at the expense of their models being highly tuned to specific patient demographics or the composition available. This greatly hinders generalizability and, thus, the marketability and clinical applicability of such tools. Care must be taken in developing protocols to avoid overfitting a model or use larger and more evenly distributed datasets.

## 15.1.6 Sensitivity and Specificity

Sensitivity and specificity are measures used to describe the accuracy of screenings, diagnostic tools, and other healthcare interventions. Sensitivity measures the number of true positives out of all patients with a particular condition or disease, and specificity describes the number of true negatives out of all patients who do not. Medical tests and technologies designed to catch diseases early are often geared toward being highly sensitive; the goal is to decrease the false-negative rate. However, high sensitivity often comes at the expense of being less specific. For example, technology and tests used to diagnose brain infections from cerebrospinal fluid are often highly sensitive given the drastic consequences of missing an infection; but may be non-specific in that a positive value can be due to many diseases, not just infection. While certain tests can achieve high levels of both sensitivity and specificity, it is more often the case that a tradeoff must be made during development toward one or the other.

## 15.1.7 Big Data and AI

The rise of "Big Data" in neuroscience, and the increasing use of AI and machine learning, come with several problems related to the underlying data and the end-use of such tools.

Big Data refers to the increasing use of sophisticated data analytics combined with huge healthcare databases in order to draw clinical conclusions and drive innovation. Increasingly, multicenter databases for certain diseases, such as the Central Brain Tumor Registry, serve as platforms on which clinical research is produced. More generalizable and "true" conclusions can be drawn by increasing sample size and diversity in such datasets.

Artificial intelligence comprises a broad spectrum of computer science technologies that employ learning techniques modeled on human learning patterns to analyze and model datasets. Artificial intelligence encompasses many technologies currently applicable in neuroscience, such as computer vision, natural language processing, and neural networks.

Several challenges impede the production of such technologies, mainly based on the conception and development process.

## 15.1.8 Dataset Quality

Whether looking at large datasets for standard statistical analysis, developing new technology based on disease epidemiological data, or training an artificial intelligence, the problem of dataset quality runs rampant. Clinical research produced at a single institution is based upon the patient data available at that institution, likely pulled from the EMR. As such, these datasets tend to be smaller and heterogeneous compared to the overall population and introduce biases into whatever analysis is performed on them. This disparity can be seen when comparing machine learning research produced in the healthcare field with machine learning research in the computer science field. The quality of machine learning tools and regressions produced from data analysis is dependent on the datasets used to produce them, so the first challenge to overcome is the lack of quality datasets for niche fields or applications. While larger national or multicenter databases for certain diseases and applications exist, they may be costly to access or not contain certain variables of interest. On the other hand, technology or protocols dealing with rarer diseases must produce new datasets, dealing with the problems detailed earlier.

### 15.1.9 Clinical Applicability

Given the wide array of technology developed and tested in neuroscience, the average developer or entrepreneur would be surprised observing a clinical neurologist or neurosurgeon. Often, the rate of introduction of such technologies into routine clinical practice is low due to a lack of clinical applicability. Healthcare professionals are extremely busy and somewhat resistant to change. New technologies must demonstrate significant benefits over current practice, be easy to use, and widely applicable to the patient population. Balancing these characteristics is vital to the development of new neurotechnology.

### 15.1.10 Collaboration

The development of new, clinically applicable technologies must be driven by collaboration between physician and engineer. It is difficult for engineers and entrepreneurs to understand the demands and intricacies of the healthcare field, and physicians may not be capable of complex technological development and marketing. Increased industry-physician collaboration is necessary to increase the availability of new technologies and target development toward salient medical issues.

### 15.1.11 Human Augmentation & Experimentation

Human augmentation and experimentation is one of the most futuristic aspects of neurotechnology. Human augmentation can range from prosthetic devices for the disabled to elective enhancements designed to increase performance. Drug research, such as nootropics, also falls under this category. While one of the most exciting fields in neurotechnology, this area also faces some of the steepest challenges in reaching mainstream acceptance and development.

### 15.1.12 Regulation

While technology can be incredibly impactful, it also involves some of the highest risks. Any sort of augmentation, prosthetic, or drug must be rigorously tested, validated, and is regulated by administrative bodies such as the FDA. In addition, human experimentation outside of regulated clinical trials is impossible, and any potential technology must have its risks analyzed against potential benefits. Neural augmentations, including ocular implants, brain-computer interfaces, and other new technologies, must be tested on animal models to monitor adverse side effects and efficacy. Only after safety and efficacy are demonstrated on an animal model can the clinical trials of newer technology take place. These regulatory investigations go through multiple phases, with each phase progressively enrolling more patients for longer periods of time, culminating in a device being approved for market use. Even after approval, long-term effects are closely monitored. The extensive regulation surrounding neurotechnology and medical devices serves to protect patients from faulty technology but also poses a challenge for developers who must expend enormous amounts of time and resources in order to demonstrate efficacy.

## 15.1.13 Cost

Cost is an issue on both the producer and the consumer side of neurotechnology. The development of new technologies can take many years, require expensive expertise, and incur prototyping and manufacturing costs. While the most common way for such production to be funded is through medical device companies, entrepreneurs in the field must work with angel investments and accelerators to push a product to market. The steep cost of research, production, and development is a large barrier to new companies seeking to break into the neurotechnology market. In addition, such products may not be eligible for national research funding, further exacerbating the problem.

Due to the high cost and the experimental nature of such technology, the price to the consumer is often exorbitant. Elective implantations and augmentations are not usually covered under insurance as prostheses might be, and the consumer market for such technologies is already niche without widespread sensational marketing. This is a problem that plagued the development of consumer Virtual Reality (VR) systems that only was solved due to further developments in making the technology smaller, cheaper, and more accessible. Likewise, neurotechnology will need to advance far past the feasibility stage before widespread consumer use can be achieved.

## 15.1.14 Computational Limitations

Neurotechnology deals with some of the most convoluted and taxing datasets in all of healthcare innovation. Computational limitations are a key challenge that developers seeking to model or store data must face. These limitations are intrinsically tied to data analysis and machine learning methods as developments often require the heaviest computational resources outside of complex neuronal modeling and simulation technology, which is not yet widely researched. While supercomputer time can be rented, and larger academic centers may have the computing resources to foster such innovation, the burden lies on the developer to raise funds and seek support from such institutions.

## 15.1.15 Neural Networks and Analytics

Artificial neural networks are a form of machine learning modeled after the way neural impulses are transmitted. Information is categorized into various nodes, or neurons, on multiple layers, and relationships are drawn between these nodes to classify objects, find patterns in data, and model complex systems. While promising in terms of applicability, neural networks require much more computational power than other, more deterministic, machine learning protocols. The choice must often be made between optimizing a model with more data and more layers or saving resources on computation costs.

In addition, big data analytics require vast amounts of computational power to condense and process the number of cases or discrete objects in a set. Relevant clinical tools can be the result of millions of data points, and the average person's computer simply cannot handle such calculations. Computational limitations again can hinder the development of applicable outcomes from novel data analytics and must be addressed to move the field forward.

### 15.1.16 Neuronal Simulations

One of the most exciting advances in neurotechnology is the ability to simulate complex neuronal patterns, including relationships and transmissions. These differ from neural networks in that such simulations are the end goal. Instead of using these networks for data analysis, scientists can use such models to understand more about how the human brain functions and model potential interventions for diseases like Alzheimer's and Parkinson's. These simulations require incredibly large amounts of computational power, often requiring supercomputer time to build and run such simulations. Given the infinite complexity of such models, even this is not enough. While computational power is increasing exponentially, the availability and cost of such power can be inhibitory to widespread progress.

### 15.1.17 Accessibility

Accessibility refers to the barriers of entry to the neurotechnology field for entrepreneurs and consumers alike. While clinical and basic science research is often perused and discussed among academic circles, the challenge lies in creating products and technologies applicable to the public at large.

### 15.1.18 Cost of Development

As mentioned before, the cost of neurotechnology development can be massive. Possible costs incurred include personnel, workspace, prototyping, materials, running clinical trials, and manufacturing. The cost of development of neurotechnology is a major barrier to entry, and needless to say, can deter many entrepreneurs with promising ideas. Also, given the lack of widespread knowledge about the field, investors are less likely to contribute to such ventures than more well-known biotechnology areas, again leading to a deficiency in funding. For-profit companies may not receive support through organizations such as the NIH, which offers grants for research. Addressing the cost of development is a key step in greatly accelerating the pace of neurotechnology development.

## 15.1.19 Information Prerequisites

Unlike other areas of innovation, neurotechnology requires not only an in-depth understanding of engineering but also knowledge of neurology and neuroscience. This barrier to entry is one of the highest, as basic neuroscience research can be esoteric and far removed from clinical applicability. The problem of such information prerequisites can be solved through strong collaboration between professionals in multiple fields. The success of companies in the medical device field, such as Medtronic, that utilize medical and scientific consultants as well as engineering staff demonstrates the need for this collaboration. In addition, entrepreneurs must educate themselves extensively on the state of the field and understand the basics of brain anatomy and physiology to synthesize new concepts and develop new technology.

# 16
# An Introduction to Neuroethics and the Neuroethical Considerations of Neurotechnology

## Sunidhi Ramesh

*Sunidhi Ramesh is an MD Candidate at Sidney Kimmel Medical College at Thomas Jefferson University. She is the Managing Editor of The Neuroethics Blog, an Editorial Intern for The American Journal of Bioethics Neuroscience, and a member of the Student-Postdoc Committee for The International Neuroethics Society. Sunidhi graduated Phi Beta Kappa from Emory University in 2018, with degrees in both sociology and neuroscience. Her writing has been featured in numerous peer-reviewed journals, and she authored "Growing Brains: Warnings from a Cell Line That Became Immortal," the winning essay in the 2019 International Neuroethics Society Essay Competition. Sunidhi works on research spanning neurology, neurosurgery, ophthalmology, and sociology, particularly focused on the intersections of science, disparity, social justice, and ethics. In her free time, she enjoys powerlifting, doodling Madhubani-inspired art, playing competitive bridge, and cooking international cuisine.*

## 16.1 Introduction

The International Neuroethics Society defines neuroethics as a "field that studies the implications of neuroscience for human self-understanding, ethics, and policy." Its place at the intersection of several rapidly advancing fields of science and inquiry puts neuroethics in a unique position to ask questions about the consequences of today's strides in neuroscience and what they may mean for the broader functioning of our world.

What is the underlying science involved, and how are we manipulating it? Does the technology have the ability to change "the self" (e.g., consciousness, identity, autonomy, and higher-order brain function)? How will we ensure the privacy of consumers? What global regulations should be put in place to guarantee the safety and security of these devices? How will these neuroscientifically-rooted technologies be marketed to the general population?

The ability of neurotechnology to formulate brain-machine hybrids makes it a major concern of neuroethics. While these technologies often hold practical and functional purposes, taking "pause" to be critical of what we do with them is an absolute imperative.

## 16.2 The "Self"consciousness, autonomy, and identity

consciousness: to be aware of one's own intellectual experience and the surrounding environment.

autonomy: to have the capacity and authority to make decisions about oneself.

identity: beliefs, ideals, qualities, and perceptions one holds about oneself and others.

Deep Brain Stimulation (DBS) is a well-known surgical treatment for medication-resistant movement disorders such as Parkinson's disease (PD). Functioning much like cardiac pacemakers and placed strategically within the basal ganglia-thalamocortical circuit (the "voluntary movements" center),[1] DBS electrodes use high-frequency electrical signals to modulate the nature of brain activity (see Chapter 10).[2] Unlike cardiac pacemakers, however, the electrical impulses generated by DBS have the potential to impact brain circuits other than those originally targeted for surgery — circuits that can alter an individual's identity altogether.[3]

The idea of identity permeates almost every form of the human experience. In the criminal justice system, we rely on the fact that each person holds only "one identity" and that one identity is responsible for its own actions. In the educational system, we invest in cultivating, developing, and praising that "one identity." In our social circles, we expect to interact with the single identities of the people we know and love. And, most importantly, our individual morals, thoughts, and behaviors revolve around our perceptions of whom we believe we are.

However, we also hold a double standard. We believe our identities are complex: "I'm a different person when I'm tired," or "That time I snapped at my brother? I was having a rough day. I just wasn't myself." We make excuses for our identity by breaking it into distinct pieces.

But, how does this play into the idea of a "true self"? Is it all these pieces averaged together into one? Is it one piece more than another?[4] With neurotechnology: do we want to engage in procedures or interventions that pose a threat to a patient's personal identity? Do these procedures involve the risk or side effect that a patient could wake up as "another person" or, effectively, a "healthy stranger"?[5]

DBS is a tricky example of this modulation of "the self" because it happens under the guise of medical intervention for a degenerative and debilitating disease. One could argue that the drastic improvements in PD tremors outweigh the potential minute changes in identity instigated by DBS.[7]

Comparatively, we must ask ourselves how this discussion changes with other neurotechnologies (especially those used solely for commercial or convenience purposes). Take transcranial direct-current stimulation (tDCS), a technique that uses non-invasive neuromodulation to deliver electric current to the scalp, for example.[6] The technology is so easy to reproduce that "Do-It-Yourself tDCS Device" videos (complete with kitchen sponges and alligator clips) are rampant on YouTube.

One could, in theory, go to a nearby convenience store tonight and make a tDCS device twenty minutes later that could strengthen or weaken synaptic transmission between neurons in the brain; one could do all this without being a neurologist or having any formal expertise on the brain. If the device was misplaced, could it interfere with brain signaling? Maybe. Could it inadvertently impact a person's identity or sense of self? Unlikely, but perhaps.

The point is this: the brain is complicated. It is so complicated that a century of dedicated research and study by millions of scientists and academics has been unsuccessful in completely and fully cracking the code of how it works. Interfering with the brain without this understanding is, at the least, risky when we are not entirely sure precisely what regions, circuits, or neurons of the brain we are manipulating (or whether we are even manipulating the brain at all). We may effectively be altering or changing properties of the brain that we cannot even begin to understand — properties that could pertain to the ambiguous "self."

## 16.3 Ownership and Consent

*Brain Imaging, Informed Consent, and Responsible Research*

consent: to permit or to explicitly agree

privacy: freedom from obtrusion

Functional scans[7] (including positron emission tomography (PET), single-photon emission computerized tomography (SPECT), and, most recently, functional magnetic resonance imaging (fMRI) are a collection of techniques beginning to infiltrate the field of forensics. These technologies assume that "disruptions in the function of discrete parts of the brain can lead to alterations in particular aspects of cognition and behavior."[8] For example, damage in the prefrontal cortex (a region in the brain critical for reasoning, planning, impulse control, and moral judgment) can imply marred decision-making abilities. Other areas such as the amygdala (involved with sudden emotions, including anger) and the anterior cingulate cortex (involved with empathy and compassion) can be studied and mapped as well.

These scanning techniques simply measure changes in blood flow and correlate changes with increased or decreased brain activity in specific areas.12 Recently, however, functional neuroimaging evidence has been used in criminal cases "in support of the insanity defense, claims of incompetence to stand trial, and pleas for mitigation in sentencing."[12]

In 2007, Peter Braunstein, dressed as a firefighter, set off a smoke bomb and knocked on a woman's apartment door. After knocking her out with chloroform, Braunstein "sexually assaulted her for the next 13 hours."[12] During his trial, his defense team used PET scans to argue that "Braunstein had decreased function in his frontal lobes," the part of the brain that controls "initiation and cessation of behavior, planning, and moral judgment." The defense contended that Braunstein was "completely unable to plan" and incapable of thinking ahead.[12] (The jury ultimately found him guilty on all charges).

The technology nestled within neuroimaging is not perfect. A simple PET or brain scan generates images that are open to interpretation and human subjectivity. Still, current research suggests that personality traits, mental illness, sexual preferences, and predisposition to drug addiction are all types of information that can be gathered from neuroimaging.[9] As this technology grows to incorporate Artificial Intelligence (AI) and other precision metrics, the amount of data that can be gleaned from these scans will only continue to increase.

So, what about tomorrow? What if brain scans disclose more than they currently do, with more accuracy and more certainty? How do we limit or control the information gleaned from brain scans, regardless of whether they are done for medical, commercial, or criminal purposes? Furthermore, how do we maintain boundaries on who has access to these technologies to limit the potential for misuse and abuse?

These questions highlight an overarching narrative of relevant concerns about ownership, consent, and autonomy. Neurotechnologies must be critically evaluated with respect to each of these privacy concerns before being made commercially available for use. This preparation must include the necessity for policies that take into account the strengths and weaknesses of the use of neurotechnology in law, most notably:

a. Understanding neuroimaging, its limitations, and its meaning: First and foremost, if this evidence is to be admissible, judges, juries, and attorneys need to be trained in the value, meaning, and limitations of these scans — that these scans yield pictures that are then interpreted. Personality traits, mental illness, sexual preferences, and predisposition to drug addiction are all types of information that can be inferred from neuroimaging. However, there are important limits to the types and accuracy of the information that can be obtained. These limits need to be openly shared and discussed before actual cases are reviewed.

b. Recognizing the slippery slope of inferring a state of mind: Although behavior can be explained by brain evidence, brain evidence cannot directly imply behavior. It is easy to find an anomaly in the brain and point to it as the source of a misdemeanor. However, we all have anomalies; they are the simple product of genetic variation. Where do we draw the line between person-to-person variation and a serious abnormality that caused a crime to be committed? Ethicists, neurologists, and legal scholars must determine where this line is drawn. What are the parameters of an "average brain?" How different is "abnormal?" Case studies should be referenced to understand how abnormalities in specific regions could impact behavior.

c. Protecting the privacy of the defendant: Only pertinent neuroimaging information should be disclosed, and only for a specific purpose. There is a wide range of personal information that can be deciphered from brain scans. Nevertheless, for example, whether or not a defendant is susceptible to drug abuse need not be included in a trial unless the information is relevant to the particular case at hand. In fact, any irrelevant information should not be disclosed lest it confers a bias for or against the defendant. Thus, this information should be concealed and protected. Also, it should only be presented to the judge, the jury, and the relevant criminal attorneys with security measures taken to prevent it from reaching the general public. Furthermore, the neurologist providing testimony should be unrelated to the case and selected by the court to prevent any bias concerning the plaintiff or the defendant.[10]

d. Identifying the reliability and accuracy of results: As the state of neurotechnology currently stands, one test and one expert cannot be enough to present this information reliably. At least two independent, separate tests must be conducted with more than one neurologist to corroborate the findings. If any inconsistencies are found, either between the two tests or between the neurologists' opinions, the information should be deemed inadmissible on the grounds of being unreliable.

e. Using lie detection vs. neuroimaging: Lie detection through the polygraph has been used since the early 1900s. Although the technique is far from perfect, many courts use it as supporting evidence. Lie detection poses many similar questions as neuroimaging. How accurate is it? Are there privacy concerns involved? When can we use it, and when can we not? To address these questions as they relate to neuroimaging, we must turn to lie detection policies and frame neuroimaging policies around them.[11]

f. Implementing neuroimaging only when necessary: A range of implications come with the consistent implementation of neuroimaging in court cases. Will criminals always rely on these technologies to bail them out? Will we get to a point where every criminal is effectively "made innocent" through neuroimaging? Perhaps. Clear guidelines as to when the use of neuroimaging is appropriate must be set. Examples could include cases where the intentionality of the defendant is uncertain or where no real evidence exists. Neuroimaging should not be open for use in every case, and protections around its use must be established.[12]

g. Avoiding neuroimaging as the "be-all and end-all": Similar to current expectations around lie detector results, neuroimaging information should be used as one piece of a larger body of evidence presented in a trial. It should not be the only evidence that decides the fate of a case. Once trained in understanding the science behind these techniques, the judge should decide on the relevancy and admissibility of neuroimaging results on a case-by-case basis. Until such a time where the technology is refined to perfection, neuroimaging should never be used as the sole evidence provided to demonstrate the mental capacity of an individual.

In addition to these policy considerations, more research and validation of neuroimaging techniques are necessary to ensure that this technology is indeed accurate and applicable to the field of law. Ideally, neuroimaging as a technology would need to be furthered to avoid misplaced conclusions or premature use in the courts.

Lastly, the ambiguity about neuroimaging in current laws and constitutional amendments requires addressing.[13] Consider the US fifth amendment and the right against self-incrimination: could neuroimaging evidence acquired from a brain scan be used against the individual?

## 16.4 Neurohype, Neuroseduction, Overtrust, and Dishonest Marketing

trust: a steady belief in the dependability of someone or something

The global availability of the internet has fundamentally changed the nature of information dissemination. A single stated thought can become pervasive in society through a simple Facebook post or uncensored Tweet. While this has made room for social belonging and collective effervescence, it has also created a niche for other schools of thought; the most notable of these is pseudoscience, defined by Merriam Webster as "a system of theories, assumptions, and methods erroneously regarded as scientific."

Pseudoscience's brainy twin is neurohype, "a broad class of neuroscientific claims . . . in the absence of convincing data,"[14] or the presumption that science rooted in the brain is, for some reason, more valid than other sciences. While the two can in themselves be innocuous, pseudoscience and neurohype have the potential to convolute information — particularly in this fragile age of "fake news."

Neurohype is incredibly prominent in popular culture. Media outlets frequently water down brain science, and click-bait inspired by ambiguous "studies" often misrepresents findings that may or may not be statistically relevant. With this, the science becomes oversimplified and the findings over-sensationalized. It is a vicious and unregulated cycle.[15]

It is also this phenomenon that renders populations vulnerable to "brain scams" (the tendency to over-value brain technology) and "neuroseduction" (the tendency to believe information more readily if "neural images, neural explanations, or both" are used as supplementing evidence). Studies have demonstrated that "irrelevant neuroscience information in an explanation of a . . . [topic can] interfere with people's abilities to critically consider the underlying logic of [that topic]." The addition of phrases such as "brain scans indicate that . . ." and "the frontal lobe brain circuitry is known to be involved in . . ." were sufficient to elicit this effect.

These issues are inherent to neuroscience, but they must be combated by scientists in general. How do we ensure that the science produced in research labs and classrooms is the same science being marketed to the general public? It is this same question that must be considered with neurotechnology.

An eerie tale of human-technology interactions (and how they may be manipulated in the near future) is nestled in a 2016 paper titled Overtrust of Robots in Emergency Evacuation Scenarios.[16] The researchers in this study conducted an experiment where "a participant interacts with a robot in a non-emergency task to experience its behavior and then chooses whether to follow the robot's instructions in an emergency."

The conclusion? They do. Overwhelmingly so. All 26 participants chose to follow the robot's instructions in an emergency, even when it "pointed to a dark room with no discernible exit." The investigators labeled this as a disturbing display of overtrust of robots — overtrust that even applied to robots that showed indications of not being trustworthy.[17]

This premise is not new. We trust technology every day. We trust our cars to stop when we hit the brakes. Our phones to stop listening when we press the lock button. So, how is this different? What does this say?

This overarching overtrust in technology suggests just how malleable we can be. Overtrust in neurotechnology, then compounded with neurohype and neuroseduction, will make us especially susceptible to its influence. For this reason, new technologies must require responsible marketing — marketing that is careful to present the benefits and limitations of products accurately. What do we know about the science? And what do we still need to learn?

## 16.5 What does this mean for neurotechnology?

In short, there is a lot to consider. The concerns covered in this chapter barely scratch the surface on what bigger resources, such as The Routledge Handbook of Neuroethics, highlight to be relevant to neurotechnology. What we have established, though, is the need for careful consideration, strenuous research, and responsible marketing of neurotechnology moving forward.

We are in a golden era. Neurotechnology is new and can be molded to be what we want it to be. Still, the most important concern remains: how do we brace ourselves for the practical, social, and ethical consequences we cannot even preemptively anticipate — the ones that will inevitably rear their heads as technology continues to outpace itself?

Neuroethics can serve as a tool to frame this question — today, tomorrow, and in the daring years ahead.

## Endnotes

1. Alexander, Garrett E., Michael D. Crutcher, and Mahlon R. DeLong. "Basal ganglia-thalamocortical circuits: parallel substrates for motor, oculomotor, "prefrontal" and "limbic" functions." In *Progress in brain research*, vol. 85, pp. 119-146. Elsevier, 1991.

2. Chiken, Satomi, and Atsushi Nambu. "Disrupting neuronal transmission: mechanism of DBS." *Frontiers in systems neuroscience* 8 (2014): 33.

3. Hariz, G. M., Limousin, P., & Hamberg, K. (2016). " DBS means everything-for some time". Patients' Perspectives on Daily Life with Deep Brain Stimulation for Parkinson's Disease. *Journal of Parkinson's disease*, 6(2), 335.

4. Feinberg, Todd E., and Julian Paul Keenan. "Where in the brain is the self?" *Consciousness and cognition* 14.4 (2005): 661-678.

5. Mackenzie, Robin. "Must family/carers look after strangers? Post-DBS identity changes and related conflicts of interest." *Frontiers in integrative neuroscience* 5 (2011): 12.

6. Gandiga, Prateek C., Friedhelm C. Hummel, and Leonardo G. Cohen. "Transcranial DC stimulation (tDCS): a tool for double-blind sham-controlled clinical studies in brain stimulation." *Clinical neurophysiology* 117, no. 4 (2006): 845-850.

7. Volkow, Nora D., Bruce Rosen, and Lars Farde. "Imaging the living human brain: magnetic resonance imaging and positron emission tomography." *Proceedings of the National Academy of Sciences* 94, no. 7 (1997): 2787-2788.

8. Appelbaum, P. S. (2015). Law & psychiatry: Through a glass darkly: Functional neuroimaging evidence enters the courtroom. Psychiatric Services.

9. Feigenson, N. (2006). Brain imaging and courtroom evidence: On the admissibility and persuasiveness of fMRI. *International Journal of Law in Context*, 2(03), 233-255.

10. Finn, David P. "Brain imaging and privacy: How recent advances in neuroimaging implicate privacy concerns." *bepress Legal Series* (2006): 1752.

11. Rusconi, Elena, and Timothy Mitchener-Nissen. "Prospects of functional magnetic resonance imaging as lie detector." *Frontiers in* human *neuroscience* 7 (2013): 594.

12. Baertschi, Bernard. "Neuroimaging in the Courts of Law." *Journal of Applied Ethics and Philosophy* 3 (2011): 9-16.

13. Appelbaum, Paul S. "Law & psychiatry: Through a glass darkly: Functional neuroimaging evidence enters the courtroom." *Psychiatric Services* 60.1 (2009): 21-23.

14. Lilienfeld, Scott O., Elizabeth Aslinger, Julia Marshall, and Sally Satel. "A Field Guide to Exaggerated Brain-Based Claims." *The Routledge Handbook of Neuroethics* (2017).

15. Caulfield, Timothy, Christen Rachul, and Amy Zarzeczny. "Neurohype" and the Name Game: Who's to Blame?" *AJOB Neuroscience* 1, no. 2 (2010): 13-15.

16. Robinette, Paul, Wenchen Li, Robert Allen, Ayanna M. Howard, and Alan R. Wagner. "Overtrust of robots in emergency evacuation scenarios." In *2016 11th ACM/IEEE International Conference on Human-Robot Interaction (HRI)*, pp. 101-108. IEEE, 2016.

17. Ramesh, Sunidhi. (2018). The Ethical Design of Intelligent Robots. The Neuroethics Blog. Retrieved on July 11, 2019, from http://www.theneuroethicsblog.com/2018/02/the-ethical-design-of-intelligent-robots.html

# 17
# The Future of NeuroTechnology

**Yannick Roy**

*Yannick is spearheading NeuroTechX – the international neurotech community, as a cofounder and executive director. He is an electrical engineer with a background in computer science currently doing his PhD in visual neuroscience at University of Montreal. He's obsessed about combining brain & tech. When he's not engaging with other neurotech enthusiasts or managing neurotech projects, he's usually in his lab working on his research. He also teaches computer science at ETS in Montreal.*

In the future, when we look back, some years will stand out more than others. For researchers, 2013 stands out as the year President Obama launched the BRAIN Initiative and the EU launched the Human Brain Project (HBP). To date, these are the biggest announcements ever made in the field of neurotechnology and introduced the investment of more money than ever before into tools to better understand the brain. In the years following 2013, many other massive government-driven initiatives followed worldwide. Then, in 2016, the neurotech headlines were stolen by Bryan Johnson and Mary Lou Jepsen, two outsiders announcing their ventures in the field.

## 17.1  Companies driving the future of Neurotech

### 17.1.1  Kernel

Bryan Johnson, who previously sold Braintree/Venmo (a payment system) to PayPal for $800M, announced that he was investing $100M in his new company, *Kernel*, to unlock the brain's potential. The initial vision was to develop a brain chip based on Theodore Berger's work to enhance memory; basically, adding an SD card to your brain. Theodore Berger has been working on memory for a few decades. DARPA also supported his work of creating a *Hippocampal Cognitive Prosthesis*.[1] However, shortly after, Berger left Kernel over some disagreements, mainly around timelines. Kernel then stayed quiet for a while before pivoting its business model completely to focus on non-invasive neuroscience as a service.

## 17.1.2 OpenWater

Mary Lou Jepsen quickly gained media attention when she announced that she was on a quest to make a wearable fMRI machine. Using a similar approach to functional MRI and functional NIRS measuring blood flow in the brain, she claimed that her new venture, OpenWater, could use Holography principles to build a light-based brain and body scanner. Though her claim could have easily been viewed as grandiose to the media and the scientific community, Mary Lou Jepsen's track record made her hard to dismiss. Mary Lou Jepsen did her Ph.D. dissertation on Holography in the early 1990s and has her name on over 200 patents.[2] She was also the co-founder and CTO of One Laptop Per Child and was an executive at Google and Facebook working on next-generation microelectronic devices. Jepsen understands the manufacturing of such devices at scale and left Facebook to work on her own project. Moreover, it is hard to argue her deepest motivation to have a genuine impact in neuroscience — she had to deal with a brain tumor and brain surgery herself as a graduate student. Mary Lou Jepsen went on to appear in several TED Talks and delivered many fascinating demos showing how light goes through the body. However, the world is still waiting to see the device.

Despite those big news items in 2016, it is 2017 that history will likely remember as an inflection point for neurotechnologies and brain-computer interfaces (BCI), thanks to back-to-back announcements from Elon Musk and Facebook revealing their BCI projects. Elon Musk announced Neuralink, whose mission is to connect the brain to the digital world to enhance its bandwidth, mainly to compete against AI and avoid being left behind. Facebook announced its vision for a non-invasive consumer BCI in virtual reality (VR) that would let you communicate directly from your brain.

## 17.1.3 Neuralink

Prior to 2017, Elon Musk started talking about neural interfaces and his personal interest in the field. In 2017, he publicly announced the launch of Neuralink, his venture in neurotechnology. He remained very secretive about the exact product and technology they would be developing, but it was clear that it would be an invasive technology for human enhancement. In April 2017, Tim Urban was the lucky one who got to document Elon Musk's vision, and he did not disappoint! His "Wait But Why" piece on Neuralink is a piece of art and should be read by everyone in the space.[3] (warning: not a quick read!)

Then, the Neuralink team got to work, and it took almost two years before their next announcement. The "official" Launch Event occurred in July 2019, when they revealed what they were working on. Aside from giving an update, the main objective was recruiting. During that Launch Event, Musk shared his vision of having a robot perform the surgical insertion of their brain implant, with thousands of channels, placing small, flexible threads (electrodes) adjacent to neurons — showing images and videos of "The Sewing Machine," as Musk described the manner of the process. He suggested that the procedure should be similar to Lasik. In 2019, they also published their white paper describing their technology.[4]

**Figure 17.1** In August 2020, in the midst of the COVID-19 pandemic, they live-streamed their progress updates with a live demo of a Neuralink device in a pig (shoutout to Gertrude, the pig,).[5]

Once again, they were clear about the goal of such a mediatic event: recruiting. "The main reason for doing this presentation is recruiting," Musk said, hinting at Neuralink seeking approval from the Food and Drug Administration to begin using human test subjects as early as the following year. "This is going to sound pretty weird, but ultimately, we will achieve symbiosis with artificial intelligence," Musk said. "This is not a mandatory thing. It is a thing you can choose to have if you want. This is something that I think will be really important on a civilization-level scale.[6]"

The event, just as anything Elon Musk does, resulted in a storm of articles and posts on social media, spurring controversy about the different claims and timelines put forward by Elon Musk and his team at Neuralink.[7,8,9]

In October 2020, I (*Yannick Roy, author of this chapter*) had the opportunity to host a panel discussion with Jonathan Wolpaw, Mikhail Lebedev, Karen Rommelfanger, and Xing Chen on *"Neural Implants - Neuralink but not only..."* as part of the BCI Samara 2020 conference.[10] The consensus was that the science presented at the Neuralink event was generally conventional and on-par with the current field of neural implants. Conversely, the technological advances presented were impressive and applauded by the neurotechnology community.[11]

As of 2020, Neuralink pivoted from a device behind the ear to removing a piece of the skull over the motor cortex to implant the device surgically. Neuralink received the FDA Breakthrough Device designation and sought to conduct human clinical trials as early as 2021 if the FDA provides the approval to do so. Still aiming at human enhancement, they will begin with a focus on physical disabilities, memory loss, and blindness.

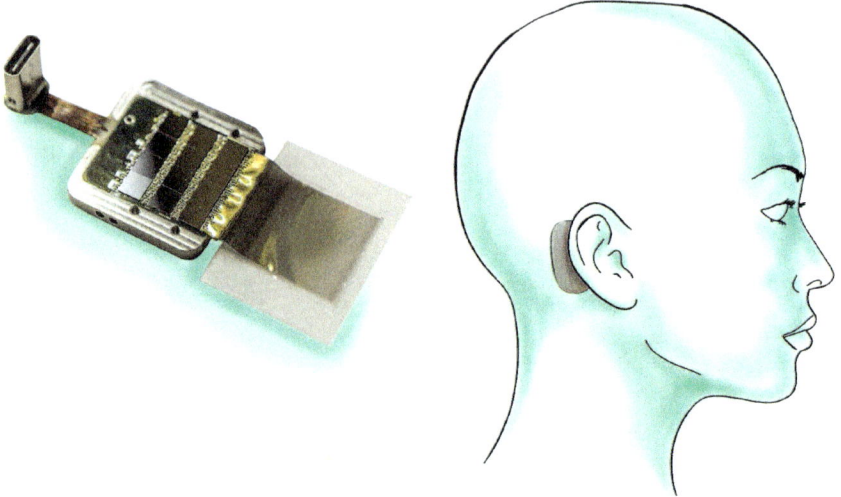

Figure 17.2 Updated device suggested in 2020 and the initial, behind the ear, device.

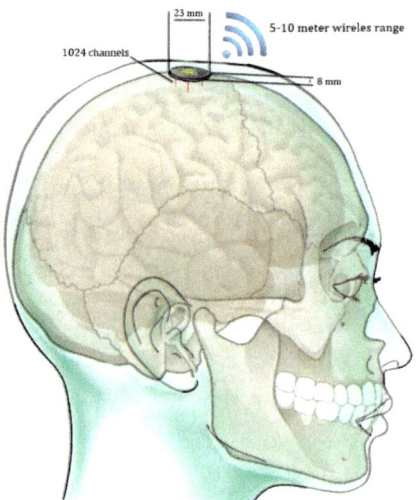

Figure 17.3 Updated Neuralink design.

## 17.1.4 Facebook

In April 2017, Facebook held its F8 conference and made a few big announcements (and claims) that would take the field of neurotech somewhat by surprise, creating a mediatic storm.

Facebook Building 8 R&D division head Regina Dugan took the stage to announce their bold vision of creating a brain-computer interface to communicate directly from the brain. The announcement itself, the idea of creating a BCI device that communicates, is nothing new or bold, as you have seen in this book. Research labs have been working on BCI devices for years. However, the claims of a non-invasive wearable device that types at a speed of 100 words per minute and controls the mouse in two years-time are what made most experts in the field very skeptical and vocal on social media.

Facebook picked the right ambassador for delivering such an announcement as Regina Dugan previously ran Google's Advanced Technology and Products division, was the former senior VP at Motorola, and a former director at DARPA. Sadly, eight months later, she would leave Facebook.

For the remainder of 2017, most of the scientific community remained quite skeptical about Facebook's BCI project (obviously, we can only judge based on what is publicly shared, without the full picture or full understanding). We must give Facebook credit for their smart move in 2018 when they accepted the invitation to join the BCI Meeting in Asilomar, addressing the most educated and critical BCI crowd in the world. The BCI Meeting is the most prominent event in the Brain-Computer Interface field. The scientific conference lasted a full week in Asilomar and attracted the top researchers in the field as well as grad students. During the conference, Facebook explained their bold vision and their roadmap, not with their typical click-bait public-facing claims as they wouldn't fly with such a tough crowd, but rather explaining an ambitious 10-year plan. They acknowledged the complexity of their endeavor and explained why they didn't need a "miracle" but rather significant improvements in multiple aspects of the technology. They mentioned that they would not be working alone and are already collaborating with many research labs. The scientific community had no other choice but to respect the millions of dollars that Facebook will pour into the field over the next decade because it will undoubtedly help the field's progress, despite whether or not Facebook reaches its goal. As you might guess, many also expressed their ethical concerns, knowing the history of Facebook. But we'll keep this for another book!

In 2018, Facebook restructured the *Building 8* initiative, and the BCI initiative was moved under the Facebook Reality Labs arm. Facebook's contribution is already paying off through their partnership with Dr. Edward "Eddie" Chang at UCSF, working on invasive speech decoding. Chang's group published a Nature paper in 2019 and then again in 2020, showing very promising results using AI for real-time speech decoding directly from brain activity.[12],[13] As for their wearable (non-invasive) device, we have yet to hear more about it. It is known that they are going down the path of optical imaging, namely via infrared light. If you would like to learn more about the FB BCI project, I invite you to read their post, "Imagining a new interface: Hands-free communication without saying a word.[14]"

Moreover, in 2019, Facebook acquired CTRL-Labs, a New-York based startup, for an undisclosed amount between $500M and $1B. CTRL-Labs had not (and still hasn't, as of 2021) delivered any device. This is a good example of their commitment to the field.

Obviously, Neuralink and Facebook, as well as Kernel and OpenWater, all sit on the shoulders of giants and so many years of research, products, and experiments; but social media prefers buzz-worthy headlines. Both Elon Musk and Mark Zuckerberg certainly fall into that category; therefore, that is the story the general public will most likely get and remember, for better or worse.

In writing an introductory book on the field of neurotechnology in 2021, we could not skip talking about these four big announcements from 2016 and 2017; however, many other exciting neurotechnologies are emerging. For the remainder of this chapter, we will give you a glimpse into a few exciting neurotechnologies to keep an eye on.

## 17.2 Researchers

### 17.2.1 Wearable MEG via OPMs

#### 17.2.1.1 Pioneers

Researchers from the Sir Peter Mansfield Imaging Centre at the University of Nottingham and the Wellcome Centre for Human Neuroimaging at University College London (UCL) have been pioneering exciting work around a portable MEG system using Optically Pumped Magnetometers (OPMs).

OPMs have been around for a few years, and many research groups have explored this avenue to measure electrical brain activity via its magnetic field (see MEG chapter). However, the collaboration between these two specific research groups, and the company QuSpin, certainly got the public's attention in 2018 when they published their paper in Nature, one of the most prestigious scientific journals. It received a lot of media coverage with a picture of a participant wearing a face mask that resembles Jason in "Friday the 13th".[15] It also got a lot of attention on social media, as it was hard to tell if clicking the image would lead to a scientific paper or a horror movie.

## 17.2.1.2 The science behind wearable MEGs

As explained in chapter 3 (Magnetoencephalography [MEG]), MEG allows the direct imaging of brain electrophysiology by measuring magnetic fields generated by neural activity. It is possible to generate 3D images of such fields in time and space using mathematical models. MEG systems use superconducting sensors (SQUIDS) that are cryogenically cooled. Optically Pumped Magnetometers (OPMs) on the other hand, leverage quantum mechanical properties of alkali metals (the first column in the periodic table).

Figure 17.4 Alkali metals.

Simply put, and without diving into the physics of it, a light of a very specific wavelength (e.g., laser) is sent through the gaseous (alkali) metal and will move some electrons to a higher energy level (i.e., pumping), aligning them with the light. Naturally, the electrons decay to a lower energy state after a while of keeping the light on. The electrons align with the light, and the gaseous metal becomes somewhat transparent to the light. The light receptor on the other side (e.g., photodiode) measures the light received (i.e., passing through the gaseous metal). With no outside magnetic field, this measure would be constant. At this point, the system is "pumped" and ready for measurement. Any variation of the light received on the other side can be attributed to the surrounding magnetic field disrupting the system, making it less transparent to the light.

## 17.2.1.3 Advantages

As seen in the MEG chapter, existing systems offer a unique high temporal resolution of brain activity but also come with many limitations, namely their size, sensibility to movements, and cost. New non-cryogenic quantum-based OPMs might be able to address these limitations while offering even better data quality.

First, as opposed to SQUIDs requiring cryogenic cooling, OPMs can operate at room temperature with no massive cooling system, making each sensor small and lightweight. Second, since OPMs operate with miniaturized wearable insulation, it allows placement of the sensors close to the scalp and can, in theory, be adapted to any head size as opposed to being in a big bulky machine with a one-size-fits-all helmet. Having the sensors as close as possible to the head matters because the MEG signal follows the inverse square law with distance, whereby the signal decays exponentially with distance. Thus, any motion of the head relative to the sensors reduces data quality significantly. Even a 5mm movement can prevent the use of the data.[16] With a one-size-fits-all helmet, the gap between the sensors and the head is inhomogeneous and increases dramatically for individuals with small heads. In 2020, Ryan M. Hill and his colleagues (many of them involved in the Nature paper mentioned above) addressed the mounting of OPM sensors by designing two new methods: a flexible (EEG-like) cap and a rigid helmet.[17] They argued that the rigid helmet offers a more robust option with significant advantages for reconstructing the field data into 3D images of changes in the neuronal current. Perhaps the Jason-like pictures we will see coming out of such research will inspire young minds to go into STEM.

### 17.2.1.4 We still need to counter out the Earth's magnetic field!

As mentioned in the MEG chapter, given the strength of the Earth's magnetic field and that generated by current technology versus the very low magnetic field produced by brain activity, such systems must be operated in a shielded room (i.e., the Faraday cage). This remains true for OPM-based systems. However, despite the Faraday cage, the remaining Earth's field within the room is still significant, and more importantly, spatially inhomogeneous. Any sensor movement through this field would result in a field change much larger than the one of interest (brain activity), therefore making the data unusable. To solve this problem, researchers are setting up bi-planar electromagnetic coils generating fields equal and opposite to the remnant Earth's field, thereby canceling it out.[18] Simply put, they use two planes of about a meter and a half square placed at about 1.5m on both sides of the subject, creating a 40x40x40cm^3 cube of interest in which the field is nullified. The head and sensors can freely move in that cube of interest.

OPMs have been shown to have sensitivities close to that of commercial SQUIDs and are now commercially available. Therefore, we might see a shift of MEG technology in the coming years toward an OPM-based system. This shift would most likely increase the general use of MEG for brain imaging in various domains while enabling its use on some populations, such as children, and new experimental paradigms where people can freely move. It is important to note that most OPM systems today have not been used with dense full-head coverage.

**Figure 17.5** Bi-planar electromagnetic coils can create a region free from the influence of Earth's magnetic field where the head and sensors can move freely.

Most published work in the last few years used only a few sensors at a specific location to answer a particular research question. A lot more research needs to be done before OPM-based MEG systems become mainstream, but the startup, Kernel (founded by Bryan Johnson),[19] announced, in 2020, a pivot from their initial business model in favor of neuroscience as a service using an OP-MEG system with the QuSpin Gen2 sensors.[20] Each module provides 15 channels from 9 OPMs, and a fully loaded system provides 720 channels from 432 OPMs.

## 17.2.2 Neural Dust

A few years ago, a group of researchers at UC Berkeley challenged themselves to "make a ridiculously small implant that goes into tissue.[21]" After looking at a few different approaches to power such a device from an outside source, Michel Maharbiz finally had his "aha" moment in 2012, suggesting that ultrasound might be the best way to go about it. The basic idea behind Neural Dust is to send an ultrasound that propagates through the body tissues. These signals then hit something that will respond to the ultrasound and bounce back with a different amount of energy (i.e., backscattering), allowing the system to measure something of interest. Using a piezoelectric crystal that transforms ultrasound into electricity and vice-versa, they can clip a tiny chip with such a crystal onto a nerve. When the device is activated by a beam of ultrasound, a voltage runs between the electrodes and is affected by the electrical activity of the tissue to which it is clipped. Therefore, the changes in ultrasound echo (i.e., backscattering) can be used to enact inference on the electrical activity happening at the nerve level.

The work initially stemmed out of Dongjin (aka DJ) Seo's Ph.D. under the guidance of Jose Carmena and Michel Maharbiz.[22] In 2019, both Professors took a sabbatical from Berkeley to focus 100% of their time on Iota Biosciences, the spinoff looking to commercialize the technology. In late 2018, Iota Biosciences raised a $15M Series A to help move the FDA application and clinical trials forward.[23] On October 16, 2020, the big Japanese pharma company Astellas announced the acquisition of Iota Biosciences.[24] As for "DJ" Seo, after finishing his Ph.D., he helped launch Neuralink as one of the founding members and is the Director of Implant Systems at Neuralink as of 2021.

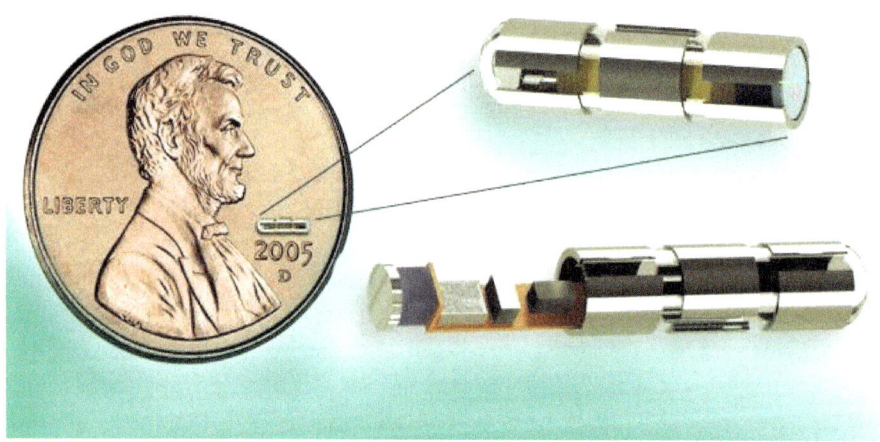

Figure 17.6 Size of each Neural Dust.

The initial and ultimate vision is to have many of these tiny sensors (i.e., motes) all over the brain. The sensors can be implanted laparoscopically or through a tiny incision. The huge potential lies in the fact that the device is wireless, battery-free, and so small that you could have many, many motes collecting information for various locations simultaneously. Moreover, by adding a capacitor to the chip, they could store enough energy to stimulate the nerve, enabling the device to also modulate the nerve's activity. of the nerve.

Adding more sensors obviously increases the complexity of properly decoding the signal since the orientation, position, motion, and many other factors will influence the signal. They use machine learning to train the system to better understand how to differentiate real signals from the noise coming from various sources.

At this point in time, the device is still too big for the brain, the current size being bigger than a millimeter cube, and they are currently focusing on applications "from the neck down" (i.e., the peripheral nervous system). If you are interested in learning more about Neural Dust, we highly recommend that you watch Maharbiz's 2019 talk.[25]

### 17.2.3 Neural Lace

There has been a fair amount of confusion around Neural Dust, Neural Lace, Neuralink, and Stentrode. It is important to note that there are four different approaches. We previously discussed Neuralink (Elon Musk's company) implanting a chip with tiny threads and Neural Dust (Carmena & Maharbiz's company) implanting tiny wireless motes. Neural Lace is the idea of deploying an electronic mesh over and around the brain. For more information, we invite you to check out the *Syringe-injectable electronics* Nature paper from 2015.[26] The Sentrode approach will be covered in the next section. To add to the confusion, Elon Musk used to refer to his project as a "Neural Lace" for the brain.[27] Musk previously said his interest in the idea partly stemmed from the science fiction concept of "neural lace" in the fictional universe in The Culture, a series of 10 novels by Iain M. Banks.[26,28]

### 17.2.4 Stentrode

A very promising approach coming out of Australia is the Stentrode™. The idea is that of a stent electrode. Since we have already mastered inserting stents in blood vessels, why not make them "electrical" to read and write to the brain? This procedure eliminates the need for brain surgery but is less invasive and destructive than other invasive devices since the stent stays in your brain's blood vessels.

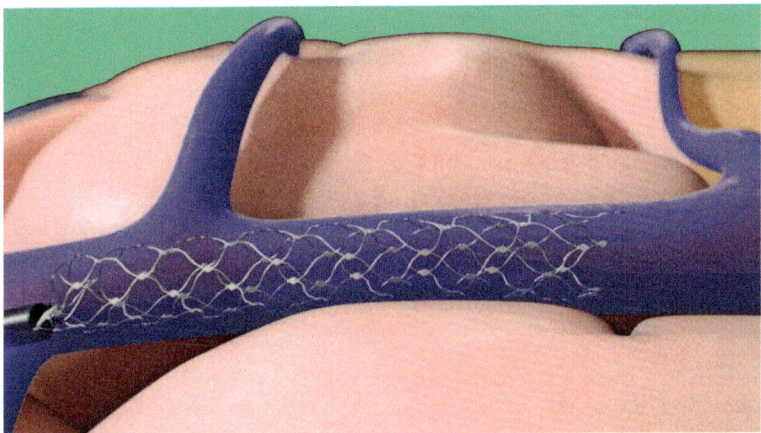

Figure 17.7 Stentrode Illustration.

As one can read on their website (as of mid-2020):

*"Synchron is a clinical-stage neurovascular bioelectronics medicine company developing bloodstream-delivered solutions for previously untreatable nervous system conditions.*

*Our flagship product, the Stentrode™, is a minimally-invasive brain-computer interface currently being investigated in a clinical trial involving people affected by severe paralysis. The system is designed to improve functional independence by enabling patients to obtain command control of external devices through thought alone."*

Partly funded by DARPA, they have published pre-clinical studies showing long-term safety and the ability to record brain activity.[29,30,31] Synchron is now conducting clinical trials with human participants to evaluate its ability to improve functional independence for people with paralysis by restoring command control of external devices that facilitate instrumental activities of daily living, such as text messaging.

In addition to their hardware, they've developed their brainOS™ BCI pipeline, converting brain activity to commands in the real world.

You should keep an eye open because they are moving fast! Here is a rough timeline:

**2016:** Initial paper showing the innovation + incorporation of Synchron.[28]

**2017:** Synchron raises a $10M Series A.

**2019:** Starts their early Clinical Trial. In December 2019, the first implant in a human (successful).[32]

**2020:** FDA Breakthrough Device designation.[33]

**Next:** Safety and efficacy data from the ongoing first-in-human clinical trial will be used to finalize the protocol for a pivotal FDA study that will guide evaluation for U.S. marketing approval.[34]

## 17.3 Government Led Initiatives

### 17.3.1 DARPA & Neurotechnology

We cannot talk about neurotechnology's future without mentioning the major and sometimes controversial contributions of DARPA (Defense Advanced Research Projects Agency). Aligned with the BRAIN Initiative, DARPA is investing massively in high-risk and high-potential technology. They see their role as a means to "de-risk" some of the potential breakthroughs that other agencies would not fund. Not only do they fund the research, but they also support and encourage its transition out of the lab toward commercialization. DARPA started working on neurotechnology in the 1970s and has doubled down its commitment over the past few years while also allocating funding to support the commercialization of these innovations.[35] DARPA is behind many innovations and companies you have seen throughout this book and many more. For example, the sewing machine of Neuralink, the memory enhancement chip of Nia Therapeutics, the invasive neural interface of Paradromics, the stentrode of Synchron, and the neural dust of Iota Biosciences.

Table 17.1 Current Darpa programs

| |
|---|
| **Electrical Prescriptions (ElectRx).** Build microscopic, injectable neuromodulation devices that can help the human body heal itself. |
| **Hand Proprioception and Touch Interfaces (HAPTIX).** Build wireless neural-interface microsystems that can deliver sensations to amputees. |
| **Neural Engineering System Design (NESD).** Improve signal resolution and data-transfer bandwidth between implantable neural interfaces and devices. |
| **Neuro Function, Activity, Structure and Technology (Neuro-FAST).** Visualize and decode brain activity to characterize and mitigate threats and improve functional behaviors. |
| **Next-Generation Nonsurgical Neurotechnology (N3).** Read and write to multiple points in the brain at once via a portable neural interface system that does not require surgery to implant. |
| **Restoring Active Memory (RAM).** Help people whose memories have been damaged to form and retrieve memories via a wireless neural interface. |
| **Restoring Active Memory – Replay (RAM Replay).** Improve memories of events and skills by better understanding how neural replay helps form and recall memories. |
| **Revolutionizing Prosthetics.** Improve DARPA-developed prosthetic systems for people who have lost upper limbs. |
| **Systems-Based Neurotechnology for Emerging Therapies (SUBNETS).** Help treat neuropsychological illnesses via implanted, closed-loop diagnostic and therapeutic systems. |
| **Targeted Neuroplasticity Training (TNT).** Improve cognitive skills training by activating peripheral nerves in ways that promote and strengthen the brain's neural connections. |

Darpa, Defense Advanced Research Projects Agency. n.d. "Our Research." Explore Neurosciene by Office. Retrieved 11/13/2020. https://www.darpa.mil/archive/our-research.

All these programs are very exciting, and all have tremendous potential. However, let's just have a look at the N3 (noninvasive) program to decipher from insights on what might be coming next.

DARPA's tweet on Sept. 6, 2018, was very exciting for the noninvasive neurotech world.

*"DARPA is at a point where we think hi-res, portable brain-machine interfaces might be feasible for able-bodied [non-disabled] people. Why? This graphic shows some of the options we could explore under our new N3 program."*

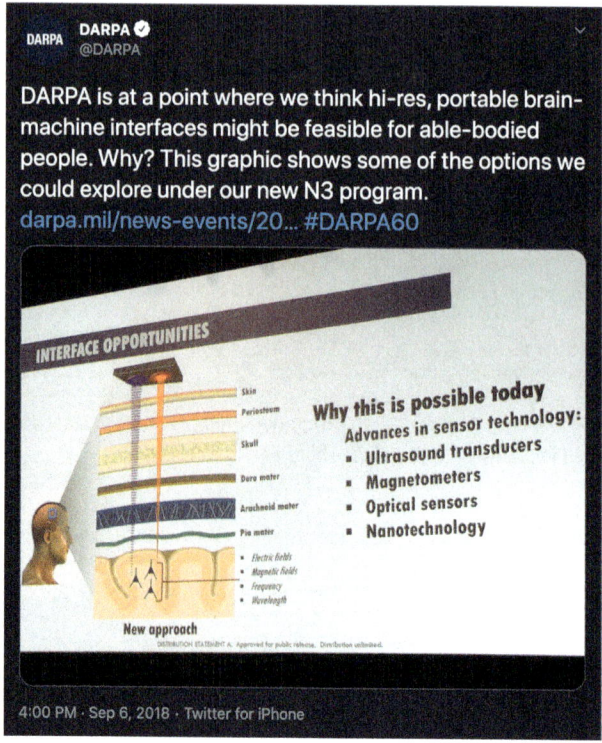

Eight months later, the DARPA N3 program would award funding to six organizations to support the Next-Generation Nonsurgical Neurotechnology (N3): the Battelle Memorial Institute, Carnegie Mellon University, Johns Hopkins University Applied Physics Laboratory, Palo Alto Research Center (PARC), Rice University, and Teledyne Scientific. Here is blurb on each of these six projects taken from their announcement on May 20, 2019:[36]

"**The Battelle team**, under principal investigator Dr. Gaurav Sharma, aims to develop a minutely invasive interface system that pairs an external transceiver with electromagnetic nanotransducers that are nonsurgically delivered to neurons of interest. The nanotransducers would convert electrical signals from the neurons into magnetic signals that can be recorded and processed by the external transceiver, and vice versa, to enable bidirectional communication.

**The Carnegie Mellon University team**, under principal investigator Dr. Pulkit Grover, aims to develop a completely noninvasive device that uses an acousto-optical approach to record from the brain and interfering electrical fields to write to specific neurons. The team will use ultrasound waves to guide light into and out of the brain to detect neural activity. The team's write approach exploits the non-linear response of neurons to electric fields to enable localized stimulation of specific cell types.

**The Johns Hopkins University Applied Physics Laboratory team**, under principal investigator Dr. David Blodgett, aims to develop a completely noninvasive, coherent optical system for recording from the brain. The system will directly measure optical path-length changes in neural tissue that correlate with neural activity.

**The PARC team**, under principal investigator Dr. Krishnan Thyagarajan, aims to develop a completely noninvasive acousto-magnetic device for writing to the brain. Their approach pairs ultrasound waves with magnetic fields to generate localized electric currents for neuromodulation. The hybrid approach offers the potential for localized neuromodulation deeper in the brain.

**The Rice University team**, under principal investigator Dr. Jacob Robinson, aims to develop a minutely invasive, bidirectional system for recording from and writing to the brain. For the recording function, the interface will use diffuse optical tomography to infer neural activity by measuring light scattering in neural tissue. To enable the write function, the team will use a magneto-genetic approach to make neurons sensitive to magnetic fields.

**The Teledyne team**, under principal investigator Dr. Patrick Connolly, aims to develop a completely noninvasive, integrated device that uses micro optically pumped magnetometers to detect small, localized magnetic fields that correlate with neural activity. The team will use focused ultrasound for writing to neurons."

In reading these projects, it is clear that light-based and sound-based approaches will see a new wave of innovation over the next decade. So, for the younger neurotech enthusiasts out there, perhaps missing your physics classes might not be the best idea for a career in neurotech!

Coming from a military department, one might wonder about the ethics, legal, and social implications of such research and the commercialization of products. On DARPA's website:

*"[...] program is informed by independent Ethical, Legal, and Social Implications (ELSI) experts to help DARPA proactively identify potential issues related to memory and neurotechnology. Communications with ELSI experts supplement the standard oversight provided by institutional review boards that govern human clinical studies and animal use.*[37]*"*

It is also important to note that given the current pace of innovation in the field, those regulators are beginning to adapt to the needs of the BCI field. In February, the FDA released "Implanted Brain-Computer Interface (BCI) Devices for Patients with Paralysis or Amputation — Non-clinical Testing and Clinical Considerations,"[38] a document aiming to guide companies on how to document their BCIs and how to design preclinical animal studies and human clinical trials.

## 17.4 Brain Data on the Blockchain?

The neurotech field has seen a growing interest in using blockchain technology (e.g., the idea behind cryptocurrency) to store brain data. Blockchain technology offers great promises in many fields and has the potential to be very disruptive. The main advantages usually revolve around a decentralized system, the integrity of the data (and the system), and traceability of data. While it might be early for the neurotech field to really benefit from blockchain, one could understand why, in 10-15 years from now, we might want such a backend platform. One of the motivations behind adopting such technology to handle brain data is that we are undoubtedly entering a *big brain data* era where we produce more data than ever before and at an exponentially increasing pace while also sharing more and more of that data to allow for data mining and levering artificial intelligence. This is a new world. Data used to be collected within a research lab, healthcare facility, or within a company, and then stay there and not "travel" or be shared to any extent. Now, we are moving toward business models where the primary currency is data. You have certainly heard the phrase "data is the new oil." This dynamic will become increasingly true in neuroscience and neurotechnology and will put pressure on data handling backend systems. The future will tell if blockchain is the best option for the job.

In 2017, Bryan Johnson gave a talk, "The Brain on Blockchain" (available on YouTube),[39] explaining how "dropping" brain data of individuals on the blockchain could allow for new models to emerge, giving examples around trust and security. In 2018, Buzsáki & Tingley proposed in their paper[40] that the hippocampus is similar to a linked list connecting events and experiences into sequences. Based on this view, Cho and colleagues wrote a paper called "Blockchain and human episodic memory,"[41] suggesting that we could share such information on the blockchain. It is important to note that the paper has not been published in a peer-reviewed journal. Nevertheless, a few examples showed a growing interest; but is this scientifically rooted, or is it simply a "shiny new object that looks cool?"

Unfortunately, many groups took advantage of the over-hyped cryptocurrency market in late 2017. We have seen many new initiatives for brain data on the blockchain and companies looking to raise money to launch ICOs (Initial Coin Offering, similar to an IPO for companies going public on the stock market). At NeuroTechX, we would like to remind the public to keep their *BS radar* on alert. As much as the technology has real potential for the field, the fact that most initiatives launched in 2017-2018 (the cryptocurrency peak) died shortly after, and many have not seen the light since, is a good indicator that this was just buzz. We predict that we will see genuine initiatives in the coming years. However, we will also see some opportunistic groups trying to make a quick buck. If you ever have doubts about such an initiative, we would invite you to join the NTX community to discuss it.

To conclude this segment, we will list a few examples for historical purposes. We are not pointing fingers. Or maybe we are. . . .

## 17.4.1 BASIS NEURO (BNST)

"Brain-computer Interfaces to train your brain, manipulate gadgets, and enjoy new VR powerful games. BASIS NEURO is a platform for creating brain-controlled gadgets and services. Our unique neural interfaces allow everyone to add super features to their projects. We have realized the technology of neural control for smartphones, VR, and games in business, education, and medicine. Join us and the new NeuroFuture!"

Status: Dead.

Source: https://icobench.com/ico/basis-neuro

## 17.4.2 Brainmab

"Brainmab's mission is to bring the effort of information transfers to a minimum. This goal can be extended to store every aspect of a person's conscious mind up in a blockchain network that can be accessed by third parties if permitted. Brain-Computer Interfaces (BCI) will sustainably alter the means of communication as we know them today, and the blockchain technology will help bring forth this change in a secure and reliable manner."

Source: https://icoholder.com/en/brainmab-21976 (Oct. 2nd, 2020)

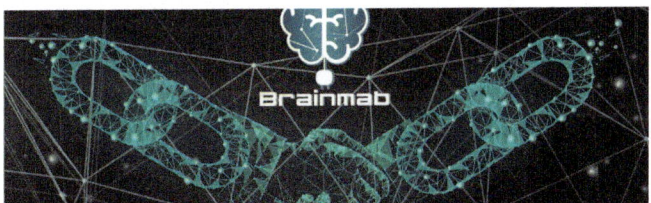

Figure 17.8 Source: https://medium.com/@Brainmab/brainmab-raises-30-million-capital-d3f8f3e2da6 [now deleted, still accessible via Wayback Time Machine as of October 2nd, 2020] https://web.archive.org/web/20181106100950/https://medium.com/@Brainmab.

Initial Website: https://brainmab.network/
Status: Dead.

## 17.4.3 RUNEURO

### RUNEURO — neurotechnologies powered by blockchain — 30% start bonus will end in 8 hours!

 runeuro (44) ▼ in #runeuro • 4 years ago

RUNEURO pre-ICO has launched successfully and is rapidly speeding. Almost $3,000 have been collected in some hours. Right now the investors are offered a special 30% start bonus.

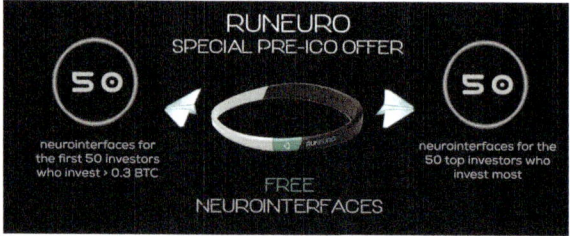

What is RUNEURO?

RUNEURO is much more than an ordinary ICO-project. It embraces both hardware and software development, manufacturing neurointerfaces outfitted with different thought-powered functions and builds a new security standard. BTW we provide the first 50 people who invest more than 0,3 BTC with a free brain-computer interface that will be manufactured three months after pre-ICO. Visit our website runeuro.net for further information.

To participate in pre-ICO you need to:

1. to fill in the form;
2. to send ETH to smart-contract address.

Participate in pre-ICO and take your share in the company that will set the trends of the future!

-------------------
Faithfully yours,
RUNEURO team

Figure 17.9 Source: https://steemit.com/runeuro/@runeuro/runeuro-neurotechnologies-powered-by-blockchain-30-start-bonus-will-end-in-8-hours (Oct. 2nd, 2020).

Initial website: runeuro.net
Status: Dead.

## 17.4.4 Neurogress

In a press release on PR Newswire from 2018, "Neurogress, an artificial intelligence (AI) based scientific software company, is raising about $ 44 million (Rs. 282 crore) growth capital in two stages (Pre-TGE & TGE) using blockchain technology. The company, promoted by a group of 12 neuroscientists and technocrats, launched its ICO (Initial Coin Offer) in the first stage, with Pre-TGE (Token Generation Event) at a 50 percent discount from February 10$^{th}$ to March 25$^{th}$, 2018."

Status: Still alive. (Not sure about the ICO and their raise… TBD)

Website: https://neurogress.site/

Source: https://www.prnewswire.com/in/news-releases/neurogress-ico-to-raise-44-mn-with-pre-tge-offer-of-50-off-674810203.html

## 17.4.5 Brainpatch: [Still Alive!!] — https://brainpatch.ai/

→ Review the Old vs New vision. Is it still about Blockchain?

Can neurological diseases be cured in a revolutionary way? At brainpatch, we appreciate that optimal brain stimulation will be complex, noninvasive, unique and different for each individual.

*We use artificial intelligence to optimize brain stimulation and achieve an unbiased objective outcome as a blockchain record of change in brain activity.*

Source (not available anymore, can be accessed via Wayback Timemachine):

Initial Website:

Wayback: https://web.archive.org/web/20190428060938/http://www.brainpatch.ai/

# Endnotes

1. Buzsáki, György, and David Tingley. "Space and time: The hippocampus as a sequence generator." *Trends in cognitive sciences* 22, no. 10 (2018): 853-869.

2. Jepsen, Mary Lou. "Holographic video: design and implementation of a display system." PhD diss., Massachusetts Institute of Technology, 1989.

3. Urban, Tim. "Neuralink and the brain's magical future." *Wait But Why* (2017). https://waitbutwhy.com/2017/04/neuralink.html

4. Musk, Elon. "An integrated brain-machine interface platform with thousands of channels." *Journal of medical Internet research* 21, no. 10 (2019): e16194.

5. Neuralink. August 28, 2020. "Elon Musk's Neuralink chip tested live in pig brains."https://www.youtube.com/watch?v=NqbQuZOFvOQ

6. Boyle, Alan. "Elon Musk Takes the Wraps off Neuralink Brain Probe and Aims for Human Trials." GeekWire, July 17, 2019. https://www.geekwire.com/2019/elon-musk-takes-wraps-off-neuralink-brain-probe-tests-rats/.

7. Regalado, Antonio. "Elon Musk's Neuralink Is Neuroscience Theater." MIT Technology Review. MIT Technology Review, August 30, 2020. Https://www.technologyreview.com/2020/08/30/1007786/elon-musks-neuralink-demo-update-neuroscience-theater/.

8. Uni, Sydney. "Media Alert Elon Musk's Neuralink Pig Research." University of Sydney, August 30, 2020. https://practicesource.com/sydney-uni-media-alert-elon-musks-neuralink-pig-research/

9. Brodwin, Erin, and Robbins, Rebecca "As Elon Musk's Neuralink prepares to draw back the curtain, ex-employees describe rushed timelines clashing with science's slow pace." STAT, August 25, 2020. https://www.statnews.com/2020/08/25/elon-musk-neuralink-update-brain-machine-implants/

10. Yannick Roy, Jonathan Wolpaw, Karen Rommelfanger, Mikhail Lebedev, Xing Chen. "BCI Samara 2020 Panel: Neural Implants – Neural Implants -Neuralink, ... but not only." YouTube, 1:45:10, December 9, 2020.

11. Marano, M and Roy, Y. "BCI Samara 2020 Neuralink Panel Discussion Overview." The Neuroethics Blog. November 17, 2020. http://www.theneuroethicsblog.com/2020/11/bci-samara-2020-neuralink-panel.html

12. Anumanchipalli, Gopala K., Josh Chartier, and Edward F. Chang. "Speech synthesis from neural decoding of spoken sentences." *Nature* 568, no. 7753 (2019): 493-498.

13. Makin, Joseph G., David A. Moses, and Edward F. Chang. *Machine translation of cortical activity to text with an encoder–decoder framework*. Nature Publishing Group (Nature Neuroscience), March 30, 2020.

14. Tech@Facebook. 2020. "Imagining a new interface: Hands-free communication without saying a word." March 30, 2020. https://tech.fb.com/imagining-a-new-interface-hands-free-communication-without-saying-a-word/

15. Boto, Elena, Niall Holmes, James Leggett, Gillian Roberts, Vishal Shah, Sofie S. Meyer, Leonardo Duque Muñoz et al. "Moving magnetoencephalography towards real-world applications with a wearable system." *Nature* 555, no. 7698 (2018): 657-661.

16. Gross, Joachim, Sylvain Baillet, Gareth R. Barnes, Richard N. Henson, Arjan Hillebrand, Ole Jensen, Karim Jerbi et al. "Good practice for conducting and reporting MEG research." *Neuroimage* 65 (2013): 349-363.

17. Hill, Ryan M., Elena Boto, Molly Rea, Niall Holmes, James Leggett, Laurence A. Coles, Manolis Papastavrou et al. "Multi-channel whole-head OPM-MEG: Helmet design and a comparison with a co nventional system." *NeuroImage* (2020): 116995.

18. Boto et al. "Moving magnetoencephalography towards real-world applications with a wearable system." *Nature* 555, no. 7698 (2018): 657-661.

19. Kernel. "Hello Humanity." November 10, 2020. https://www.kernel.co/hello-humanity

20. QuSpin; An Atomic Devices Company. 2020. https://quspin.com/

21. Devin. 2018. "Iota Biosciences raises $15M to produce in-body sensors smaller than a grain of rice." 1:26 pm pst - December 27, 2018. TechCrunch.com. https://techcrunch.com/2018/12/27/iota-biosciences-raises-15m-to-produce-in-body-sensors-smaller-than-a-grain-of-rice/

22. Seo, Dongjin, Ryan M. Neely, Konlin Shen, Utkarsh Singhal, Elad Alon, Jan M. Rabaey, Jose M. Carmena, and Michel M. Maharbiz. "Wireless recording in the peripheral nervous system with ultrasonic neural dust." *Neuron* 91, no. 3 (2016): 529-539.

23. Devin. 2018. "Iota Biosciences raises $15M to produce in-body sensors smaller than a grain of rice." 1:26 pm pst - December 27, 2018. TechCrunch.com. https://techcrunch.com/2018/12/27/iota-biosciences-raises-15m-to-produce-in-body-sensors-smaller-than-a-grain-of-rice/

24. Astellas. 2020. "Astellas Completes Acquisition of iota Biosciences." https://www.astellas.com/en/news/16151

25. Maharbiz, Michel. "Recent Advances in the Neural Dust Platform: Can we target many motes, deep in the brain and through the skull?" IEEE.tv, 50:02, January 21, 2019. https://ieeetv.ieee.org/recent-advances-neural-dust-platform-ieee-brain.

26. Liu, J., Fu, TM., Cheng, Z. et al. Syringe-injectable electronics. *Nature Nanotech* 10, 629–636 (2015). https://doi.org/10.1038/nnano.2015.115.

27. "Neuralink," Wikipedia. Wikipedia Foundation. November 12, 2020. https://en.wikipedia.org/wiki/Neuralink.

28. "Neuralink." Wikipedia. Wikimedia Foundation, October 26, 2020. https://en.wikipedia.org/wiki/Neuralink#:~:text=Musk%20said%20his%20interest%20in,novels%20by%20Iain%20M.%20Banks.

29. Oxley, Thomas J., Nicholas L. Opie, Sam E. John, Gil S. Rind, Stephen M. Ronayne, Tracey L. Wheeler, Jack W. Judy et al. "Minimally invasive endovascular stent-electrode array for high-fidelity, chronic recordings of cortical neural activity." *Nature biotechnology* 34, no. 3 (2016): 320-327.

30. Oxley, Thomas James, Nicholas Lachlan Opie, Gil Simon Rind, Kishan Liyanage, Sam Emmanuel John, Stephen Ronayne, Alan James McDonald et al. "An ovine model of cerebral catheter venography for implantation of an endovascular neural interface." *Journal of neurosurgery* 128, no. 4 (2018 [online, 2017]): 1020-1027.

31. Opie, Nicholas L., Sam E. John, Gil S. Rind, Stephen M. Ronayne, Yan T. Wong, Giulia Gerboni, Peter E. Yoo et al. "Focal stimulation of the sheep motor cortex with a chronically implanted minimally invasive electrode array mounted on an endovascular stent." *Nature biomedical engineering* 2, no. 12 (2018): 907-914.

32. Cision PR Newswire. 2019. "Synchron Initiates First-ever Clinical Trial to Evaluate Thought-to-Text™ Brain-Computer Interface Technology in Patients with Severe Paralysis." April 8, 2019. https://www.prnewswire.com/news-releases/synchron-initiates-first-ever-clinical-trial-to-evaluate-thought-to-text-brain-computer-interface-technology-in-patients-with-severe-paralysis-300826068.html.

33. Businesswire. 2020. "Synchron's Stentrode Brain-Computer Interface Receives Breakthrough Device Designation from FDA." August 27, 2020. https://www.businesswire.com/news/home/20200827005748/en/Synchron's-Stentrode-Brain-Computer-Interface-Receives-Breakthrough-Device-Designation-from-FDA.

34. NIH, U.S. National Library of Medicine. 2020. "STENTRODE First in Human Early Feasibility Study (SWITCH)." ClinicalTrials.gov. Updated June 22, 2020. https://clinicaltrials.gov/ct2/show/NCT03834857.

35. Miranda, Robbin A., William D. Casebeer, Amy M. Hein, Jack W. Judy, Eric P. Krotkov, Tracy L. Laabs, Justin E. Manzo et al. "DARPA-funded efforts in the development of novel brain–computer interface technologies." *Journal of neuroscience methods* 244 (2015): 52-67.

36. SharpBrains. 2019. "Six DARPA-funded research teams aim at revolutionizing noninvasive brain-machine interfaces." May 22, 2019. https://sharpbrains.com/blog/2019/05/22/six-darpa-funded-research-teams-aim-at-revolutionizing-noninvasive-brain-machine-interfaces/

37. DARPA. 2018. "Nonsurgical Neural Interfaces Could Significantly Expand Use of Neurotechnology." March 13, 2018. https://www.darpa.mil/news-events/2018-03-16.

38. U.S. Food and Drug Administration. 2019. "Implanted Brain-Computer Interface (BCI) Devices for Patients with Paralysis or Amputation - Non-clinical Testing and Clinical Considerations." Draft Guidance for Industry and Food and Drug Administration Staff. February 2019. https://www.fda.gov/regulatory-information/search-fda-guidance-documents/implanted-brain-computer-interface-bci-devices-patients-paralysis-or-amputation-non-clinical-testing.

39. Bryan Johnson. "The Brain on Blockchain." YouTube, 15:51, October 31, 2017. https://www.youtube.com/watch?v=uyAgz08_uaE.

40. Buzsáki, György, and David Tingley. "Space and time: The hippocampus as a sequence generator." *Trends in cognitive sciences* 22, no. 10 (2018): 853-869.

41. Cho, Seong Hah, Cody A. Cushing, Kunal Patel, Alok Kothari, Rongjian Lan, Matthias Michel, Mouslim Cherkaoui, and Hakwan Lau. "Blockchain and human episodic memory." *arXiv preprint arXiv:1811.02881* (2018).

# 18 Where to Start

## Sydney Swaine-Simon

*Sydney is a Montreal native with a strong desire to grow the cities innovation ecosystem. Having completed his studies in Psychology and Computer Science he developed a strong passion for Biotechnology, AI, and Open Innovation. In 2012 Sydney became one of the co-founders of District 3, one of Quebec's largest innovation centers.. His responsibilities as the AI Fellow included supporting and recruiting teams for the AI XPRIZE, helping to organize the AI for Good Summit which is hosted by the ITU, and supporting AI startups. Sydney also co-founded NeuroTechX, a non-profit organization which has built the largest international network of neurotechnology enthusiasts. The organization has created a community of over 10,000 people worldwide and has supported multiple open source neurotech projects. In his spare time, Sydney is a core organizer of the DEF CON Biohacking Village, a conference which brings biohackers from across the world to share their projects and experiences.*

## Jen Wang

*Jen Wang is a recent graduate from McGill University where she studied neuroscience and computer science. She has a passion for science communication and strongly believes in making scientific concepts accessible to everyone, whether that be through articles or educational infographics. Having joined the NeuroTechX community in 2018, her interests vary between AI, neurotech, and mental health.*

One of the peculiarities of the field of neurotechnology is its inherently interdisciplinary nature. Its rapid growth over the last few years can be partially attributed to its ability to draw people of different levels and disciplines. Software developers, hardware developers, educators, product managers, physicists, artificial intelligence and data science experts, neuroscientists, designers, ethicists, and more all bring essential and unique perspectives to the field.

Wherever your interests or skill sets lie, there is a spot in the neurotechnology community for you to get involved.

Additional links and resources for any of the following sections can be found on the NeuroTechX BCI GitHub repository: https://github.com/NeuroTechX/awesome-bci. If you have a good resource that has not been linked, feel free to submit a pull request as we are always seeking to expand the list.

## 18.1 Getting started with hardware

As the field grows, previously inaccessible hardware becomes cheaper and more widely available. Whereas just a few years ago, brain imaging machines were reserved for hospitals and labs, the rise of neurotechnology and BCI startups put powerful and portable hardware into the hands of the average consumer.

For now, electroencephalogram (EEG) and near-infrared spectroscopy (NIRS) are considered the cheapest and most accessible.

Some affordable EEG initiatives include:

- OpenBCI sells and ships hardware bundles and kits for the average enthusiast. Some of their products include EEG headsets, biosensing starter kits, and neurotechnology starter kits. Also included in their store are products from OpenEIT, which contain extensive documentation, tutorials, and software.
- Olimex's EEG-SMT is a low-cost and open-source EEG device that uses a USB interface with comprehensive documentation.
- The FreeEEG32 is an affordable and open-source 32-channel EEG sampling board.
- The OpenEEG project is aimed toward beginners in the field of electronics and neurotechnology and provide plans and software for DIY EEG software.
- In addition to EEG, OpenNIRS provides documentation and files for NIRS and has an analogous OpenfNIRS site for functional NIRS.

## 18.2 Data and Software

Though neurotechnological equipment is getting cheaper, it is not a requirement to get started in the field. As scientific and technological fields converge towards open-source, open neuroscience data has become more widely available. Some of the sources mentioned above have their own open-source data sets, and even more can be viewed in the provided GitHub repository.

Once you have the data, the average neurotechnology enthusiast can find several open-source software online to aid in the exploration, organization, and visualization of data.

- One favorite amongst data scientists is Jupyter Notebook, a beginner-friendly and intuitive web application for live code that works with your favorite programming language.
- MNE is an open-source MEG + EEG Analysis and Visualization software. It is versatile and efficient at "exploring, visualizing, and analyzing human neurophysiological data."

## 18.3 Hackathons, competitions, and conferences

A great way to set aside some time for your neurotechnological whims and practice your skills is to participate in events like hackathons and competitions, both in-person and online. It is a great way to meet new people interested in neurotechnology.

Kaggle is a data science community that regularly hosts data science-related competitions, often with prize money. Among these are EEG or BCI, and past competitions are available for you to peruse and try out yourself.

Hackathons are events that span multiple days, can be off- or online, and bring together interested parties to collaborate on creating functional software or hardware products. Generally done in groups, neurotechnology-related hackathons can range from small (the annual NeuroTechX hackathons, for example) to large (IEEE hackathons) events.

Conferences and other events can be smaller and less formal or large and academic. Some of these include the BCI society's annual conference, the ACM Conference on Human Factors in Computing Systems (CHI). Again, the provided GitHub Repository keeps a more up-to-date version of the list.

## 18.4 DIY Projects and the Neurotechnology Community

With the plethora of resources available online and on the market, even beginners can get started with their own projects.

- Know the variety of technologies and resources available and decide in which area you'd like to devote some time and interest. Online forums like OpenBCI are filled with enthusiasts, just like you, with whom you can collaborate, learn, and build.
- Google (Scholar) is your friend. If you cannot find a solid starting point for your project, look for papers online, too such as articles on EEG, and try to replace its hardware with ones available to you. For example, if the researcher used a 16-channel EEG system and your own has four, note the areas that the researcher identified as having the strongest signals and attempt to reproduce a coarser version of the study. Accessibility and convenience will only get easier in the next few years, as more researchers are starting to adopt the use of consumer EEG in their research to make it more accessible. Focus, especially on the methodology section.
- Join online communities.
    - ✓ Check out the projects on NeuroTechX, detailed further in the next section.
    - ✓ Github

## 18.5 NeuroTechX

### 18.5.1 Chapters

Though we do have online communities, the strength of NeuroTechX resides in its local chapters around the world. NeuroTech works year-round on various online and offline events and activities to build a stronger neurotechnology ecosystem. Please see https://neurotechx.com/community/ to search for communities in your city.

### 18.5.2 Student Clubs

Start early! Student clubs are a great way for undergraduates to get involved in the community and meet other students with similar interests and skillsets.

### 18.5.3 Slack

NeuroTechX has an active Slack community (which you can join via NeuroTechX's website) to keep up to date with announcements or share your latest projects.

Printed in Great Britain
by Amazon